It's Just Cheeseburgers, Honey

It's Just Cheeseburgers, Honey

IT'S JUST CHEESE BURGERS, HONEY

A MEMOIR OF LOVE, FOOD, AND THE TITANIC

JUDITH B. GELLER

GFORCE
PUBLISHING

ATLANTA, GEORGIA

GForce Publishing

Atlanta, Georgia

Copyright © 2025 by Judith B. Geller. All rights reserved.

Library of Congress Control Number: 2025927022

Paperback ISBN: 979-8-9937890-0-2

Hardcover ISBN: 979-8-9937890-1-9

eBook ISBN: 979-8-9937890-2-6

Book design by Christina Thiele

Editorial production by KN Literary Arts

For Arnie Who Gave Me The World

Prologue

rnie and I were living in New York City in the mid-1970s—
when telephones were mainly beige, their handsets tethered
to a box on the wall, with a spiral cord that could strangle you if
you tried to move around—when one morning my phone rang. It
was my friend Katherine calling from Tokyo. Hearing her voice was
unsettling; calls from abroad were not the norm at the time. The first
words she whispered were, "Jack has left us."

I thought: divorce, abandonment, serious disagreement? None
of that made sense. It had been less than a month since Arnie and I
had had dinner with her and Jack on their visit to the city, and their
relationship seemed normal. "Can't you get him back?" I asked.

Exasperated, she said, "No, no. He's gone. He passed away. Judy,
he died!"

How stupid I was, how insensitive! It never occurred to me that
a young healthy man, Arnie's age, could have died. Katherine had
been trying to tell me it was so without actually using the word *dead*.

Euphemisms like "passed away," "in heaven," or "in a better
place," are used by the well-meaning to soften the edges of reality.
I didn't understand how painful it must have been for Katherine to
say, "He died" until I "lost" Arnie and could not bring him back, no
matter how fervently I wished it to be so.

I tried meditation, therapy, tarot cards, spiritualism, and a bog-
gling amount of wine and wishful thinking. I read books on how the
brain is modified when grieving—searching, searching for a way to
internalize the concept that Arnie was no longer here. To this day, I
wake some mornings, expecting him to be by my side. And it's not
unusual for me to wake in the middle of the night and walk the
apartment to see why he isn't.

Arnie's shirts, still in their plastic sleeves fresh from the cleaners, are hanging in our closet. His black leather dopp kit sits ready for travel under his side of the sink in what was once our shared bathroom. His bubbly Topo Chico still chills on the upper shelf of our refrigerator in line with his Welch's grape jelly, French's mustard, and Heinz ketchup. His favorite Hershey's bars are stacked on a shelf in the freezer. I have yet to internalize that none of these kept items will bring Arnie back.

This book is my attempt to make peace with the concept of his passing in some meaningful way by revisiting his multiple achievements, his creative mind, his acts of kindness, and the gentle and loving way he dealt with me and our daughter, Samantha, as he stood, arms around us, on our family journey through this world. In hospice, shortly before his death, Arnie said to me, "All I ever wanted to do was take care of you and Samantha."

To which, along with Winnie the Pooh, I say: "How lucky am I to have something so special, that makes saying goodbye so hard."

PART I

Long Fine Life

Venice, More Than a Few Years Ago

Venice appeared to me as a recurring dream, a place once visited and now fixed in memory like images on a photographer's plates so that my return was akin to turning the leaves of a portfolio.
—GARY INBINDER

Arnie and I had flown into Marco Polo Airport multiple times, but this time my memory portfolio was telling me it might be the last, at least together. Arnie, not well, was exhausted and anxious to get to our rental flat. To settle in. To rest from our long journey.

I felt myself switching to in-charge mode, trying to protect him from dealing with the arrival details of luggage, customs, transport—when I discovered that Delta Airlines had lost our luggage. Handling life's aggravations had always been Arnie's forte, but now that responsibility had shifted to me. I had slipped into the role during his illness. There was never a verbal handoff; it simply evolved.

Ultimately, we were forced to leave the Marco Polo airport minus our luggage but with the consolation prize of two Delta T-shirts, white, medium and large, and a few toiletries to hold us over until when—or if—our luggage showed up. They couldn't predict.

No matter: The minute we stepped onto the water taxi that the Venetians call a *motoscafo* (everything sounds better in Italian), we entered another world as we sped full throttle from the airport across the open lagoon toward the city. And for the first time since boarding the plane in Atlanta, Arnie started to relax.

The waterway was cordoned off on both sides by a line of wooden support posts, *bricole*, buried deep in the lagoon's seabed, outlining the watery highway leading to Venice—the Long Island Expressway but with waves. Seagulls, perched on top of each bricola like guards at Buckingham Palace, made sure we didn't run off course.

And there she was, *La Serenissima*, rising up before us in all her majestic Renaissance glory. Our captain, in his aviators, wearing a navy-and-white-striped Gucci polo, collar up to signify he was one cool dude, pulled back on his throttle and maneuvered us through a narrow canal, following its path as it wound its way between the ancient buildings, depositing us directly into the boat traffic on the Grand Canal. The wake created by all this action caused a spray of water that sparkled in the sunlight. It was refreshing and glorious; Arnie and I grinned at each other as it touched our faces.

Cutting across the stream of gondolas, vaporettos, and tugs loaded with the necessities that keep the city alive, the captain again pulled back on his throttle. Spinning his steering wheel, he left the Grand Canal and navigated his motoscafo into a smaller canal, a *rio*, finally depositing us on a brick-paved *fondementa* in a less-hectic, fewer-tourists area of the city where we had rented a small apartment in one of the palazzos. This was our first stay on this side of the Grand Canal, and we were looking forward to this new perspective of Venice—and maybe of our life along with it.

The next morning, while Arnie slept in, I walked on the fondementa around the corner from where we had disembarked to a bakery on my places-to-go-list to secure three chocolate-filled *cornetti* (Italy's answer to the croissant) for Arnie's breakfast, and three *tramezzini* for me.

Ahhhh, tramezzini. They're triangular sandwiches built on what my mom always called "junky white bread." You know, the squishy type that traps your fingerprints when you pick it up. Something to do with the high mayonnaise component in the fillings as they mixed with the pillowy bread they sit on. Fillings of prosciutto and mozzarella, tuna and egg, mini shrimp and mayonnaise, make them addictive little buggers.

On my way back to our palazzo, I write with a grin, I slowed my pace, realizing I was back in Venice—time to regroup, to take in a day that no chemo infusions, blood tests, or radiation could interrupt.

It was a true-blue-sky day, the water in the rio an emerald green. Its opacity provided a canvas for the shimmering reflections of the muted terra cotta, ochre, and peach stucco of the ancient buildings that had stood on both sides of the rio for centuries. The perfect place to stop and assuage the voices calling "eat me, eat me" from the bakery bag in my hand. *A tuna and egg, perhaps, Signora?*

As I lifted my treat out of the white, grease-spotted bag, a harsh screeching noise, accompanied by a furious, disorienting fluttering, swirled around my head. It took me a few seconds to grasp that a flock of seagulls had swooped down from the roof of one of those buildings across the rio. Beaks deployed; they were fighting over my head to see who would be the first to snatch the tramezzino from my hand. The winner, very large, very aggressive, and very loud, not only took my tramezzino, but a sizable chunk of the forefinger on my right hand along with it.

Seeing blood and thinking infection, I hurried back to the palazzo and woke Arnie for help. Having been a medic in the army, of which he often reminded me, he calmly suggested that a dab of Neosporin and a bandage should do it.

"But if that doesn't work," he said, "I spotted a pharmacy on the other bank of the rio when we arrived." And then he fell back to sleep.

No luggage.

Bitten by a seagull.

What next?

With a little Googling, I discovered these feathered bandits are not to be messed with. They're mean, smart, opportunistic little bastards—inbred with transgenerational knowledge informing them that hapless tourists are the bearers of good eats. Could these be the same birds who had spied on us as we sped across the lagoon? Had they followed us, reasoning that we were ripe for the picking? *Oh, come on!* Arnie's diagnosis had caused me to overthink everything.

Those of us of a certain age remember the more civilized seagulls written about in the 1970s by Richard Bach in his New Age book of inspiration, *Jonathan Livingston Seagull.* The book sold more than forty million copies, one to me. And I read it multiple times. Jonathan the Seagull discovered that "boredom and fear and anger are the reasons a gull's life is so short, and with these gone from his thoughts, Jonathan lived a long fine life indeed."

Mr. Google further revealed that seagulls have enjoyed spiritual symbolism in every culture reaching back to Egyptian times. Despite my tangle with the ravaging flock that morning, through the ages, gulls have been considered harbingers of good luck, of resiliency, of fearlessness, of perseverance. The only negative comment I found was Deuteronomy 14:15, which warned: "Ye shall not eat them because they are unclean." It said nothing about their not eating you.

This anointing by bird was not new to me. A pigeon had pooped on my head in London's Trafalgar Square in 1973, during the first European trip Arnie and I made. Pigeon poop was then considered good luck, or so we were told by the persistent hustler who had snapped a photo of that event. So, was it still good luck when that seagull stole my tramezzino? Or maybe it simply meant one less tramezzino.

It was imperative that I control my neuroses and enjoy every precious minute of this holiday—and concentrate on: *Long fine life. Long fine life. Long fine life.*

July 27, 1969
Bashert

Sitting on the desk in front of me is a rectangular brass box. Inside are Arnie's ashes. On top of the box, I've placed a pale-green, highly polished piece of marble engraved with one word: Remember.

July 27, 1969, is one of those days I could never forget for two significant reasons, Arnie being number one. His mustache and goatee were the first things I noticed, below which was a dark-gray suit, definitely not off the rack at the local Sears & Roebuck. It reminded me of a suit George Peppard would have worn in Truman Capote's movie *Breakfast at Tiffany's*, in which Audrey Hepburn (Holly Golightly) meets tall handsome George Peppard (Paul Varjak), and they fall into a never-to-be love.

Love of any kind was not on my agenda at the time.

The suit the intriguing man across the room was wearing was tailored within an inch of what I estimated to be his six-foot-plus frame—three-button jacket with double vents, trousers that ended with just the correct amount of break. (I never knew you should give pants a break before I met this man.)

To be truthful, I didn't grasp those details at first glance, but they came into full view soon enough.

The occasion was a birthday party, and I was there under duress. The host, the birthday boy, owned the housing provided for students attending the career school where I taught English, public speaking, and business etiquette. Is business etiquette—or any kind of etiquette, for that matter—taught anymore? If not, it should be. How to shake hands, don't show your bra straps at work, answer the phone with no gum in your mouth, look people in the eye when you speak with them—that now-passé stuff.

Our school, a career school for young women, was currently in negotiations with Birthday Boy over whether the quality of the living conditions he provided for our students were commensurate with the rental fees he was charging. They were not. I was there to rectify that situation by making nice. I can't remember if I did or did not make nice. Wrong person to send; negotiations are not my strong suit. I am not always logical and can easily be pushed over.

As the evening wore on, I periodically noticed the dark-haired man with the mustache-goatee glancing my way. It appeared he was in charge of the girl singer hired for the event. Actually, it appeared he was in charge of everything—he had that demeanor. He made me self-conscious, and I kept looking away.

It didn't elude me that he was the most intriguing man in the room. However, I was too physically and, most definitely, too emotionally exhausted to follow through with that thought because of the second significant reason to remember July 27, 1969.

A scant few hours before, I had been in Lansing, Michigan's divorce court, standing before a judge, dissolving my nine-year marriage—a sad mutual choice. I remember having to make up some cockamamy reason for the divorce. Husband and I had drifted apart? Unreconciled differences? Infidelity? Infertility? Ah, that may have been it. The emotional ache of infertility.

I wasn't happy to be at this party. Perspiration was dripping down my back, and I felt chilled at the same time. My dress was drooping on top because my boobs were not as big as my sister's, whose dress I had borrowed at the last minute. It was not a dress I would ever have purchased, because it had lace outlining the neckline and down the front to the hem. To me lace belongs on brides, not divorcées. Bad choice all around.

Underneath the droop, my chest felt tight from the smoke in the air—or more likely from the razor-sharp emotional severance I had agreed to a few hours before. All I wanted to do was get out of this smoky crowd and into my apartment and my bed. I was in the middle of an existential breakdown over how I would manage the rest of my life. For the first time in my twenty-nine years, I was entirely on my own and scared out of my ever-lovin' mind.

School business attended to, I was maneuvering through the smoky crowd for an early getaway when the dark-haired man in the gray suit, with the facial hair and a break in his trousers, literally materialized, poof, in my path. Maybe he came out of the smoke from his cigarette that was circling up from his left hand as he surreptitiously palmed it low by his side.

His demeanor was calm, not pushy or intimidating. However, his eyes had an unreadable intensity, and he bent his six-foot-plus frame so those eyes looked directly into mine.

"Hi. I'm Arnie Geller."

Thinking back, I realize we never shook hands. That was OK, as my palms were a sweaty mess along with my back.

To appear calm, I concentrated on his mustache and goatee, thinking it must be difficult to blow his nose. I felt as if I were little Red Riding Hood meeting the big, bad wolf. He unsettled me—bending over that way—but intrigued me as well.

Also on my desktop is a framed photo of that exact moment Arnie Geller came into my life. He had hired a photographer to snap publicity shots of the singer that evening, and the photographer managed to snap our first encounter as well. It is a black-and-white profile shot, taken from a distance. How young we were that night, eyes wide open, bodies slim, jawlines taut, and Arnie with that ubiquitous cigarette in his left hand. I look naive and surprised. He looks—well—sophisticated and in control. Oh, and I still had cheekbones at the time, which appear to be also shining with perspiration.

Seems to me that photo might have been a sneaky move Arnie had arranged before walking over to me. Planned or not, it's a treasure to have that shot now, taken so many years ago at the exact moment we met. How it came about, I never thought to ask him. Over the years since then, there are multiple things I never thought to ask him; they simply happened.

The exact words of our first conversation have vanished, filed somewhere in the section of my brain that never remembers if I paid my property taxes.

What I do remember clearly is acquiescing when he asked for my phone number. With only the slightest hesitation, I gave it to him. Sixty seconds before, I would have sworn giving my phone number to any man, no matter how intriguing, was the absolute last thing on earth I wanted to do. What nutcase divorces one man in the afternoon and gives her phone number to another in the evening? An irrational one, Your Honor! My immediate need for home, sleep, and wallowing in my predicament didn't seem quite as tragic or imperative. Arnie Geller slammed into my life like a ten-ton Mack truck, and I never saw him coming.

Later I would learn the Yiddish word for our meeting was *bashert*: an unavoidable situation, our destiny, a meant to be, a preordained encounter you can't escape.

A Fifty-Year Phone Call

The next day, as I entered my apartment after work, my landline was ringing. I knew it was Arnie Geller. I had given him my phone number, after all, but how had he figured out when I would be home to answer? I guess that was one of those things that simply happened—Arnie always had ways of getting what he wanted.

Those phone calls soon became a nightly event.

Night after night, we revealed more and more intimate information about our backgrounds and situations. He was temporarily in Lansing to jumpstart his life after his treasured project had fallen through. I, a permanent resident, had ended my not-so-permanent marriage and didn't know how to jumpstart anything. Arnie and I were in the same uncertain emotional space, both at loose ends, both searching for a direction.

Arnie had apparently done this phone courting business before. With his comforting voice and persuasive technique, he was a grand master of the telephone. In his soft tone, which one of his female associates later described to me as being smooth as Tupelo honey, he kept the conversation going and asked just the right questions at just the right time. It was a technique that continued for his entire life: The phone his device of choice to pursue and to persuade in both personal relationships and business.

Those calls were the start of a lifelong telephone conversation. We talked every day for fifty years no matter where we were in the world or even when both of us were home on opposite sides of our apartment. It would mostly be Arnie calling me. His call may have been as simple as, "Honey, would you please come here, I want to show you something I'm working on." Or "I'm leaving the office now.

I'll pick you up in front. Chinese or pizza?" or "I'm at the airport in [wherever], will call you when I land in New York."

Oh, how I wish I had access to all the years of calls so I can hear over and over: "Hi, honey" or "Judy, are you there?"

When we progressed to a face-to-face date, Arnie picked me up in an impressive dark blue Jaguar convertible XKE, a low-slung, sexy personification of a man on the move or making moves, both of which were true. Jaguars had always been his vehicle of choice. He told me that throughout his teen years he kept a magazine clipping of a red two-seater under the glass on his desktop. During our married life he had at least four. One was a British racing green XJS with a hole in the exhaust pipe—the fumes nearly wiped us out the first time we rode in it. If we had been wiped out, I guess I wouldn't be writing this chronicle and would have missed one helluva life.

Strangely enough, Arnie's last car was not a Jag. It was a vintage, low-slung red Mercedes convertible SL500 with a cushy leather caramel interior and a matching caramel-colored convertible top. Purchased when he was in his early seventies, the car was the worse for wear, but he adored and babied it.

I believe he secretly enjoyed the attention it brought him as he drove his silver-haired-self around town, as much as he enjoyed recounting the story of being approached by an aggressive shall we say "lady of the parking lot" outside a Publix supermarket, asking him if he would give her a ride home. Yeah, right. I'm sure he didn't take the bait, but I'm also sure he rolled down the window to kibitz with her for a while. Arnie loved women. He hired them, championed their endeavors, challenged and protected them. Me included.

Back in 1969, I didn't know any of this, as I was enamored more by his persona and, let's say, sophistication, rather than his automobile choice. My family drove safe middle class (used) cars. My first car was cobbled together by my grandfather Hon from junkyard parts. It, too, was a convertible, blue, with doors that didn't lock properly.

One day when I was showing off by slightly speeding around a ring road called the Oval at Lake Michigan, the passenger door flew open, and my then twelve-year-old sister, Korkye, flew out of the passenger seat, coming to a bruising stop on the tarmac. Thank God she was OK and never told our parents or I would have been grounded for a year.

When I told Arnie that story, he fessed up that his cars had not always been so terrific either. The one he drove while in college only went backward. That must have been memorable and nauseating for his dates.

And then there was Arnie's cigarette case. Save for the 1940s shiny-floor movies I had seen with my mom during World War II, Arnie was the first man I had ever encountered who carried his cigarettes (Pall Malls were Arnie's choice) in a black, silver-trimmed, leather case that made a dramatic snapping noise when it closed. That cigarette case, along with his cellphone and the night-we-met photo, sit with his ashes in front of me now. I touch them every day for comfort and strength. Sometimes, I'm sure I feel Arnie's energy reaching out to me.

Mr. Geller, as I occasionally called him in later years as we worked together in office settings, was back then a man who wore tailored suits and carried his bills in a silver clip in his front right pocket. Not a common style in small-town Michigan. Men there usually stuffed their bills into a bulky wallet, which they wedged into a rear pants pocket, thus creating a bulge on their backsides. Call me shallow—you would be correct. Blame it on my being absolutely gobsmacked by this man.

At the beginning of the relationship, I was working full-time at that career school, acting, making commercials, and directing children's plays at the local community playhouse. Arnie would come by the rehearsals—I think I was directing *The Wizard of Oz* at that time—and after, we would go to dinner. We would drive around

Lansing in Arnie's Jaguar, stopping to continue our conversation over steak at the New Hut Steak House on Michigan Avenue, or cheeseburgers in the car from a fledgling fast-food chain named McDonald's on Larch Street. It was one of the first McDonald's in the country. When Arnie moved to Lansing in the late 1960s, no doubt he was instrumental in keeping that franchise up and running.

His order was always the same: one hamburger, cheese only, French fries hot from the fryer. Don't forget the Heinz ketchup. And a large Coca-Cola. Sometimes I would have the same, enticed by the greasy good smell. Consequently, my diet as well as my life quickly took an entirely different turn.

In my first marriage, eating out was not the norm. I had always cooked, experimenting with different recipes for the fun of it and often calling my Italian grandmother for help with my red sauce. I enjoyed experimenting in the kitchen, and one fall I hosted a party for the Michigan State University football coaches and all the players. (My ex worked for the university.) I served huge trays of paella, which I had never made before. Michigan State played the next game, so obviously it didn't kill them. Poisoning a football team would have been a more dramatic excuse for our divorce.

A few weeks after we met, Arnie suggested that he would buy steaks and cook for us at his apartment. It was not hard to know what else was on his menu. I was nervous and tentative at first. Was I ready for this, whatever it was? You would never call me worldly. My life experience with men had been limited. I was brought up in the 1950s: no sex before marriage, a minor amount of dating, early marriage before I graduated from college. Seeing my mistake with that last choice, I rectified it quickly by taking courses at multiple universities as my then-husband and I moved from city to city. A long way around the barn.

(At one point I took classes at a small midwestern college where I was taught by a Franciscan friar in full regalia: brown woolen habit, corded belt, hood, and sandals, who suggested I become a cartographer. But I persevered.)

Arnie, trying to sort himself out after high school, enlisted in the Army. When he was discharged, he put himself through college, graduating with a degree in business and advertising. He went to work for J. Walter Thompson in Detroit in their sales promotion and merchandising group. His focus was Ford Motors and his territory was the Eastern Seaboard. It was his first exposure to New York City and the Palm Restaurant. He was at JWT for their hundred-year anniversary and, no matter where he worked after that, he kept the oval bronze paperweight on his desk, minted in commemoration of that event.

He had every intention of remaining with the firm, but his entrepreneurial self and love of music pulled him away. He preferred working alone over being a corporate creature, no matter how well he did as the latter.

Seeing his apartment for the first time, it was hard to tell if he had recently moved in or was moving out. In his living room was a dark green couch and a bamboo bar with no glasses or bottles of anything. Why he had it, I don't know. He was not a drinker. Maybe he thought the bar was a bachelor thing to own. He had no coffee table and no lamps; the only light in the room was coming from the ceiling light in the open kitchen. At first it didn't make sense to me—he drove a Jag, but couldn't afford furniture? Soon I would understand. Arnie's surroundings weren't a priority for him; his focus was on work—preferably in an office, with a desk, a yellow legal pad, and a telephone.

That night the steaks were delicious; he had prepared each to the right temperature—mine medium well and, of course, he was a rare man. Along with the steaks, he made fried potatoes as good as my grandmother's and even bought lettuce and a salad dressing for me. As the night progressed, I became aware of how comfortable and easy it was to be in his company and decided whatever followed our steaks would be OK with me. Let's just say, dessert was absolutely delicious.

Food was always a dominant element in Arnie's and my marriage; reconciling our different palates and upbringing by eating out—a lot—in restaurants that provided each of us a variety of selections—mine preferably with something from the green section of the menu. Arnie had a sweet tooth and we often ended our evenings with Big Boy's cherry pie generously covered with their no-doubt fake whipped cream: "More please, and thank you very much, ma'am." And I mustn't forget the fresh-baked donuts from Bill Knapp's Restaurant, where we went on Sunday mornings. Arnie would go in alone to purchase two glazed for him, one plain for me. I stayed in the car, not wanting to be seen by my small-town neighbors as the recently divorced hussy already out on the town with a tall dude they didn't recognize.

Arnie and I spent untold hours riding in his car, comfortably talking and listening to music from two different points of view. His preference was rock 'n' roll and mine was old school—well, old school now—Nat King Cole, Frank Sinatra, and many a Rogers and Hammerstein score in the mix. Broadway show tunes were my guiding light.

My exposure to pop music was at the Fruitport Pavilion, a popular outdoor venue in southwestern Michigan owned by my best friend's father. She was a Judy also. We Judys would stand in the first row, in our highly starched crinolines and bobby socks, screaming along with crowds that came by the hundreds on those warm summer nights.

It was a well-known stop on the summer circuit and attracted the top artists—from Lawrence Welk and Louis Armstrong to Buddy Holly and the Crickets, who played there only a short four months before Buddy died in a plane crash with the Big Bopper and Ritchie Valens. Why do I even know that? Because Arnie reminded me of their history during one of our rock 'n' roll discussions.

Arnie loved rock 'n' roll. So, I burnished my credentials with him by boasting I had been kissed by one of the Beach Boys backstage at the Pavilion. I don't know which Beach Boy, can't remember. He was blond—though weren't they all blond?

That was about as close to pop music I got until Arnie introduced me to the business and the artists it created—including Little Richard, who promptly gave me an extraordinarily sweaty kiss on the cheek after a concert. What is it with these music people? Gotta love 'em!

Swing Lively

While I married and dreamed of being on the Broadway stage, Arnie had been listening and dreaming of pulling the strings behind the curtain in the business side of music. But it took him a while to get there.

Times were tough and money was tight for Arnie after he left the army, so he stayed in Detroit with his Grandma Lena until he could afford his own apartment. Periodically, his older cousin, Nat Tarnopol, would stay with Grandma Lena when he swung through town and the two became close. (Nat's mother was Grandma Lena's sister, so Arnie's Grandma Lena was Aunt Lena to Nat.)

In the '50s, '60s, and into the '70s, Nat was a force in the music world of soul and R&B. He managed Jackie Wilson, Brunswick Record's lead talent, whose first eleven singles made the top ten charts between 1959 and 1963. And in 1970, Nat became president of Brunswick Records, leading the label to become a serious Motown rival.

It was Nat who, during the Grandma Lena years, introduced Arnie to the Detroit music scene and the seduction of the record business. Rock 'n' roll was new and enticing. Teens on both sides of the Detroit River—all over the country for that matter—were listening to hits by the greats: Little Richard, Chuck Berry, Aretha Franklin, Marvin Gaye, the Temptations, and, of course, Jackie Wilson. It wasn't surprising that Arnie would become involved in the music business. And it happened in 1967, when Detroit was the music place to be. The automobile industry was pushing the economy, Motown was the center of all things musical, and the 20 Grand club was the place where the top music stars of the era played their gigs.

One night at the 20 Grand, Arnie heard an R&B singer named

Spyder Turner sing the soul song "Stand By Me," written by B.B. King, Jerry Leiber, and Mike Stoller. Spyder's take was to imitate other singers as he sang the lyrics: Smokey Robinson, Chuck Johnson, and B.B. King himself were mimicked. Not only was that a refreshing take on the song, but Spyder was so right on with his imitations that Arnie immediately recognized a hit.

He negotiated a record deal for Spyder with MGM Records in New York, and in 1967, two years before we met at the birthday party, "Stand By Me" sold 10,000 copies in the first week of its release, received a gold record, made the top fifty singles lists on both Cash Box and Billboard charts, and Arnie was recognized as one of *Billboard*'s Notable Independent Record Producers. I learned this particular detail while doing research for this memoir. Never one to brag about his achievements, Arnie had only told me bits and pieces of that era in his life.

Having come off that huge success, Arnie was also working on another project, scouting the state of Michigan for a central location to open a non-alcohol nightclub for the eighteen and under crowd. The demographics told him Lansing, a college town, was the place and in 1968, he and a partner opened a nightclub named The Incline, mainly because the club was in an old warehouse and the floor actually had an incline.

As entertainment, Arnie booked up-and-coming young bands to play live, while teens danced along with white-booted go-go dancers on a stage. He parlayed that into a dance show called *Swing Lively* on WJIM, a local Lansing TV station. Occasionally, I would appear on that channel with a fashion show or a makeup segment, but for some reason we never met.

Arnie was fixated on a larger market than Lansing. He wanted to produce *The Tom Shannon Show* on CKLW TV, an internationally known top forty station in Windsor, Canada. Tom Shannon was one of the top DJs in the country, and his television show was a mix of teenagers dancing to the latest hits, interspersed by interviews with top recording stars in the nation. Arnie finally got his wish approximately a year before we met.

During our first drive-arounds, Arnie displayed unabashed joy as he told me stories of his seven-days-a-week trip over the Ambassador Bridge from Detroit to Windsor to decide the show's lineup, book the talent, pre-interview the guests, and ready the show for broadcast. In Detroit, being the home of Motown Records, talents seeking exposure were always available, and the show attracted names such as Smokey Robinson and the Miracles, Marvin Gaye, Four Tops—and who can forget Aretha Franklin, who was at the beginning of becoming her fabulous self.

It was Arnie's dream job, one he was undeniably suited for with his calm demeanor, advertising skills, and ear for musical hits.

All that came to an end quite abruptly when the Canadian government, headed by the newly elected Prime Minister Pierre Trudeau (Justin's father) and his cohorts, in a shortsighted surge of nationalism, at least from Arnie's point of view, passed a law that Canadian television and radio content had to be at least 80 percent home-grown. Arnie's show on CKLW was not. It was all American R&B and pop. Consequently, it was canceled, and Arnie's days of crossing the Detroit River two times a day in his dark-blue Jaguar came to an abrupt end. Frankly, he was devastated.

Meanwhile, I was living the married life, had moved four times, finally ending up in Lansing, working at the career school and on my own theatrical obsession by auditioning for everything that came down the pike. I was serious about acting as a profession. I made national commercials and acted in plays: *Take Her, She's Mine*, and *Tea House of the August Moon*, to name a few. I played the part of Millie Owens in *Picnic* with Burt Reynolds in summer stock. This part earned me entry into Actors' Equity, upping my hopes for a professional career.

(Hey, Barbra . . . Ms. Streisand . . . darling, call me, we should talk. I know when you were my age, you also played Millie Owens in *Picnic* and a child in *Teahouse of the August Moon*. In that production I played the lead female character, Mariko. We can compare notes.)

Back then my dream was to live in New York with Barbra—someday becoming one of the lights on Broadway.

Enter Arnie stage right.

His television show had been pulled off the air, and I had ceased to have either a husband or the get-up-and-go to become anything. All my theatrical lights had gone out. When we met, both Arnie and I were living inside disrupted dreams—two stumbling souls in emotional upheaval, in the same small city, operating in concentric circles, yet we had never met. Not until the day of my divorce, July 27, 1969.

As the title of a song our friend Marty Cooper wrote in 1976 says, "A Little Bit Country, a Little Bit Rock 'n' roll." Guess who sings the country part?

Arnie and I were an unlikely pair, but apparently bashert knew something we didn't.

Chuck Berry

From that first ride, cocooned in the warmth of Arnie's delicious car, it all seemed so right. I had been married for nine years to a very sociable, talented, witty guy, but had never felt such an instant emotional and physical connection to anyone as I did from the very second my eyes met Arnie's and he swept me into his world.

One of our early dates was a concert he produced with Chuck Berry as the headliner. Chuck was the granddaddy of rock 'n' roll and one of the first ten to be voted into the Rock & Roll Hall of Fame in 1986. Back then, getting Berry to do a concert in a small venue in Lansing, Michigan, was a coup. Arnie pulled it off, but not without drama.

He masterminded the whole event. Cold-called Chuck, who agreed to the gig—perhaps lured by Arnie's mentioning his success with Spyder—borrowed the money to pay Chuck, booked the venue, and organized the pickup band. Being an ad man, Arnie's pre-show planning was so successful that he had a sellout crowd of two thousand exuberant MSU students.

That was the first time I experienced Arnie in action. The night of the event, he patiently stood on the steps of the venue, occasionally glancing at me waiting at the entrance, or taking a furtive glance at his watch as he waited for Chuck to show up. Arnie didn't seem to be overly anxious except for his occasional pacing back and forth and his tentative grin as he glanced my way.

But I was anxious enough for him. Five minutes, three minutes, one minute before curtain time, with the crowd inside the venue yelling "Chuck, Chuck," and when Chuck should have been in the wings ready to take the stage, Arnie still remained unruffled.

Chuck finally pulled up at the very last second in a beat-up white clunker, rolled down his window, and called out, "Ernie! Ernie, I'm here!"

Arnie hustled him around the venue to backstage where he had a quick discussion with the band about the set list. And with that settled, Chuck stuck his hand out to receive his money in cash, jammed it in his pocket, picked up his guitar, and went on to bring the house down! Arnie had his first big success in concert production. But not exactly. I only heard the real story years later and recorded it.

On the tape, Arnie chuckles as he tells our daughter, Samantha, and me the end of the story: "Yes, it was a success and yes, I pulled it off by myself. But in the final settlement, the venue, the band, and Chuck all got paid; however, I had forgotten to carve out money for myself. And I was known as a numbers guy. Go figure."

After that concert, Arnie and I had dinner with his cousin Nicki, during which Arnie never let on about his loss or show any distress. That was before I knew him well and at least ten years before Dry Idea antiperspirant and their commercial, "Never let them see you sweat!" Arnie was that guy. He hadn't made a dime that night, but rather than dwell on it, he took it as a learning experience, a cautionary tale. And he moved on.

"Hey, I was young and new at the game." He winked at Samantha and me and said, "But you can bet it never happened again."

Four Months

It wasn't too long into our dating that Arnie began spending more time at my apartment than at his own. I must admit, I was disconcerted when I came home after work one day to find him sitting in the same chair, at the same small table where I had left him that morning—cigarette in his hand, Coca Cola within reach, working on a partially finished puzzle I had arranged on a side table with no intentions of ever finishing. To me it was purely decorative.

Seeing me, Arnie looked up and said, "I had to finish this before I left, but it took longer than I thought it would. Sorry."

Something I would never have had the patience to do. But Arnie did. He was not only calm and kind, but tenacious. Having come from a line of essentially nine-to-five men and never having met someone who had latitude to take a day off work to finish a puzzle, I had some adjusting to do if I were to continue in this relationship. It was apparent that dating Arnie was not going to be a normal, everyday experience.

One of the other first things Arnie did when we began dating was to buy four new tires for my old Chevy Malibu, declaring mine unsafe. And soon thereafter, when he found out I had gone to the doctor by myself for a minor surgery, he was disturbed that I hadn't asked him to go with me. I found both gestures unbelievably generous—above and beyond thoughtful. I would soon learn that was just who he was.

It didn't take me long to understand that wherever Arnie was, or what he was doing, such as buying me tires, his brain never rested. He was always considering his opportunities, most in his element sitting behind a desk, phone nearby, covering a yellow legal pad with columns of numbers, then sentences and ideas, which would eventually become projects—an entrepreneurial, driven, gentle man with a phone addiction. His tenacity and attention to detail were traits that held him in good stead throughout his life. From our first date, he seemed larger than life to me, but often indecipherable.

During the early days of our courtship, his working project was a TV pilot about Otis Redding, the soul singer–songwriter who had died tragically in a 1967 plane crash at age twenty-six. The soundtrack of our courtship was Otis Redding's soulful voice coming from the Jag's speakers, singing "Try a Little Tenderness" and "Love Man." Can you tell why I was gobsmacked?

Four months, *four months*, into our relationship, Arnie asked me to marry him. Talk about indecipherable—I never saw it coming. Divorced and still adjusting to that single life, forget being gob-smacked, I was speechless. The concept of marrying again—so soon after my divorce—had never entered my mind. I had yet to determine who I was and how to go about finding out. But as easily as I had given him my phone number that first night at the birthday-business event, I inhaled and, on the exhale, said, "Yes," with a disclaimer.

There was one thing Arnie had yet to learn about me, and it had the potential to put an end to our perfectly beautiful relationship. If he wanted a family—a few tiny, high-strung, theatrical beings with an ear for music—I could not be the vehicle to take him there, as I was unable to conceive.

The 1950s idea of the perfect nuclear family, man+woman+at least one child, was still the norm in the 1960s, pushed along by the concept that women, still considered second-class citizens, generally did not work outside the home. Back then women couldn't open a bank account or get a credit card without their husband being a cosignatory. I was one of them.

I wasn't an all-out feminist, even if we were in the women's lib era and my role models were its leaders, Gloria Steinem and "Battling Bella" Abzug. Bella was an attorney and a woman's advocate quoted as saying, "I began wearing hats as a young lawyer because it helped me to establish my professional identity. Before that, whenever I was at a meeting, someone would ask me to get coffee."

So, I wore hats too. Especially when, on behalf of my school, I was speaking to young women around the state of Michigan, espousing my beliefs on femininity and explaining a new federally funded program designed to prepare underprivileged women to enter and conquer the workforce. I enjoyed my work, but was on the fence, not knowing what I would become if there were ever children involved.

Arnie had to know I couldn't have children and, even if that were possible, I could not fathom staying at home with them after years of working. I wanted to be the lone signatory on my credit cards with my own money in my own bank account. It was imperative that I knew Arnie's position on a potentially childless marriage.

Having, in my previous life, endured the anxieties and indignities inherent in the struggle to conceive, a gut-wrenching experience for both me and my then-husband, I did not want Arnie to endure the same emotional and physical pain that comes with the curse of infertility, especially since the blame lay in my reproductive house. IVF, donor sperm, and artificial insemination were not yet the talk of the town unless it was on a farm among sheep breeders.

After all, ours would be a mixed marriage to begin with—Arnie was Jewish, I was not—and all the problems that might arise from our different backgrounds, during that more conservative era, could only be exacerbated by my physical inadequacies. I was the biblical Sarah in Genesis who could not bring forth a son for her husband Abraham, so she asked Hagar, her Egyptian maid, to do the deed for her and "sleep" with Abraham on her behalf to bear him that son he so wanted.

By the way, Hagar didn't have much to lose for doing so, except her low-paying housemaid's job in the Abraham-Sarah tent. God had already promised that son to Abraham. Wow, it just dawned on me that God could promise a son to Abraham, but he couldn't make Sarah fertile, or me for that matter. *Oh my god, God! You are a misogynist! . . . Let it go, Judy, let it go.*

Since I am not the type to share my husband or the food on my plate with anyone—Don't you just hate that? People poking at your food with their fork? Without asking?—I had to be sure that Arnie understood the whole situation. My infertility may well have been one of the reasons for the divorce from my ex-husband, and I could not, would not, take the chance of pushing the burden of infertility across the barren landscape of another marriage. It was not easy to say and, presumably, not particularly uplifting news for Arnie to hear, having just asked someone to marry him.

He sat in front of me, calmly holding my hands, listening to me rattling on about my situation, asking him questions about how he felt about that issue, how his family would take it, how they would respond to my not being Jewish and having been married before.

Arnie was quiet; he never flinched or asked questions, just took me in his arms, then said, "Don't worry about all that. We'll work it out."

Remaining steadfast in his proposal, we set the wedding date for the next May. May 24, 1970, to be exact—301 days, 7,224 hours, after my divorce. It all seemed so right, except I continued to worry about our very different backgrounds.

Room Service and Rationing Cards

Our one commonality was we were both born in 1940, at the beginning of WWII. I entered the stage in January and Arnie followed in October. Later he would tell everyone he had married an older woman.

Arnie's nuclear family was intact. They were the Gellers—a mother and father and an older sister, a clean throughline back to his ancestors on both sides, all having emigrated from Eastern Europe. All raised with the dictates and customs of Judaism and all with the same physical characteristics: tall, fair-skinned, dark-haired, commanding postures. If you observed them walking toward you on a Detroit sidewalk (people walked back then), you would recognize them as members of the same family. When Arnie spit into an Ancestry.com test tube, out came a total Ashkenazi, a descendent of Jews who had lived in Central and Eastern Europe from at least the eleventh century.

Arnie's grandfather on his mother's side, Nathan Agree, had immigrated with his brother, Charles, from Petropavlovsk district, Southern Ukraine, near the Russian border, disembarking on January 2, 1904, in Philadelphia. On his immigration papers, Nathan listed plumber as his occupation, Russia as his country of origin, and his birthdate as January 1, 1891, or 1892 depending on the source.

Grandma Lena, Arnie's adored maternal grandmother, had also emigrated from Vilnius, Lithuania, with her family in 1904 at the age of nine. It was a time of great migration when more than 1.5 million Eastern European Ashkenazi Jews fled to the United States, away from fear and toward freedom for them and their future offspring.

Nathan Agree married Lena Chemovitz in 1911 and they had five children, Flossie Geller, Arnie's mother, being the eldest.

Arnie and I had a more personal look into Grandma Lena's background when we went to Vilnius on business early in our marriage. We flew in from Dublin in a small plane through a blinding snowstorm on a death-defying flight. We landed on a precarious runway lined on both sides with towering banks of snow, into a cold that literally and figuratively took our breath away.

It surprised me that the first thing Arnie wanted to do was visit Vilnius's old quarter, a UNESCO World Heritage Site. Not one for breath-stealing cold or heritage sites, he was determined we walk the streets where his grandmother had walked before she and her family immigrated to the United States.

Bundled up in our Nanook of the North weather gear, we braved the elements to walk Pylimo Street, the main street in the old quarter. Vilnius had been a center of Jewish culture and learning since the 1500s, with more than 100 synagogues to serve the population's needs. In 1941, the Nazis put an end to that by burning, looting, and destroying most of the synagogues in town. Remarkably, the main area of Vilnius had been turned into a ghetto by the Nazis, allowing it to remain intact.

On Pylimo we found a synagogue, which according to the plaque on the façade, had been built in 1903, a year before Lena and her family left. The plaque also informed us that in this synagogue we might be able to view the records of families who had lived in Vilnius around that time. Sadly, the archives were only open by appointment, which we didn't have.

However, being in Vilnius's old town, walking up and down the hilly, snow-slippery streets, its yellow and red gothic medieval buildings emerging out of the snow as if from history, was sufficient. We had slipped into another era, before pogroms and war and death had arrived, and when everyone knew each other as they went in and out of the small shops during their daily errands. *Hello, Mrs. Chemovitz. It's nice to see you. How's Lena?*

Down the hill from the synagogue, we stopped for tea at a small corner café in one of the old narrow buildings that lined our route. The tea was served not in a cup, but in a small clear glass encased in a filigreed Russian holder with a demitasse spoon holding a sugar cube balancing on its rim. Arnie told me that was how Grandma Lena aways drank her tea, holding the sugar cube between her teeth, absorbing its sweetness as the tea passed her lips.

We did the same as we toasted Grandma Lena and all our ancestors from not only Lithuania, but also from Russia, Hungry, Italy, Denmark, and Holland as well, all brave enough to leave their homeland to forge a better life for themselves and thus, their decedents.

Later that day, we fought the blizzard and again; slipping from the old world into the new, we climbed through the snowbanks to have a cheeseburger at McDonald's across from our hotel. The young Lithuanians behind the counter were charming, and the one on the grill made that hamburger exactly as Arnie had ordered—cheese only, with French fries hot from the fryer. He swore it was the best McDonald's cheeseburger he'd ever eaten.

• • •

Arnie most definitely got his entrepreneurial tendencies and aspirations from his grandfather Nathan, who had worked his way from Philadelphia to Detroit, progressing over thirty years from plumber to real estate investor, builder, and hotelier. In the 1930s, Grandaddy Nathan owned the New Yorker Hotel, which still stands at 481 Eighth Avenue, all renovated and now a Wyndham property. In later years, when Arnie and I lived on and off in New York, every time we walked or drove by the hotel, Arnie would proudly point it out in admiration.

Nathan also owned the Detroiter Hotel in, of course, Detroit. During the 1940s, when World War II raged globally, and all the men in the family, including Arnie's father, were away at war, Nathan had gathered his grown daughters and their children, Arnie and his mother and sister included, into the Detroiter so they would have the comfort of family as the war raged on.

The Detroiter was famous for the movie stars who frequently stayed there as they toured the country selling war bonds. Arnie, who had an amazing memory, told stories of meeting the movie stars and hearing the Andrew Sisters sing "Boogie Woogie Bugle Boy of Company B" on one of their visits. And he would sing it to you if you asked.

Only a toddler at the time (I believe he was three), Arnie was sent to a sleepaway camp for fresh air, I presume. This was a concept unfathomable to cosseted me. Who separates you from your mother at that early age? I always wondered if the stress of that experience had laid the foundation for Arnie's quiet composure and strength of will. His mother told me that, even as a three-year-old in camp, he refused to eat anything green when the counselors tried to force it on him.

I learned quickly that Arnie had mastered the technique of slow rolling you until you gave up or he could finesse you in another direction: his direction. And another thing I learned about him is he rarely, if ever, raised his voice. In fact, one time when I introduced him to a friend of my sister's, a psychologist, she remarked as Arnie walked away, "I bet that man never has to raise his voice." He projected that aura of quiet authority.

When I spit into my Ancestry.com test tube, out came a slurry of genes with no relationship to Arnie's whatsoever. My DNA was more peripatetic, perhaps foreshadowing my visceral need to travel. Could that be right? My genes began their journey in Southern Italy (my grandmother) to Northern Europe (my Dutch father and Danish grandfather) where they finally collided when my grandfather married my grandmother. Eventually leading to me—a Scandinavian type with reddish-blonde hair, green eyes, and, so I have been told, the intense personality of a Sicilian Mafia boss.

My grandfather Thorwald Nielsen, whom I called Hon, mimicking my grandmother Nanny, sailed the Great Lakes with his father, a Danish immigrant. They were itinerant carpenters working for the US government, building housing and schools for the Indian tribes that ringed the Great Lakes. During one of their port stops in Muskegon Harbor, Hon, a young dandy wandering the streets looking for something to do, caught a glimpse of my grandmother through a window, working behind the counter in her father's Italian alimentari shop.

She was a tiny little Italian stunner with olive skin and deep-set, dark-brown Sophia Loren eyes staring at you from under strong dramatic eyebrows. She was Armenia Agnes Vento, born in 1896, the second of seven Vento children—all first-generation Americans born to Italian immigrant parents.

Hon's version of meeting Nanny was biblical. He swore, cross his heart and hope to die, that he had rescued her from a burning basement and felt an obligation to take care of her forever and ever, amen. And he never wavered from that story.

I call BS to that! He simply adored her at first sight. Well into his eighties, he would sneak up behind her to nuzzle her neck and steal a kiss. With a coquettish smile, she would push him away, whispering under her breath, "Go away, you old fart." Theirs was a sixty-five-year love affair until Nanny passed away, and Hon slipped into what I know in my heart was love-lost dementia. Growing up, my sisters and I longed to find such love.

My WWII years were so very different from Arnie's. My birth father, George Brouwer, had died of pneumonia at twenty-one, just before the war broke out, leaving my mom a widow with an eighteen-month-old daughter to care for. She was young, grieving, scared, and with only a small stipend from the government to live on. So, just as Arnie's grandfather had brought Arnie and his mother into the

Detroiter Hotel for the duration of the war, Hon and Nanny brought my mom and me into their home, where we stayed for over six years.

Hon was a manager at Campbell, Wyant and Cannon, a gray iron foundry producing camshafts for the military. We had rationing cards, and, to augment what we could not buy with the cards, Hon grew sweet corn, potatoes, tomatoes, strawberries, anything he could, in a victory garden on the empty lot next to our house. I always kidded Arnie that he grew up with room service, and I grew up with rationing cards.

But Arnie and I did have one thing in common besides being WWII babies: We were both introduced to "show business" early on. Arnie to the stars and their music at the Detroiter Hotel; me at the movies playing at the Michigan Theater on Western Avenue in downtown Muskegon. My mom took me there as a diversion from her responsibility of being a single parent, the loss of her husband, the world's collective tragedy, and her fear for the fighting men in her family now scattered around the globe.

My great-aunt Lillian played the organ at that theater, and I was mesmerized when she rose from the orchestra pit, playing her Wurlitzer as the red velvet curtains parted, and the wizard in the projection booth focused his magic beam on the silver screen. Technicolor shiny-floor musicals were my mom's favorite and mine to this day, especially the ones where Fred Astaire whirls Ginger Rogers, marabou flying, across a glossy floor. It was magical—so dramatic, so exciting. The family always said that I was theatrical like Great Aunt Lil. I never played the organ, but I was told that I climbed into her casket during her wake because I wanted to take a nap. Theatrical enough for you?

Hon was the first man in my life, and I measured those who followed by his example of loving and caring. "And doting on you," mom always said.

When I met Arnie, I felt as if I had found my "Hon." Both made me feel safe, secure, and cared for, and both did that in a quiet unassuming way. As with Hon, I felt confident Arnie would also rescue me from a burning building if he had to, God forbid!

Hon was a master of tall tales. His cross-my-heart-and-hope-to-die story was he was Jewish, born in Alsace-Lorraine, that small area between France and Germany that switched back and forth between those two countries with every European territorial war. To put a stamp of authority on the story, Hon and Nanny named my mom Lorraine when she was born. I guess that's better than naming her Alsace.

Jews in the diaspora from the Levant had indeed been passing through the Alsace-Lorraine area since before Roman times. And it is remotely plausible that one of Hon's distant ancestors—on his or her way across the European continent from the Middle East—could have been a breakout Israelite momentarily stopping in Alsace or Lorraine for a rest and a little hanky-panky, which multiple generations later produced my grandfather, my mom, and eventually me.

We will never know that truth. But as a child, hearing Hon's stories of his being Jewish over and over may well have been the genesis for my interest in that faith. I was one of those all-American kids with a mixed genetic makeup and no fixed religion—open to any and all spiritual explorations.

Where There's Smoke, There's Fire

Arnie and Hon were similar in another way—both at all times had something smoking in their hands or between their lips. Arnie's was a cigarette and Hon's was a White Owl cigar. When I was maybe four, I remember asking if I could puff one of Hon's White Owls, which he casually handed over. Taking a puff, I gagged and promptly threw up on the living room floor, an immediate inoculation from ever wanting to smoke as an adult.

The only difference between Arnie and Hon was Hon smoked both in the house and in the car, making it inevitable that I would turn green and throw up virtually every time we went for a ride.

Arnie was thoughtful about never smoking inside, but he did smoke in the car, always keeping the window cracked so the smoke would be sucked out and not drift my way. Early in our relationship, it was not my place to chide him, so I bit my tongue whenever I found myself on the verge of commenting on his habit. But it's hard to forget the searing, ugly taste of a nasty, brown, White Owl burning the roof of your mouth.

My silence lasted until one of Michigan's crisp, colorful fall days, when Arnie and I set off to enjoy the turn of the autumn leaves upstate. We had gone shopping the day before, and Arnie, on my urging and to please me, had reluctantly purchased a pair of red tartan pants for the outing. That was the era of Ralph Lauren and his sophisticated country gentleman look, something definitely out of Arnie's comfort zone. Settling in the car in his new pants, Arnie lit a cigarette, inhaled his first puff, held his cigarette so the smoke would do its thing, and stepped on the gas.

Without thinking, out of my mouth came, "Arn, have you ever thought of quitting?"

Arnie jerked his Jag over to the side of the road, slammed on the brakes and, visually trying to control himself through clenched teeth, he ever so softly said, "Please don't tell me what to do!"

My timing had been impeccably bad. Arnie had planned a romantic weekend in a chalet near Traverse City where the leaves were at the peak of their color—and I had blown it. I was taken aback by his sudden change of temperament and nervously said sorry multiple times. It took quite a few miles of heavy silence to break the wall that had risen between us. Driving through the colorful riot of fall leaves as they dropped from the canopy of branches and swirled around the car was no longer cinematic or romantic.

That was the one and only time Arnie ever expressed such an outburst of anger toward me. I can only imagine how many other times he may have wanted to over our half century as a couple.

The upshot was I learned that always-calm Arnie had a temper, if you told him what to do. He would not eat anything green, and he would smoke if he damn well wanted to.

It was then I adopted Maya Angelou's position: "If you don't like something, change it. If you can't change it, change your attitude."

I silently changed my attitude, at least about the smoking issue, and tried to pick my battles. Arnie knew the dangers of smoking, but he was a risk taker.

Ralph Lauren's plaid pants went to Goodwill.

PART II

A Ham Sandwich in a Corned Beef World

Meeting the Machatunim (AKA the In-Laws)

In the fall of 1969, soon after our trip to the autumn leaves, Arnie and I rented an apartment in Bloomfield Hills, a northern suburb of Detroit. It was his hometown, and he had family, friends, and more business connections there than in Lansing, which had been a temporary move for him anyway. It was OK with me, as I needed a new environment away from old wounds and sad memories. A blank slate to inscribe a new life on.

Arnie had already told his parents about our plans, but I had yet to break the news of our move—or our pending marriage, for that matter—to my family. They knew I was dating Arnie, but that was all. So, I took a solo trip home to Muskegon to break it to them face-to-face.

Their responses were short and incredulous. My mom's deep brown eyes opened even wider than usual, but she offered no comment except a *harrumph* from deep in her throat.

My father put his hands in his pockets and said, "I hope to hell you know what you're doing! Divorced in July and planning to marry again within a year's time. Really?" I never told Arnie about that comment.

We rented a U-Haul for this first of many schleps in our life. I brought the detritus of my previous marriage: silver, china, Nanny's tablecloths and crystal goblets, sheets, cookware—you know, domestic stuff. I had the sense that all my "stuff" unsettled Arnie, and I wondered if he might be rethinking what he had gotten himself into.

All he brought was his car, a few pieces of his furniture, minus the bar, and the obligation of the care and feeding of another human.

Before my boxes were unpacked, he took me to meet his parents for a *Shabbos* dinner at their apartment. I remember how nervous I was and that the roast chicken was dry—and the conversation absolutely nerve-wracking.

Flossie, Arnie's mother, positioned me at the head of the table with his father to my right. His name was Robert, and with his immaculately groomed mustache and slicked back hair, he looked much like the 1940s movie star Errol Flynn who, by the way, died in 1959 in the arms of his mistress. Apparently, he had been sleeping with her since she was fifteen. Hopefully, Arnie's father was no Errol Flynn, and if he were, I hoped Arnie would not be a like-father-like-son guy. I was not interested in any monkey business. Remember, I am not a sharer.

Arnie sat on my left at the other end of the rectangular French country-style dining table, leaving two chairs between us. Behind him was a large faux Ficus tree, which I focused on to calm my nerves. Arnie's mother sat close by on his left, directly opposite me at the other end of the table. Obviously an intentional placing, seating chart etiquette denied. It felt similar to a tribunal. She was a lovely woman, with silvery blonde, each-strand-in-place hair, and with the same penetrating dark eyes and translucent skin that had drawn me to her son.

She was gracious and imposing in her quietness. Similar to Arnie, she talked little and listened intently. The only time she became animated was when she told me that when Arnie was a child, she had nicknamed him Boston Blackie, as he was always wanting to help people. For those of you under sixty, Boston Blackie was a suave 1940s movie detective who drove a convertible and was characterized as "an enemy to those who make him an enemy, friend to those who have no friend." An apt description of Arnie for his entire life.

Beyond that, I remember that mother and son observed me intently during that dinner, hardly talking at all while I talked too much. When I'm nervous, I have this penchant to explain things in meandering paragraphs, and I remember doing just that as I talked about my family and my upbringing. I wish I had a tape of that conversation. Oh, not to forget, they showed me the family album with the photo of Arnie at his *Bar Mitzvah* in his tallis, standing with his family and Cantor Tulman. Not a subtle move, to be sure.

Later, most surely, the Geller family discussed not only my faith or lack thereof, but also my fertility issues and the intermarriage business, as it was not as acceptable in those days for the only son from a Jewish family to marry outside the faith—especially to a barren divorcée. Arnie was the carrier of their name, the master of their eternal fate. The one who would fulfill God's first commandment to the Jews: "Be fruitful and multiply" or words to that affect.

I never sensed that Florence and Robert Geller were opposed to our marriage; maybe they reacted negatively in private conversation, but Arnie was too old to need their permission. Their blessing would be sufficient.

Gribenes and Grandma

There is no sincerer love than the love of food.
—GEORGE BERNARD SHAW

Gribenes is delicious and addictive. How could you not like thin slivers of onions and chicken skin fried to a crisp in chicken fat? Early on in our getting-to-know-you period, Arnie had told me he loved this crispy brown Ashkenazic goody, especially when made by his Grandma Lena. So soon after the dinner with his parents, we went to visit her.

She met us at the door, where she surprised Arnie with a plastic bag (which in her Eastern European accent, she called "plaster" bag) filled with newly fried gribenes. She told me that when Arnie was a child, every time she made gribenes, she would hide some in a plaster bag in her bedroom, just for him, to keep it from the hands of his rambunctious male cousins who lived in the apartment above.

Because it was one of Arnie's favorite things, I was determined to learn how to make it myself—though it could never be as good as Grandma Lena's. Nonetheless, I gave it a go one day when Arnie was out at an appointment of some sort—I think buying a TV for our new apartment.

I put strips of chicken skin into my Italian grandmother's heavy cast iron skillet, symbolically joining the two ethnicities; truthfully, it was the only pan I had big enough to do the work. And we're not talking kosher here.

I rendered the chicken skin until it was golden brown and crispy and had given up its fat, aka *schmaltz*. Then I used the remaining schmaltz to crisp up the onions and gribenes a little more and put the final result in my own "plaster" bags, tying them with silky red ribbons.

(I never knew what to do with the leftover schmaltz. Later someone told me that it is delicious on toast and in frying potatoes. That was before we had to worry about clogged arteries.)

When Arnie came home for lunch that day, I met him at the door dressed in an enticing red nightgown, with a red beribboned "plaster" bag of gribenes in my hand.

When he finally stopped laughing, we had the tastiest lunch. (I had also scattered a few of those "plaster" bags on our bed.)

The Other Side of the Machatunim Equation

Arnie didn't physically meet my clan until just before Christmas 1969, after our move, when they all gathered to sell Christmas trees on the empty lot beside our family's coal office in Muskegon Heights. It was a yearly family event and somewhat of a command performance. I thought it a good time to get it over with and introduce Arnie to the whole lot of them at one time: Mother, Father, Korkye, her husband, Joe, and younger sister Jan, who was still in high school. The Christmas tree selling was a family tradition and that year the proceeds were to help fund Jan's college tuition.

This time, Arnie and I together made the three-hour winter's drive from our new apartment in Bloomfield Hills to Muskegon Heights on the other side of the state. I entertained him the whole way with a resume of the kinfolk waiting for him at the end of that road—assuring him they were a nonjudgmental, good lot.

I filled him in on my father's family, who had owned the coal business we were headed to, for more than 100 years. And bragged, rightly so, that it had been a stop on the Underground Railroad during the Civil War. Out in the way-way backyard, hidden by fifteen-foot-high piles of black lumpy coal, was a dilapidated old house where the Southern runaways had been sheltered during their journey north. I remember my father telling my sisters and me that story as he rolled back the house's cracked and yellowed linoleum to reveal the dirt crawlspace beneath the kitchen floor where the fugitives had been sheltered until it was safe to move on. My family was a proud inclusive lot.

When Arnie stepped out of his low, sleek, Jaguar that icy frigid day, to meet a phalanx of strangers lined up as if they were a Russian firing squad in their quilted jackets and fur-lined, rubber-soled work boots, he lost his footing and fell hard on the ice-packed snow. I had warned him to bundle up, so he *was* wearing "boots." Unfortunately, the only ones in his closet were soft leather, French riding boots with slippery leather soles, fit for stirrups—not for snow.

My family, bless their irreverent hearts, tried not to laugh but couldn't help themselves, especially my brother-in-law, Joe. I could see what he was thinking by the look on his face: *This city guy hasn't got a snowball's chance in hell.* I was tempted to grab a coal shovel and bash them all over the head.

Meeting a family of gentiles selling Christmas trees in a snow-covered coal yard must have been as uncomfortable for urban Jewish Arnie as the dry Shabbos chicken dinner in an apartment in Detroit had been for small-town, gentile me. Fortunately, as with Arnie and his parents, I was too old to need permission for my new relationship. Having already had one husband, all they had to do was hope this time I was making a better choice, one that would last.

As with everything in our life, Arnie weathered that storm with grace. Pitching in that day, he helped off-load the mound of prickly firs, pines, and spruce trees from the back of the flatbed truck, setting them up neatly under the string of twinkling Christmas lights strung across the lot, ready for the sale. He had survived his trial by ice and lived to see another day to become a beloved member of my family and vice-versa.

Unfortunately, the "pratfall on ice" incident remains one of those family stories that continues to be told and embellished year after year after damn year. And I continue to wish I had a coal shovel every time they bring it up.

Good lot, my tush!

Guidelines for a Conquering Jewish Warrior

*You shall not intermarry with them; you shall not give your daughter
to his son, and you shall not take his daughter for your son. For he will
turn away your son from following me, and they will worship the gods
of others, and the wrath of the lord will be kindled against you, and he
will quickly destroy you.*
—DEUTERONOMY 7:3–4

Or, to grossly misquote a Sondheim lyric from *Westside Story*: A *goy*
like that will kill your mother. Stick to your own kind! Sorry Mr.
Sondheim, up in the music in the sky. I truly love your work.

Arnie was a grounded human. He understood that his faith had a
biblical dictate against mixed marriage, intermarriage, marrying out
of the faith—no matter which way you slice it, for Arnie's ancestors
it wasn't bologna, it was verboten. It was their way of keeping their
faith strong, of not letting it be watered down by messy procreation
practices.

Arnie's grandfather Nathan was a prominent figure in Detroit's
Jewish community. In October of 1921, he and his brother, Charles,
along with extended family members, established the Issac Agree
Memorial Society in downtown Detroit to carry on their father Issac's
charitable commitments and to honor his legacy. Issac was Arnie's
great-grandfather, and Arnie's Hebrew name is Itzhak in his honor.

The memorial society soon morphed into the Issac Agree
Downtown Synagogue, which began as an orthodox place of worship
and still stands as the last synagogue in downtown Detroit. It has now
branched out and welcomes Jews of all denominations, but by the
original bylaws, a family member must still remain on the governing

board. If Arnie had worshiped at the Orthodox Agree Downtown Synagogue, chances are excellent he would have been on the board, and we would have never met. But the Gellers were Reform Jews, a sect, some say, developed to make it easier for Jews to live in a modern society, if they chose to do so.

On January first of every year, the entire Agree family congregated to celebrate Grandfather Nathan's birthday. Arnie revered his grandfather and painted him as larger than life, a venerated member of the family, a man to be respected. And a man's success Arnie hoped to emulate.

On January 1, 1970, in anticipation of our upcoming marriage, Arnie felt it important that we attend the celebration so he could introduce me to Grandfather Nathan and the extended family. Another command performance—an audition, if you will—and my heart was doing flip-flops in my chest. I kept counting my breaths to calm it down.

Am I dressed correctly? Who's going to be there? What should I say . . . or not say? Will I see Cousin Nicki? The one I met at the Chuck Berry concert?

Enter Arnie's older sister who had brought her young son. As soon as she stepped into the room, she stopped, bent down, and pointed me out to him in a very obvious way. She had a loud voice, and everyone heard when she shouted, "Look! There she is, right over there!"

Apparently, I had been discussed before.

She was followed by multiple aunts and uncles, cousins with and without their spouses, Nicki (thank goodness), and so on and so forth, all gathered to wish Granddaddy a happy day. Some quite obviously now peering out of the corner of their eyes to have a look at the non-member-of-the-tribe woman whom longtime bachelor Arnie, eldest grandson, had asked to marry him. I felt as if I were one of the puffed-up show dogs at the Westminster Kennel Show being trotted out every New Year's Day for a look-see by the assembled crowd.

I became not only embarrassed, but overcome with that being out-of-place sensation, not dissimilar to my childhood when I visited my friends' churches where the congregants were welcoming and kind, but where I was definitely an outsider.

Arnie must have felt equally nervous as he schlepped Christmas trees with my family, but, far more self-possessed than I, he had carried on with calm and kept to the trees as a diversion. At this birthday party, I had only to stand and smile while I was being examined, not yet understanding the family relationships, the inside jokes, the Yiddish words bandied about, the who-got-along-with-whom stuff that resides in every family.

Though I was accustomed to auditions and appearing on stage before groups of people I didn't know, these people were to be a part of my new life. Arnie's family would become my family, one whose rituals were different than mine, who celebrated their religious holidays with as much vigor as my family celebrated theirs. I wondered if I would ever fit in.

They went to temple, and Arnie went to religious classes, though there was an urban legend that he spent most of his time there kissing girls in the temple bathroom—which he swore was not true. He became a Bar Mitzvah in the coming-of-age ritual binding him to his faith and requiring him to be responsible for his actions. I wonder how he handled kissing girls in the bathroom after that.

Arnie grew up in a Jewish neighborhood and went to a Jewish high school where he made lifelong friends. After his stint in the Army (the only Jew in his platoon), where he survived on bread and peanut butter he kept stashed under his bunk, he decided college was the way to go. He chose a secular college, Ferris State in Big Rapids, Michigan, but belonged to a Jewish fraternity. It was there he began his exposure to non-Jewish girls when he led a successful promotion for twin Scandinavian blondes to become the prom queens. (The ones in the car that only drove backward.)

I corresponded with one of his cousins recently who told me that Arnie had been a role model when they were kids. Following in Arnie's footsteps, he had gone to the same college, joined the same fraternity, Sigma Alpha Mu, where Arnie had been elected the chapter's prior. He said he would never forget how Arnie looked out for him when he joined the fraternity, even changing the fraternity's hell week into "help week" to make his younger cousin's hazing less rigorous.

He vividly remembers one of their conversations, when he was thirteen and Arnie was seventeen. Arnie gave him tips on dating and said, "If you're nice to people, they will be nice to you." A statement so simple, so golden rule, perhaps some would call trite, but something teenager and grown-up Boston Blackie Arnie had definitely adhered to his entire life. Only later would I learn that Boston Blackie held grudges; if you were not nice to him, you were toast. Kaput.

Through it all, Arnie's essence remained Jewish; some might call it a soul—a *Yiddish kop*, an unspoken state of thinking and being. As a Reform Jew, his beliefs remained rooted deep in the middle ages but were definitely growing in twentieth-century soil. Thus, Arnie seemed to have no qualms about taking me into his world.

According to Arnold Schwartz, a researcher who wrote in the 1970 edition of the *American Jewish Yearbook*, "though the admonitions against those unions still exist in some branches of Judaism, in the reformed movement they had been tempered by the American ethos, which places primary emphasis on the individual—his will, his choices, his personal well-being." In other words—Arnie. And I felt a moral imperative not to upset his balance even though societal restrictions were starting to mellow.

Schwartz further wrote that the number of Jews marrying non-Jews in 1970 when Arnie and I married was estimated to be only between 10 and 15 percent of the total United States Jewish population. I had moved into Arnie's world; he hadn't moved into mine. Statistically, we were both outsiders. Today intermarriage between Jews and non-Jews has risen to 45 percent.

Our union would be a mixture of cultures and religions. A bagel and spaghetti, cream cheese and red sauce mash-up. Or as my Nanny would call it, a "mishkabish," which spoken aloud sounds like a perfect description, though I have yet to find any reference to its etymology. (Maybe when I finish this tale, I will contact the *Oxford English Dictionary* people and ask them to consider it.)

But never mind; it's enough to ponder that we were indeed of different beliefs and traditions and food preferences with no intuitive understanding of each other's backgrounds—all of which had the possibility to run amuck and upset the status quo. We both felt strong ties to our family traditions; but, in my case for sure, not as much to our family's religious beliefs.

Stand By Me Under the Chuppah

Though many Reform rabbis in the early 1970s were still reticent to marry couples of different faiths, Rabbi Robert Syme, then head rabbi of Temple Israel in Palmer Park, a suburb of Detroit, agreed to officiate at ours. It was at Temple Israel Arnie had become a Bar Mitzvah, and just maybe Rabbi Syme was pleased that Arnie had finally decided to settle down.

Arnie and I met with Rabbi Syme several times over our courtship, during which he asked kind but direct questions regarding our relationship; one being the religion our children would be raised in. I recall being the one who spoke first, looking at Arnie as I said, without hesitation, "Judaism," knowing full well how complicated producing those offspring would be.

For our wedding, remarkably all four of our grandparents were still alive and able to attend: Hon and Granddaddy Nathan with their cigars and Nanny and Grandma Lena, both frail with illness in their eyes. Theirs was the generation with a foot on each side of the divide that had transitioned us, their descendants, from the old world to this new one, where mixed marriage was becoming more common. All four of them seemed to be happy for us.

When I arrived that day at the Geller's apartment, accompanied by my family, the *chuppah* was in place, and the crystal goblet was at the ready, properly wrapped in a pristine white napkin, waiting to be stomped on. Having not participated in the preparations, let alone knowing its exact rituals, I was stupidly not aware these traditions would be honored at our wedding. I was nervous and embarrassed by my lack of knowledge when they were brought into use. I had agreed wholeheartedly to having a Jewish ceremony for Arnie's sake, along with my promise that our children would be raised in the faith. What

I had failed to do was have the sense to learn how it was to be done.

Because of my previous marriage, I had requested that Arnie and I have a small quiet ceremony, thinking it inappropriate to have a grand event. I wanted to keep my second simple: no long flowing white, only above-the-knee beige. It was an intimate gathering with only close family and friends in attendance and where our family members met for the first time. My maid of honor was my sister Korkye (pregnant with my niece, Jody). Arnie's best man was Joel Fenley; they had been friends since they were eleven, which only ended with Joel's death in 2018 at age seventy-eight.

Besides cousin Nicki, Arnie had not invited any of his other friends due to my request that it be a small affair. Now I so wish I could tell him how sorry I am about that. Feelings were hurt—as well they should have been. This was Arnie's first marriage, and he deserved to celebrate it to the fullest. Instead, he had agreed to all my choices, though later I learned he would have preferred a bigger event. It wasn't the first time he calmly acquiesced to my wishes and would not be the last.

Recently, looking at the yellowed and faded photos of that day—taken by Arnie's willing Uncle Marvin as I had also nixed the professional photographer—I noticed an uncanny resemblance between my grandfather Hon and Arnie's grandfather Nathan. They were of the same age and height, hovering on different sides of five-feet, five-inches, both of the same stocky build, thinning gray hair, both chewing on unlit cigars. Maybe, just maybe, my grandfather was correct in his belief that he was Jewish, not in religion, but perhaps in some traveling bloodline kind of way.

Arnie's Grandma Lena, then quite ill with cancer—which Flossie had told me "is something *we* don't discuss" so I never knew her exact diagnosis—was sitting across the room from the father of her five children. They'd been divorced for many years, and it may have been one of the few times they were in the same room; both had come for Arnie, their eldest grandson. Seated next to Lena was Flossie, and in the kitchen were Arnie's four aunts: Trudy, Dorothy, Margie, and their sister-in-law, Shirley. They had made all the arrangements, prepared the food, ordered the cake, chilled the champagne. And of course, provided the chuppah and the goblet.

I now know that being married under a chuppah represents the new religious and physical home the couple will create together. The groom's shattering of the glass with his right foot symbolizes the destruction of the First Temple, the one built by Solomon more than 10,000 years ago. In more modern times, the shattering of the glass has also come to symbolize something more immediate: the wife's parting with her virginity. As with the chuppah, that had already been covered.

It's sad to think that other than Nicki, only my youngest sister, Jan, my brother-in-law Joe, Korkye's husband, and Jody, all other family members who were there that day have passed away. Our wedding ceremony now only kept alive by Uncle Marvin's photographs framed on the wall behind me as I remember and write. I have the belief that photographs of family and friends must not be destroyed. To do so seems an obliteration of their life on this earth, of their legacy—their souls. And more importantly, the love they gave us.

Crossing Borders

Arnie hadn't brought up a honeymoon. Why? I don't know. Maybe because we'd been living together for six months and that ritual seemed unnecessary. But neither had I, perhaps having a bout of negative déjà vu.

My first honeymoon had landed on the front page of the *Chicago Herald Tribune* with the headline: "Thief, Have a Heart." After that ceremony, my then husband and I had naively parked on a side street in Chicago, where our car was broken into and our wedding presents and luggage stolen. They also took my diaphragm, but the *Herald Tribune* was discreet enough to leave that out.

What followed that wedding was a divorce. So maybe I was wary of the honeymoon concept and what it might portend. Or maybe I was selfish.

After the flurry of our ceremony, the hugs, congratulations, and goodbyes exchanged, Arnie and I went back to our apartment in Bloomfield Hills, looked at each other, and to quote a lyric from a Peggy Lee song, said, "Is that all there is?" Both of us were feeling the need to celebrate the event with an exclamation point of some sort!

Arnie said, "How about Toronto? I've been there once and enjoyed it, and it's only a short flight from Detroit." And I agreed.

It would be the first flight in our married life, a prelude to the hundreds we could not have known would follow as we began our lifelong adventure as Arnie and Judy Geller. Back then the rules of etiquette dictated it was proper to put the woman's name first. To my then ears, it sounded better to put Arnie first. It projected stability and potential, and I still feel that way to this day.

Toronto: Somewhere during the hour-and-fifteen-minute flight over the United States–Canadian border, I was overtaken with the realization that I had also crossed a personal border, one between life as I had known it and life as I didn't know what. The crossing between the two countries had yet to require a passport, but it did require a personal commitment on my part that went beyond the heady, romantic experience of our courtship. I was overcome with emotions: scared, anxious, and wondering if I had made too hasty a decision.

I admit now that I was not thinking clearly—about anything. On the seat beside me, holding my hand was a handsome, sexy, gentle, intelligent man. What was there to question? The fact that I had only known him for ten months? The realization that I was still sifting through the physical and emotional remnants of a previous marriage? I had been known to be impulsive, but this was a whopper—one Arnie didn't deserve. Here was my uncertainty of place questioning my decision: That "Did I belong? Have I made the right decision?" thing was rearing its ugly head.

A numbing fog of realization engulfed me, and I was unable to carry on a decent conversation with my newly consecrated-under-the-chuppah husband. Intuitive Arnie certainly sensed it, but he never said a word. Surely, he must have had his own questions: *Where is the joy? Where is the celebration?* Or more to the point, *What the hell have I gotten myself into?*

Landing in Toronto, Arnie forged ahead in his quiet determination, chose a restaurant, ordered our wedding dinner with a celebratory wine, and carried the conversation throughout the meal. We were on our honeymoon, holding hands, sitting shoulder to shoulder on a curved and tufted red leather banquette. The lighting was soft and the air heavy with aromas from the steaks on the grill and the cigarettes in the room. But there was more at "stake" than those on the grill. I did love this man and was determined we would have a long fine life together. But back then, I guess I was scared and unsure if I had made the right decision.

It was the first day of our marriage, May 24, 1970, only 301 days since our serendipitous meeting. From that day forward through all the uncertainties and craziness that followed in the fifty years we shared, Arnie never failed to "stand by me."

PART III

It's Just Cheeseburgers, Honey

Getting to Know You

—ROGERS AND HAMMERSTEIN, 1951

In *The King and I*, two lovers from opposite sides of the globe sing "Getting to know you, getting to know all about you. Getting to like you, getting to hope you like me."

During our three years in Detroit, I made an effort to get to know Arnie and the world that had created him. (I sensed he had my number from the get-go.) He seemed to have a protective shield that kept him calm, steady, and with that unreadable aura. He was also the king of compartmentalization. He would focus on one thing and when that was completed, he would move to the next. Always closing one door before he opened another. And there were many doors in our future.

We were total opposites in our thinking: He plotted and planned. I was impulsive. If I got excited about an idea, I would jump in, never considering the way to pull it off or the ramifications if I didn't. And I worried about everything, everywhere, all at once, or something to that effect. In later years, I was the one with high blood pressure. Arnie's blood pressure always remained in the healthy range, even though stress piled on as the years went by and he became everyone's fixer and problem-solver. He had adapted quickly to the new husband business: He gently gave advice, quick to jump in if I had a problem, and always operated on an even keel no matter the crisis. He was an "It will be OK" husband, and I was an "Oh my god, we're going to die," wife. It balanced out.

We were in his hometown, and he was anxious to show me around, especially to his favorite eating establishments. As a thirty-year-old bachelor, he had been eating out for years, and we easily slipped right into his pattern of doing the same every evening. It was a tacit compromise: I didn't cook what he ate and he generally wouldn't eat what I cooked.

One of the first restaurants he introduced me to was Checker Bar, a hamburger institution in downtown Detroit that had been open since 1954. That could easily have been the number of cheeseburgers Arnie had eaten there over the years.

We would sit at the bar and watch the maestro on the grill talk to the burgers as he cooked, "You're rare, you're medium, and you're a cheeseburger." It was mesmerizing. I couldn't figure how he could keep it all in his head and not make a mistake.

One night I asked Arnie, "How does he remember which hamburger needs what?"

Arnie's response was: "How difficult can it be? It's just cheeseburgers, honey."

For the rest of our married life, every time I couldn't figure out how to do something, Arnie would smile and say, "It's just cheeseburgers, honey. It's just cheeseburgers."

Bagels were almost as important as cheeseburgers. The best bagels were from the Bagel Factory, and Arnie's instructions were: "Be there exactly when they come out of the oven." He must have had bagel radar because I could never figure that out. He wanted hot, salty bagels—with an occasional poppyseed thrown in the mix. If he picked them up, which was usually the case, he would hurry to our apartment with the still-hot bagels and call from the hall, "Set the table. The bagels are here." As if we were having guests for brunch.

He taught me how to make fluffy scrambled eggs by adding a half teaspoon or so of water per egg when you whip them, then scramble them in butter over a low flame, continuously moving the pan, being sure they were not too runny or too firm. Another radar.

And then there were my lessons in fish mongering. My knowledge of fish was simple: the perch my father caught fishing in his icehouse on Twin Lake or the trout he reeled in from a stream somewhere in Northern Michigan, all of which we mostly grilled. Nova? What is nova?

Jewish delis have fish in all its permutations: lox, nova, hot-smoked whitefish, white fish salad, mackerel, trout, and sable, which is actually black cod—most of which I hadn't known existed. And then you have your tuna fish salad and your red salmon roe, and if you want a good piece of nova, ask Al on the left behind the counter, he has the best technique: He slices it so thin you can see through it! Cram that in your brain and scream!

We ate nova.

Star Deli was Arnie's favorite sit-down delicatessen; their corned beef sandwiches were the best. The first time we went, he suggested I order the corned beef thinly sliced, marginally fatty, on rye, with American mustard. As I got bolder, I ordered mine: no fat, thinly sliced, with coleslaw, and Thousand Island dressing. I can see Arnie shaking his head at that desecration even now.

But going to a deli counter alone to place my to-go order was one of those not-so-delicious feelings of not belonging. Arnie had told me to buy nova and not lox, but I could never calculate the amount I needed—it's a numbers thing, I'm allergic to it. Used to a normal grab and go grocery, I was still reticent to ask questions and call attention to myself in this new environment. I was intimidated by all the women around me who were assertive and knew exactly what they wanted. Eventually, we either shopped together or Arnie did the shopping alone, especially for the items he liked.

• • •

During that "getting to know you, getting to know all about you" period, I managed to be "given" a position at Kingswood, one of the Cranbrook Schools in Bloomfield Hills. It was a day and boarding school for girls, and I was hired as the advisor for the middle school girls in grades seven through nine. I say "given" not to be coy, but because it was a privilege, a gift, one I never thought I deserved.

I was introduced to the head mistress by Nina Studebaker, a college sorority sister of mine, who had become the musical director at Kingswood. That must have held some sway.

Besides our regular duties, Nina and I decided to introduce opera to the girls; she knew music and I knew theater, so why not? Our first production was an all-girl's production of Puccini's *Madama Butterfly*. Take that, Shakespeare. And in a theater designed by Eliel Saarinen! It was such joy, something I shall never forget.

I'm going to digress and brag here: Kingswood was and remains a visual joy. On June 29, 1989, it was designated a National Historic Landmark, one well deserved. Designed by Saarinen, a noted Finnish architect, and finished in 1931, it is considered to be his masterpiece, a perfect example of the Arts and Craft Movement and Art Deco, right down to the cutlery, rugs, and the stained glass windows behind my desk. When I arrived in September of 1971, the Kingswood building with all its original contents was in pristine form and in use—as if Saarinen had just signed off and left the building, like Elvis after a standing-room-only concert.

The school is situated on 319 manicured acres of a campus renowned for its architecture not only by Saarinen, but by Albert Kahn and Frank Lloyd Wright as well. It is an art museum and gardens where sculptures by Carl Mills and Marshall Fredericks greeted me each day as I arrived in a modern-day sculpture—Arnie's XKE. He insisted I drive it to work, and it definitely boosted my cred with the girls on campus; they thought I was "groovy." This was love on so many levels.

Meanwhile, Arnie put out an album of 1960s pop hits, and we began our peripatetic lifestyle: We moved from our first apartment in Bloomfield Hills to a bungalow in Birmingham (where Arnie, for the first time to my knowledge, raked leaves and shoveled snow), finally landing in a high rise on the northwest side of Detroit, in an area called Southfield. It was there we began working together on various ideas.

We opened a bookstore, a hot dog stand, which Arnie named "Benjamin Frank," and a shop where we served lunch in the back garden during the warm summer months. I had always wanted to own a bookstore, and Arnie obliged. He rented an up and running bookstore in a late nineteenth-century clapboard house in Farmington Village. It was named the Rocking Horse for some now-unknown reason as it was neither rockin' or horsey. Where's Arnie? He would know the answer to that. He never forgot a thing. Anyway, as soon as we took over, the bookstore morphed into a lingerie shop, and we added a small picnic area that served lunch. Books, lingerie, and lunch—a ridiculous concoction.

Our entire menu consisted of egg salad sandwiches infused with black olives, chocolate cake to die for or that would, indeed, eventually kill you because of its rich fat content, and chocolate chip cookies that would do the same. Whose idea was such a cockamamie combo? Actually, both Arnie's and mine, trying to accommodate each of our palates. Arnie chose the sweets, and I chose the egg salad sandwiches. Well, we had to have a protein, and I thought it would be easy to do.

Luckily, my sister Jan was living with us during that time, and every morning her job was to boil fourteen dozen eggs. She still talks about the godawful sulphury smell that trailed her wherever she went. Turns out we were overboiling the eggs, which caused the yolks to release their iron and the whites to release their cysteine, which, presto chango, became hydrogen sulfide, which stinks. Who knew?

Our concept of food and lingerie was so off the wall and so out of our areas of expertise that we should have changed the shop's name to Whose Idea Was This, Anyway?

It was our first serious endeavor as a couple, built on pure chutzpah and laughter. And quite successful, if I say so myself.

Our lunches were presented in red boxes with red-checkered napkins, and our guests sat on bright red chairs at tables with red-and-white-checkered tablecloths under the shade of ancient oak trees. Arnie and I had stripped and sanded the twenty-four secondhand spindled chairs we found at a thrift store and were in the process of painting them red to match. One day during the process, I had an errand to run so Arnie carried on alone with the painting. Flossie chose that exact time to pay us a visit.

As Arnie told the story: "When you left, I was on my knees painting the chairs when my mother came by to see how we were doing."

"Oh, yes; what did she say? Did she think the place was looking pleasant? Delightful? Awful? Tell me!"

"No. First words out of her mouth were, 'Where's Judy, Sonny Boy? Shouldn't she be helping? You surely can't be painting all those chairs yourself!'" Those two had a mutual protection society.

I finally resigned from Kingswood because I had applied to Wayne State University Law School. My intent was to study entertainment law so I could become knowledgeable about Arnie's preferred business, which he was itching to return to. And I was waiting to hear if I had been accepted.

Meanwhile . . .

Arnie opened a franchise of an avant-garde maternity shop, perfectly named Lady Madonna, after the Beatles song of the same name. Though designed for wearing during pregnancy, the clothes followed the fashion of the time: patterned, 1970s bohemian chic. Arnie found a restored Victorian house in a perfect location on the main thoroughfare in Birmingham. It had a large three-section Victorian window projecting out onto the busy street, perfect to display our obviously pregnant mannequins; Arnie had searched for and found the prosthetic bellies in Sweden.

He asked me to design the interior. Brown was in at the time, and

I went crazy. Following the vibe of the 1970s, I painted the showroom walls dark brown and papered the dressing rooms with a loopy, silver metallic abstract design on a matching brown background. The furniture was luxurious and curvy, covered in caramel-colored velvet, standing on chrome legs in front of giant palms. There was no overly female vibe here, just relaxed sophistication, or so I thought.

In an article written in the *Birmingham Eccentric* on the opening of the shop, the female reporter (who was quite obviously taken with Arnie) hung on his every word as he explained that our clothes were being purchased by both pregnant and nonpregnant women alike.

In her article she wrote, "As handsome Geller said: 'My wife Judy wore an ankle-length Challis number for our Labor Day ice cream, pickles, and champagne opening. She also wore one of our pendants inscribed with *Bellies are Beautiful* . . . everyone loved it.'" (Note to reader: I was not pregnant.)

It would have been a more interesting newspaper piece if Arnie had told the reporter his new wife, Judy, who had designed the boutique, couldn't conceive no matter how beautiful the maternity clothes were.

Lady Madonna was a success so, again, we sold it and moved on, this time for a holiday in Europe. Arnie had no business to worry about, I loved to travel, and we were in young love. Eating buttery roast chicken, sitting on the back of a top-down convertible on the Grande Corniche overlooking the Mediterranean Sea may be the singularly most memorable experience of all our travels.

During that holiday, Arnie, as always, was thinking about needing an income and getting back to the music business that was more than a name on a shop. And we had long discussions about adopting a child. But even so, on this holiday, he appeared as relaxed as I had ever seen him, and the holiday was joyous. On the last line in his travel journal, Arnie wrote: "Arrived Det. at 11:45 Detroit time—4:45 Paris time. Got home and passed out. Sort of hoping we'd wake up tomorrow and still be in Paris."

Our life had taken on a pattern, which we held to for fifty years: peripatetic both in business and in life.

Shiksa—Bugs We Don't Eat

It was our first party in Detroit with a group of Arnie's longtime friends and their wives; for Arnie's benefit, I was trying my best to be happy we were going. During my previous marriage, our social life had been sparse. I can't remember ever having a dinner date with friends or a party, except the one we gave for the football team.

So, when Arnie said we were going to a party to meet his friends, I was extremely nervous. He assured me we wouldn't stay long, as he was not a partygoer either, but he wanted me to meet them. Or them me is more exact.

This group had grown up together in a tight community. Arnie had known most of them since grade school and religious school. They all had gone to Mumford High school, with a predominately Jewish population, and ranked as one of the best high schools in the state. When I was at the University of Michigan for undergrad, these kids from Mumford were known to the rest of us as the smart guys, our biggest competition for scholarships. When Arnie and I started dating, and I found out he had graduated from Mumford, I was duly impressed. He seemed to shrug it off, but when I asked him if he knew "so-and-so" who went there, as I had dated him at Michigan, Arnie looked at me as if I had dropped from outer space. "That guy? Why did you ever date that guy?"

I told him that it was only once because "that guy" had tried to make me put my hand on his genitals.

Arnie said, "Figures, I wouldn't put it past him."

I hoped "that guy" wasn't going to be at the party we were going to.

He wasn't, but when Arnie started introducing me to the group standing by the door, some other guy in the back called out: "Hey

Geller, you got a *shiksa*, huh? With a *schwartz* tush!" He congratulated Arnie as if he had just reeled in a sizeable, prized trout on a fishing expedition.

The room became quiet and heads turned in our direction. Here was the family birthday party all over again. Was this a ritual, or was I that much of an anomaly? I tried not to react, but how could I not as I got the uncomfortable feeling it was a disparaging slur and I didn't belong.

Not missing a beat, Arnie bent down and whispered, "We're leaving," and piloted me out the door, all the while apologizing and muttering, "What an ass!"

Eventually, I did meet most of Arnie's other friends in different situations and many became good friends, but that was an unsettling experience. I purchased Leo Rosten's book the *Joys of Yiddish* to keep on my shelf in preparation for whatever else might come my way. Sadly, I no longer have that book as a reference for the meaning of Yiddish words, but if a newer online version in the *Cambridge Dictionary About Words* blog works for you: on February 2, 2013, Hugh Rawson wrote:

> **shiksa (shicksa, shiksah, shikse, shikseh)**. *A female* **goy**, *and not at all complimentary. The term derives from the Hebrew* **šiqṣâ**, *detested (feminine) thing. A secret fear of many a Jewish mother is that a blonde, blue-eyed shiksa is lying in wait for her son.*

I have green eyes so that wasn't me.

I wish I could remember where I also read that shiksa literally means "bugs we don't eat," an abomination, something to avoid like a hot stove—look but do not touch! Nice, right?

Philip Roth, the prolific and widely read Jewish writer, went a long way to perpetuate its pejorative use when he generously sprinkled it throughout his 1969 bestseller *Portnoy's Complaint*. Alexander Portnoy, Roth's juvenile protagonist, spent a substantial chunk of his adolescence and imagination chasing after those shiksas, and it wasn't to buy them ice cream, I tell you that. Maybe the guy at the party was a Philip Roth fan? Nah . . . too stupid.

Yiddish words were relatively commonplace in Arnie's family. They mainly used them as descriptors. I myself found them addictive, like salty potato chips, once you get that pleasurable taste in your mouth, you keep dipping into the bag of words like *mensch, schlep, tush, chutzpah, mishigas*. They became benign everyday words in my vocabulary. I love to say *mishigas*; it belongs with *mishkabish*.

I will admit that since I was first called a shiksa at that party, the word has become more mainstream and less of a pejorative. Literally, as I am writing this memoir, I heard it used in a fluffy new rom-com on a Netflix series called *Nobody Wants This*, when a young conservative "hot" rabbi is dating a gentile girl and his blowhard brother throws the word *shiksa* in her direction.

When the girl turns to the rabbi and asks, "What does that mean?" the rabbi blows it off with: "It used to mean impure, detestable, but these days it means a hot blonde non-Jew."

Can you tell that I have a negative reaction to that shiksa word? So, I'm compelled to tell you another time that word assaulted me.

Don Rickles, one of the popular comics in the Catskills, had been one of Arnie's favorites when he waited tables there to pay for his college tuition. When we were living in LA in the early 1970s and Arnie was working for MGM, we went to see the Rickles show in Vegas at the MGM Grand Casino. On our drive from LA to Vegas, a surprise desert storm engulfed us in a red flurry of sand obliterating our vision. We pulled to the side of the highway until it passed and then we proceeded directly into another surprise experience at the Rickles show.

A voice boomed from backstage, "Ladies and gentlemen, let's give it up for Don Rickles."

Rickles bounded on stage, stepped to the mic, and immediately scanned the audience searching for an innocent mark to humiliate for his comedic warm-up. There we were, third row center, two shiny poker chips ready to be played.

Pointing to Arnie he said, "You're Jewish right?"

When Arnie nodded affirmatively, Rickles said, "Come on up here."

In good humor, Arnie made his way to the stage, knowing full well from his Catskill experience he was about to be skewered. Rickles shook Arnie's hand, kissed his neck, patted his cheek, and told him what a good-looking Jewish boy he was. Then pointing to me, Rickles continued with a smirk, "You have a beautiful shiksa there, lucky guy."

People laughed, catching the salacious innuendo, and I blushed, squirmed, and tried to smile.

That was the second and last time I have ever been called a shiksa to my face. Most likely, some of those who laughed at Rickles didn't know the word's original negative meaning as it has gone through years of obfuscation until its exact Yiddish meaning has become sanitized. But they got the innuendo—a Jewish guy with a fair-haired shiksa on his arm is up to—wink, wink, nod, nod—*shtupping*. Look it up.

If you will allow me to flash my inner Catskill comedian and tell you a joke that Arnie told me one time and I read recently on The Accidental Talmudist's website:

A priest and a rabbi are sitting next to each other on a long plane ride, and they get to talking. After a couple of hours, the priest says to the rabbi, "Tell me, Rabbi, did you ever in all your years succumb to temptation and try a little ham?"

The rabbi says, "You know what, Father? I will confess. I was so curious about it; I once had a ham sandwich."

Another hour goes by, and the rabbi feels comfortable enough to ask the priest, "Father, tell me, in all your years, did you ever succumb to temptation and see what it felt like to be with a woman?"

The priest says, "Rabbi, I'm going to tell you the truth. Yes, one time I gave in and experienced the joys of the flesh."

The rabbi says, "Beats the heck out of a ham sandwich, eh?"

Faith or Tradition—Good Question

In all the working and moving and traveling, Arnie and I had only touched on religion in the most cursory of ways, both agreeing that if it didn't matter to either of us that we had a marriage of mixed cultures and religious backgrounds, what followed was nobody's business.

Growing up in my grandparents' house, I heard stories of the Catholic church not quite excommunicating my grandmother Nanny but exerting more than a little pressure that they would do just that if she didn't follow the rules of her faith. They used not-so-subtle statements similar to, "Don't come back until you change your ways, young lady."

So, she never did. Having fallen in love with my cigar-smoking, dapper, irreverent, storytelling, possibly Jewish grandfather in 1917, there was no turning back. The pope lost a congregant, but a love match was found—one that lasted beyond the grave.

Nanny may or may not have discarded her religion's code of beliefs, but she held tightly to the traditions of her Neapolitan Catholic holidays. So, Mom and I continued to do the same. As a child, it was less about religion and more about the traditions of colored eggs and candy in baskets left by the Easter Bunny or presents under the Christmas tree left by Santa Claus.

The only religious sign of note in our house was the intricate miniature crèche my "Jewish" carpenter-grandfather had made for Nanny in his off-limits workshop behind our house. It was an important tradition of a Neapolitan Christmas brought by my great-grandmother Theresa, when she emigrated from Naples.

As a child, I enjoyed moving the miniature figures of Mary and Joseph around inside that crèche as they sheltered from the elements and kneeled before a swaddled baby Jesus asleep on real straw. Outside, in front of the manger, Hon also placed colorful figures of the frankincense and myrrh guys sitting on their camels as they shivered on the cotton-batting snow, waiting to pay homage to the newborn child. Remember we lived in Muskegon by cold Lake Michigan and not in Bethlehem by the warm Dead Sea.

One year in grade school, I was chosen to recite the story of that auspicious occasion in a school assembly before all the students and their families, which is, I believe, what fostered my serious entry into show business. I found it exhilarating to stand before the crowd to say my passage: "Today in the town of David a savior has been born to you; he is the Messiah, the Lord." But I never stopped to think of what it meant or the religion behind it. At that point I doubt I even knew there were multiple religions. These words were just the traditions of the season.

Unlike Arnie, who had grown up in the Jewish faith and had attended a reform temple, I was left to attend any church I wished, for any reason. Heady stuff for a child in grade school. This usually turned out to be the church of my best friend of the moment. One of those grade school friends was the daughter of a Dutch Reformed preacher, Pastor Ringinoldus.

Initially, his wife would not allow their daughter to play with me, thinking my mom was a divorcée. There would be no harlots in their congregation. But learning she was a widow made it all OK? These were not warm and fuzzy people. Their small stark white clapboard church was representational of their rigidness, with its wooden-shingled peaked roof, but it was within walking distance of our house, so I went.

I have often wondered if being called a "wop" or other egregious names, or losing a husband at a very young age, my mom just figured God was not on her side. She never mentioned a faith, never attended church, and never appeared at all pious. However, hedging her bets, she made sure that among the more than numerous books she read to her daughters, many were of a biblical nature in which a balayaged, blond-haired Jesus, crook in hand, guided a flock of scruffy sheep over a distant hill followed by his apostles in coats of many colors.

Mom, who seemed neither happy or unhappy about whether I went to church at all, would stand on the front stoop of Hon and Nanny's house waving goodbye as, first alone and later with my middle sister, Korkye, we went off to the Dutch Reformed people for Sunday school.

All that remains of those childhood toe dips into religion are the first lines to the song: "Jesus loves me this I know, for the Bible tells me so," and the time I spent coloring line drawings of Jesus and his sheep during Sunday school in the basement of that white clapboard church—and throughout my life, being overly concerned about fitting in and anxious about what I should wear in new situations.

In my teens, I switched from Dutch Reformed to Episcopalian, the religion of my friend Judy, both of us from the Judy Garland, Yellow Brick Road generation. She was the one whose father owned the Fruitport Pavilion. The warmth and beauty of her church, as the light filtered down on the congregation through stained glass windows, was in stark contrast to the bleak, pristine-white Dutch Reformed experience. Episcopalians' taste in architecture was more suited to my sense of design and the dramatic. This too also passed.

Thus, I grew up with no religious imperatives. Except for the dreadful prayer Mom made me and my sisters say before bed:

Now I lay me down to sleep
I pray the lord my soul to keep.
If I should die before I wake,
I pray the lord my soul to take. Amen.

At the University of Michigan, my religion was to worship at the altar of Konstantin Stanislavski and his acting techniques. Broadway, not redemption, was always my goal. Always searching for a suspension of disbelief.

I did take a class in comparative religions, only to find the geographical settings of the religions far more interesting than the dogma. My more than a little agnosticism was, if there were a God, he was a white guy, with a Santa Claus beard reminiscent of the God portrayed by Michelangelo on the ceiling of the Sistine Chapel. Colorful but far, far away.

I soon opted out of religious classes altogether and went on to others in democracy versus communism, from which I learned the phrase, "From each according to his ability; to each according to his needs." My needs then were learning and soaking up new experiences. It wasn't religion I was seeking; it was adventure. Or so I thought. Now I see it was my searching for something larger than myself, a philosophy or belief that makes me comfortable to embrace.

Becoming Ruth

Arnie was the man I loved—the one I wanted to build a life with. Judaism was the faith that had helped make that man. When I brought up the idea of my converting, he emphatically responded: "Don't do it for me. It's your choice."

We were of two different cultures, vocabularies, cuisines, and even ways of thinking—all chock-full of subtle innuendos we were learning about each other every day. Arnie was pragmatic, trying to figure out what worked and how to do it. I was idealistic, thinking only of what could be and let's get at it. I came to believe that if I understood the faith that had made Arnie who he was, and I chose to belong, ours would be a tighter bond, forged by a spiritual glue of sorts. Then I could put to rest the religious wandering I had been doing since my childhood. So, yes, I was doing it for myself, but equally for Arnie and our future; one that would, fingers crossed, include children.

Conversion—well, not exactly a conversion, maybe a "joining up" as I had nothing to convert from—became an imperative when I learned that "being Jewish" flowed through the maternal bloodline. I didn't have that bloodline, but in Reform Judaism, conversion held the same weight as that bloodline. (At least that was a reformed rabbinical interpretation in the 1970s, maybe not an everybody interpretation.) And since it was unlikely that any child would hop over my physical inadequacies and wiggle their way into Arnie's and my life, having a Jewish family could only come first by conversion and then adoption. Two life-altering commitments.

It was time for me to wrap myself around that core belief, one bigger than myself, one I had never had. I couldn't stand in the street as Mary Tyler Moore did, throw my hat in the air and say, "Hey there! Look at me! I'm Jewish now." I had to go through a process similar to being born in one country and immigrating to another and having to live by their laws—I had to study to qualify for citizenship.

Obviously, my grandfather's insistence that he was Jewish, whatever that meant to him, made me amenable to the concept. The attraction was strengthened by my Jewish roommate in college, my Jewish friends in my childhood neighborhood, by the guy named Levy who bit his nails and had a crush on me all through high school and into college, and by the fact that my ex-husband was born to a Jewish father, a weak precedent as his mother was a nonconverted gentile, but nonetheless, a pattern.

I was being pragmatic, a state of being I generally did not ascribe to. Michelangelo had revealed David in all his power and glory when he freed him from a faulty slab of marble for all to see. My goal, however many faults I had, was to turn the Star of Bethlehem, a celestial phenomenon lighting my family's crèche, into a Star of David, the symbol of the biblical king and the religion he fathered.

Rabbi Syme, who had officiated at our wedding, oversaw my conversion classes at Detroit's Temple Israel. There is a passage in the Hebrew Bible (Ruth 1:16), in which Ruth, thought to be the first convert, tells her mother-in-law, Naomi, "Where you go, I will go, and where you lodge, I will lodge; your people shall be my people, and your God my God."

As a goodwill gesture, I invited my mother-in law, Flossie, to attend the classes with me whenever she wished. She came quite frequently and would sit beside me, posture erect, purse in her lap, listening intently, whispering quietly under her breath the prayers she had known all her life. Prayers I was just beginning to learn. I could sense her acceptance of my conversion developing—especially for her sonny boy Arnie and her future grandchildren.

During the classes, I ingested a modicum of Hebrew, at least enough to know I didn't have a clue what was being said or how to pronounce it. Eventually, I learned enough to say and understand the major prayers and to light the Shabbos and holiday candles. It quickly became apparent that Judaism would be a lifelong learning experience. And speaking Hebrew? TBD.

On the day of my conversion, Arnie put a protective arm around my waist as Rabbi Syme motioned for us to step up to the bimah at Temple Israel to embark on our spiritual journey together. It has now been more than fifty years since I came out of wandering in that proverbial religious desert, and Rabbi Syme gave me my Hebrew name—Ruth—as he welcomed me to the fold.

Jews never proselytize to gather new members into their fold but are known to welcome with open arms those who knock on their door—unlike the Catholic church that had not been accepting of my agnostic grandfather when he wanted to marry my Catholic grandmother. Arnie's family welcomed me with hugs, cookbooks, Shabbos candlesticks, and family lore about Arnie's eating habits, though I am sure their warning me of "no green sh*t" was not a tenet of the faith, but an inherited trait passed from his father's side along with his height and gorgeous head of hair.

At first, I learned by viewing and listening and then trying. It was not a *mikvah* in the ritual bath immersion sort of way, but by participation in the rituals and foods of religious holidays with Arnie's extended family, and from the rituals of joy as one after another of the cousins married or became a Bat or Bar Mitzvah. Behind all this remain the deeper tenets of the faith to more fully understand and to integrate into my world.

Over the fifty years of our marriage, it wasn't unusual for Arnie, when asked about a ritual or prayer, to say, "Ask Judy. She knows more than I do about that." I am not sure that is entirely correct, but I know he was happy that I made the decision to convert.

Once a shiksa, not necessarily always a shiksa, Mr. Roth.

Funny, You Don't Look Jewish

Arnie and I didn't make our first trip to the Middle East until we were in our late sixties. Our initial plan was to tour Egypt and then Petra in Jordan. By the way, did you know that as you exit Petra, there's a shop called the Titanic Snack Shop, selling soft drinks and ice cream? At least there was then. Anything with *Titanic* in its name always caught our attention. More about our relationship with that ship later.

It was our last night in Jordan; we were staying at a resort on a hill overlooking the Dead Sea. We were enjoying dinner on the terrace when I looked across the pitch-black sea and spied a wide expanse of lights blinking in and out of the darkness. My geography was mixed up as we had been driving all day from Petra to Amman, 150 miles across a mountainous sandstone landscape, punctuated with scruffy patches of green, with no road signs or biblical references to tell us where we were. Occasionally, our driver would throw out a line such as: "To your right, on that hill over there, is where Sarah was turned into a pilar of salt," or "Moses got the Ten Commandments up there" or some other supposed fact that we had no way of knowing if it were true, though suspected it was not. We could have been anywhere; we wouldn't have known the difference. But as we sat at that table by the Dead Sea, I had a suspicion about those beckoning lights in the distance. Confirming with the waiter what I was thinking was correct, he responded with, "Yes, that's Jerusalem."

"That's Jerusalem," I said as I levitated out of my chair. "Let's go there, Arnie! We have to go there. Arnie, Arnie we must go there!" It wasn't unusual for me to double up his name when I felt intense about something I knew he might not be interested in. Why Jerusalem wasn't on our original itinerary remains a mystery but seeing those lights, I was determined we were going, even if we had to swim the Dead Sea. (Can you swim the Dead Sea with that density of salt in the water? Maybe we could float?) Anyway, we were going to Jerusalem before we left the Middle East.

Arnie was not at all interested. His response was, "You understand our plane leaves from Amman's airport tomorrow evening. We have only one day left on our itinerary, and I thought we were going to rest here and maybe take a dip in the Dead Sea."

I started to laugh because he hadn't been in a bathing suit since the 1970s. Taking a dip in any body of water had never been his thing, especially in salt water, no matter how therapeutic it might be.

He finished with, "Besides, it will be too expensive to change our tickets now."

And then I knew he was looking for an excuse not to go. He was tired of being a tourist and just wanted to go home. Seeing the crestfallen expression on my face and knowing I would pester him for the rest of the evening to change his mind, he said, "All right, OK, if you can manage to arrange a one-day trip by tomorrow morning, let's give it a go."

Seeing him work over the years, I had learned that if you want something badly enough, there is always a way. I also was reasonably sure if I didn't come up with a plan, he would jump in and make it happen. Actually, I was counting on that.

I left the table immediately and did manage, with the help of the resort's impressive concierge, to do just that. It was the *Mission Impossible* television show: I had presented the concierge with a mission, which he chose to accept, and did magnificently.

In a short time, he had arranged an early morning taxi to take us from our hotel on the Jordanian side of the Dead Sea to the King Hussein Bridge that crosses the Jordan River into Israel. (On the Israeli side of the Jordan, it is called the Allenby Bridge.) The Jordanian taxi driver wasn't allowed to go any farther but would keep our luggage in his trunk and pick us up when we returned to Jordan that evening, at the exact place he had left us that morning, after we crossed back over the bridge with two names.

For our day in Jerusalem, the concierge had booked another driver to be waiting on the Israeli side of the bridge. His mission was to guide us around Jerusalem and then bring us back to the crossing in time to make our late night flight home.

I was so fixated on packing and on the notion that we were going to Jerusalem that I have absolutely no recollection of the Jordanian driver or of that first crossing from Jordan into Israel. None. I was just excited to get there.

However, the driver in Israel I will never forget. He was a native Israeli, aka a Sabra, aka a prickly pear—an apt description of his personality. He packed a gun, wore a weathered brown-leather jacket, and a wide-brimmed felt fedora with a leather band—also brown, and was quick to tell us he had fought in the 1967 Six-Day War.

First, he sped us through Jerusalem, pointing out the high-security fencing, in some sections thirty feet high, and other sections of thick concrete walls, covered with provocative graffiti. Even the famed British street artist, Banksy, had painted peace symbols on the walls, and others had painted huge holes that were so realistic it looked as if you could step through into the West Bank. Israel had been constructing these barricades since 2002 to protect its citizens from intrusions by suicide bombers sneaking in from the Palestinian Territory on the other side—each population was living in fear of the other.

We made a hurried ride to the Mount of Olives for an overview of Jerusalem's Old City, the Jewish Cemetery, and in the distance, the Dome of the Rock. And then he drove us through the Jewish Quarter, which he told us he wasn't supposed to do, and which to me, at least, looked much like Borough Park in Brooklyn on a busy day, minus the ancient buildings and labyrinth of streets. He then dropped us at the ancient Lion's Gate to explore the Old City on foot. Neither Arnie nor I knew where we were but meandered the Via Dolorosa with the masses of people from around the world doing the same. We acknowledged to each other that we must return, as this visit was similar to a drive-by shooting. Get it over and get out. A *shanda*.

This was followed by a quick standup lunch at a deli, where everyone was jostling for position at the counter. Arnie, who felt much at home, ordered a steak sub, Prickly (as I was referring to our driver) a corned beef sandwich, and I, my first chicken shawarma. I can taste it now; it was that good. Food is always a priority on our travels.

Arnie was going with the flow, but I asked to visit the Church of the Nativity, not knowing it was in Palestinian-held Bethlehem, a conclave on the Israeli-occupied West Bank. I had seen it on numerous travel shows, and it was on a list of UNESCO World Heritage Sites. I wanted to check it off.

Prickly gave us pushback at first, telling us as Americans we were able to go to Bethlehem, but he, an Israeli citizen, was not—unless he had approval from the Israeli Civil Administration. I am not sure if he had the proper credentials, but he was obviously a tough guy with a gun and supposedly a tour guide so, with a little persuasion from Arnie, he acquiesced to drive us there anyway.

Arnie and I were not prepared for this journey. Normally, I buy the guidebooks ahead of a trip and get a sense of what we should see. Arnie counted on me to make the choices. In this case, neither of us knew exactly what we wanted to see or how complicated the political situation was if we went. But as the day wore on, we began to get an idea.

Jordan had governed the West Bank until it was occupied (all 2,185 square miles of it) by Israel after the 1967 Six-Day War, but there were areas still under the Palestinian National Authority. Perhaps the reason Prickly had given us pushback about going there.

Along the road we encountered way-too-young Israeli soldiers of both sexes, IDF forces of some sort, standing a few yards apart in their khaki uniforms and berets, holding ominous-looking long guns. Prickly pointed out, in obvious disgust, the fields left fallow by what he called the lazy Palestinian citizens, and over and over praised the luscious fields maintained by the industrious Israelis. They were indeed luscious, reminding me of the phrase in the Bible of land flowing with milk and honey. But the venom in Prickly's presentation unsettled me, and I couldn't wait to get out of the car.

Prickly deposited us at the foot of a staircase leading to the Church of the Nativity, said to have been established by Constantine in AD 330 over the manger where Jesus was born, and where the seeds of Christianity were believed to have incubated, and tersely said, "I'll wait for you here."

Arnie and I climbed the stairs and did a hasty walk around, during which I read snippets of the church's history to him from a quickly grabbed pamphlet. It is still a working house of worship, overseen by three Christian denominations: Greek Orthodox, Roman Catholic, and Armenian Apostolic, and where every day hundreds of pilgrims come to pray under amber and gold hanging oil lamps that have been burning for more than 1,000 years.

When I think of 1,000 years ago, which I don't do regularly, I visualize thatch huts and muddy beleaguered peasants. Maybe I'm thinking Middle Ages in England. This church, though obviously ancient, remains a magnificent edifice of limestone, golden tiles, alters, paintings, intricate mosaics, and merits its UNESCO designation. The day we visited, the church was filled with hundreds of pilgrims praying before ancient relics of Christianity and lined up to enter the cramped underground cavity, the location of the manger where Jesus was purported to have been born. Hon's crèche came to mind.

Our visit to the West Bank was short, but in only a few hours we had driven through layers of history—BCE, CE—centuries of ancient tribes, the birth of religions, and world-shaping wars; all in the confines of a compressed geographical location, the crucible for much of what the world thinks and believes now. It was mentally overwhelming.

At the Western Wall, both Arnie and I felt the profound spirituality of the space as the prayers of untold numbers, who had entered before us, permeated the air. This vestige of a wall, an expansion of the Second Temple built by Herod in 19 BCE, is in a vast open space where its ancient limestones blocks tower above those who enter. For a moment my nagging sense of *I don't belong* rose to the surface, and I hesitated as I covered my hair with a scarf, not knowing the wall was open to all who wished to pray there. So, no matter what they thought of me, I belonged.

Arnie, sensing my apprehension, took my hand and whispered, "Are you OK?" Taking Arnie's hand has always been for me as if I were being wrapped in a soft, comforting blanket. And I was OK.

But quickly, a grumpy Orthodox gatekeeper separated us—Arnie to the left and me to the right, as is done in most Orthodox synagogues to this day. All to prevent either sex from being distracted from their prayers. To my way of thinking, women are not that weak; it's the men they should worry about.

Alone at the wall, as the pilgrims before me, I wrote my prayers on slips of paper and secreted them into the divine presence that existed between the limestone blocks. Those millions of prayers are gathered twice a year and taken to the cemetery on the Mount of Olives to be given a proper Jewish funeral.

One of my supplications was: Before the scraps of paper are collected from the Wall and buried on the Mount of Olives, they are read by someone with clout. I had prayed for the health and safety and peace for my husband and my daughter and our families.

• • •

During that day in Jerusalem, our driver kept glancing at me through his rearview mirror. Finally, he couldn't stand it anymore and, taking his eyes off the road ahead, turned to me in the back seat and asked that old bromide of a question: "Are you Jewish?"

When I said yes, he followed up with a snort and honest-to-God, said, "Funny, you don't look Jewish." And turned around.

There was that territorial, judging-a-book-by-its-cover thing again rearing its ugly head. Arnie, sitting by my side, glanced at me but never said a word, which I thought strange. Maybe he was tired and not up for a chat with a contentious sabra totting a gun. Or maybe he knew I could handle myself. Or maybe he had heard it one too many times.

On reflection of that day, having been disturbed by our driver's obvious prejudices, what I should have said when he asked me that question, was: "Yes, I am Jewish and so is my Chinese mother who adopted me, and the biblical convert Ruth, and the entertainer Sammy Davis Jr. And what in this modern world does being Jewish look like, may I ask?"

But of course, I didn't.

We ended the day with a mad dash through the occupied West Bank to the Allenby Crossing into Jordan, thinking if these folks can't agree on the name of a bridge, no wonder they can't agree on anything else.

All day, our driver had made his opinion of the region's issues, and of me, quite clear. When we finally saw the light of the Allenby Bridge, Arnie and I were grateful to have had that day in Jerusalem, but now a little tentative, concerned about how rigorous the border crossing might be. Our driver's sense of us versus them had been troubling.

What we did not know was in January of 2009, Israel had conducted air strikes into Gaza in response to rockets coming from that direction. We were there in March, fewer than three months later, unaware that Bethlehem was under the complete control of the Palestinian Authority, and Israel had limited ability to protect its citizens if they went into the "other's" territory. Probably why Prickly carried a gun.

Leaving Prickly and his gun, Arnie and I walked through a security fence into an Israeli holding room to wait until we were cleared to leave, paid our exit fee, and moved on through customs where we were escorted to a bus to take us to the Jordanian side. It was late, and besides Arnie and me, there was only one other passenger on the bus. The lighting was bright and harsh—looking out the window, we could see nothing but our own reflections staring back at us from a pitch-black night. This was an area of the world that was illuminating, fascinating, complicated, and where anything could happen. And we held hands again and felt vulnerable.

Exiting the bus, we were processed through customs and were again under Jordanian rule, relieved to see a man holding a sign with our name on it, ready to take us to Jordan's Queen Alia International Airport for the flight home.

Sadly, religious prejudice still hides in the back alleyways of misunderstanding where some continue to not understand that people of different religions, political ideology, and ethnicities can peacefully unite under the umbrella of any one of those categories.

Centuries had not changed that; but maybe more intermarriages might.

No Green Sh*t!

My conversion to Judaism had been much easier than Arnie's conversion to different food groups. His initial attempt at a "foreign" food began on his first Thanksgiving with my family. Everything he chose to eat was white: a slice of turkey (white), mashed potatoes (white), Parker House rolls (white).

When dinner ended, graciously thanking my mother and my grandmother for the meal, Arnie disappeared, claiming he was going out for a cigarette; true, but it was also a cover for driving around to locate an open restaurant (usually Chinese) where he could find something in the few food groups he would eat. Chicken broth and fried egg roll.

I had been raised on an Americanized, high-carb mix of Neapolitan and Northern European foods. Our mainstay was pasta with red sauce, salads, vegetables of many colors, pork roasts and beef cuts Arnie had never seen, and hot dogs filled with an unidentifiable meat product—writing the latter gives me a rigor.

Arnie was raised, as we know, on a steak and fried or baked potatoes diet with an occasional side of roast chicken, chicken soup (no carrots), brisket on Passover, and, of course, bagels with cream cheese, nova, and a slice of tomato. Anything red besides those tomato slices, cherry pie, and Heinz ketchup on McDonald's fries never crossed his lips. Even his pizzas were ordered cheese only. And green?

"No green sh*t!" became a running joke. When eating out with his business cohorts and employees over the years, which he did frequently and enjoyed immensely, they would say in unison to the server before Arnie could even make his request: "Please, no green sh*t!"

The only variance happened in Mexico when we dined in a restaurant in Ensenada that had been touted as having created the Caesar salad. Not wanting to say he had been there but hadn't eaten the salad, Arnie felt the pressure, ate it, and enjoyed it enough to eventually make his own recipe for Caesar dressing with garlic croutons.

That's when I learned that telling a recalcitrant spouse, "Just try it once," was a waste of breath. Similar to that old bromide about leading a horse to water: You can lead a husband to pasta sauce or green beans, but you can't make him put them in his mouth and swallow unless it's his own idea. And in reality, taste is partially an inherited trait and one of parenting or exposure, worked on over the years. A difficult thing to change.

When we ate dinner at home, which was not often, Arnie mostly did the cooking—because he knew what he wanted and prepared it better. He made a mean cacio e pepe, grilled salmon, and a delicious shrimp dish pilfered from Mosca's Restaurant in New Orleans that was to die for. And of course, he grilled cheeseburgers, making sure he left a thumb print in the center of each burger so the fatty juices would stay in the meat and not run off into the pan. Any time I attempted to make one, it automatically was over- or undercooked, because I was nervous and trying too hard to get it right.

It was inevitable that the more we traveled, the more Arnie's palate became adventurous. He tasted caviar in a market in Kiev—mainly because the voluptuous blonde behind the counter took a liking to him and plied him with samples. Eventually, he added wee pieces of Iberico ham when we were installing an exhibition in Madrid; Moroccan lamb, well, in Morocco; and a variety of cheeses. One time he even came home from the Netherlands with a gigantic wheel of gouda.

I, on the other hand, never came across a dish I didn't care for, save for that lamb, which conjured up all those woolly sheep being herded by Jesus in my coloring books.

Mostly, Arnie remained true to his beef-and-potatoes self, with an occasional Chik-fil-A sandwich or a hot dog for lunch—well done-kosher, skinless, with regular mustard, from Nathan's, or Sabretts at Gray's Papaya in New York City, or Pink's on La Brea in LA with their Hoffy brand made with natural casings. Believe me, I have a doctorate in hot dogs.

In 1996, we rented a house in Positano, Italy, to introduce my eighty-year-old mother to her Italian origins and indigenous food. A few days after we settled in, Samantha, our daughter, and Allie, our niece, were to join us to share the experience with their grandmother. Their schedule was to fly from Atlanta to New York to Milan to Naples. The price of their trip was to schlep the Hebrew National hot dogs.

Mind you, bacteria multiples rapidly at temperatures between 40°F and 140°F; hot dogs should be discarded if left at room temperature for more than two hours. Arnie's hot dogs had a comfy cool journey in the plane's forward galley—until the cousins missed a connection and had a sixteen-hour, no-refrigeration delay in Milan's Malpensa airport.

When Samantha and Allie finally showed up in Positano in the middle of the night, still schlepping the hot dogs to prove their good intentions, they smelled like a kosher deli and the hot dogs were way beyond lethal. And Arnie was one disappointed puppy.

Arnie's Caesar Salad Dressing

Mix the following ingredients in a blender until smooth.

– 1 garlic clove

– ½ cup olive oil

– 2 tablespoons lemon juice

– 1 cup Parmesan cheese, grated

– 1 teaspoon Worcestershire sauce

– 5 anchovy fillets

– ½ teaspoon salt

– ¼ teaspoon pepper

– ¼ cup blue cheese, crumbled

Toss dressing over romaine lettuce, sprinkle with additional Parmesan cheese.

Add homemade croutons. (Occasionally, I made them.)

———————

Nanny's Red Sauce (Or as Close as I Can Get)
AKA, the sauce AMG wouldn't eat, which goes nicely
with the salad he would eat.

– 1 pound spaghetti

– 1 28-ounce can of San Marzano peeled tomatoes, squeezed by hand
into a bowl

– 4 tablespoons olive oil

– 2 onions, sliced

– 1 clove garlic

– 2 ounces grated Parmesan cheese
(Nanny used Romano cheese made from sheep's milk)

– ¼ teaspoon sugar

– 2 fillets of anchovy or anchovy paste—optional (½ teaspoon paste
equals approximately one fillet)

– Salt and pepper to taste

Sauté the onion and garlic until soft (approximately 5 minutes).

Remove garlic, add tomatoes, cook for 5 minutes.

Lower flame and simmer for 1 hour or until ready to serve.

Add anchovies and sugar.

Cook slowly for 10 minutes.

Lift the pasta from the boiling pot, shake off any dripping water,
add the pasta directly into the sauce, toss together, serve in individual
bowls. Sprinkle with Parmesan cheese to taste.

I add fresh basil near the very end; remove it before the leaves turn
brown to preserve their flavor; any longer and they become bitter.

———

PART IV

The Los Angeles, Connecticut, New York, Atlanta Turnaround

On the Road Again

Back to our early days in Detroit: I had finally been accepted to Wayne State University Law School. In my application letter, I played the woman card; quoting Bella Abzug, I wrote: "The test for whether or not you can hold a job should not be the arrangement of your chromosomes." At that time women made up only 8 percent of the lawyers in the country, and I had assured Wayne State Law that I was dedicated to becoming one of them. Then, without hesitation, I bailed. Because . . .

Arnie returned to the record business full time as director of operations for MGM Records, located in Los Angeles. The MGM record division was part of MGM Studios, whose logo, Leo the Lion, roared at every movie opening and had since way back in the 1940s when my mom took me to the movies during the war.

It was at that studio where Judy Garland, Clark Gable, Greta Garbo, Fred Astaire, Mickey Rooney—all the greats from my youth—had held court. And it was thrilling to be a minuscule part of it all.

Arnie and I drove our few possessions to LA in a U-Haul and rented an apartment in a two-story stucco house in the flats of Beverly Hills. It was a railroad apartment where one room followed another, front to back, and where I made our bed's headboard out of plywood covered with cotton batting and sheets because we couldn't afford to buy one. I had already lived in a railroad apartment when I acted in summer theater in Traverse City in my mid-twenties. It was on the third floor of an early nineteenth-century Victorian house with all the required towers and turrets, a prototype for every spooky house ever built. Remember the one in Hitchcock's *Psycho*? It looked exactly like that. I would enter the dim foyer and run like hell up the three flights to my apartment for fear of being stabbed.

But this railroad apartment in Beverly Hills was welcoming and charming. I loved it at first sight, and I *utzed* Arnie that we rent it. Moving to California had been a mutual choice, but over the years where we lived in a city was usually left to me. I have always had the best nose for locations, and Arnie usually acquiesced. It wasn't that he didn't care; he just wanted to make me happy.

The apartment was smack in the middle of Beverly Hills on the second floor of a two-family 1920s house. The clincher was that it had a screened-in porch where we could smell the scent of star jasmine wafting up from the garden below. We took it immediately for its charm, and it was less expensive than a normal apartment in Beverly Hills due to its quirky design.

One of the best parts for Arnie was our landlady, Mrs. Zinance. She had messy dyed black hair, a lot of energy, and looked to be about seventy. She loved Arnie from the get-go. Every time she stopped to speak with him, she would poke a finger into his chest and say in her Eastern European accent, "If you are going to live in Beverly Hills, you have to drive a Porchy."

Arnie loved her back because she sounded like Grandma Lena.

Living in Beverly Hills is everything you think Beverly Hills should be. Birdsong fills the air, and Japanese gardeners on every street groom the lawns for their closeups. We were only a short distance from the farmere's market, the Pacific Ocean, and the glitz, glamor, and hoopla of Rodeo Drive where the glamorous people were paying beautiful prices for unnecessary items. And it was in LA we found the Dolores Drive-In and began our love of eating our cheeseburgers al fresco, with birds chirping on the hood waiting to snatch a bite.

Another of Arnie's necessities was a good deli, and Beverly Hills had Nate'n Al's, which he zoned in on soon after our arrival. The famous faces were ubiquitous, and the prices were ridiculous, but we would splurge on an occasional corned beef sandwich. And Arnie had the added benefit of MGM's offices being on the Sunset Strip not far from the famous Tower Records—where we would go to check what placement MGM's records had in their bins—and to Pink's, the Hollywood landmark for all things hot dog since 1939. It was there I learned hot dogs can be good, if you put lots of sh*t on them.

Because of his position, we were able to take my parents to MGM Studios to see the premier of *That's Entertainment*, a compilation of all the wonderful musicals my mom and I had seen during the war years. We walked out of the theater arm in arm singing, you guessed it, "Singin' in the Rain." Much more fun than law school.

I got a California driver's license. Registered to vote. And tried to figure out what was next for me, since Arnie had finally settled into his milieu. Should I apply to a law school in LA or return to acting? So many possibilities, so many forks in the road to ponder. Trying to make up my mind, I took classes at UCLA.

My only memory of UCLA is how lovely the campus was and an incident when the teacher in one of my classes asked *the* question: "Are you Jewish?" (Why did people keep doing that?) when she read my name on the list of students in the class. I know she was just trying to match a name with a face, but I was startled by her chutzpah and bad manners. I can't remember what the class was about, but her question stirred up that old feeling of where I belonged. Apparently, I was still wandering in some desert, looking for a place to pitch my tent. I ignored her rude question, as California was a good start, and I loved it there.

But that carefree existence didn't last long. Within six months of our arrival, MGM Records was purchased by Polydor, a German company, and were moving their headquarters from the Sunset Strip to 810 Seventh Avenue, New York, New York. Arnie had been asked to go along in a new position as director of artist relations.

He accepted, and we began our preparations to move to New York City—when the God of Bashert joined hands with the God of Chaos and presented us with another offer—one we couldn't refuse.

• • •

Through all the adjusting, opening and closing businesses, and moving, Arnie had made it a priority to pursue all the possible ways for us to adopt. He knew that I had gone through the anguish of the tests and procedures in my previous marriage and adoption was our only hope. We thought about the agency pathway, but that would take too much time. Arnie and I were in our thirties, and neither of us were patient people. When we made up our minds to have something we wanted, it was in both of our natures to have it as soon as possible. So, before we moved to LA, Arnie had contacted every lawyer he knew in Detroit and enlisted them in the search for our child through private adoption.

We were well into the packing for our move from LA to New York City, when one of the lawyers called to inform us that a baby girl would be born in three months. She could be ours if all the logistics and official paperwork could be worked out.

Of course, we said, "YES!" followed by "pooh, pooh, pooh" to ward off any evil spirts who might be hanging around to gum up the works. Or as I learned later when living in the South, if you're presented with a life-changing experience, you say: "God willing, and the creek don't rise."

Short discussion, quick decision, and we changed the idea of an apartment in New York City to a country house in Cos Cob, Connecticut, on 15 Carriage Road, to be exact: an idyllic location to start a family.

A Short Back Story, If You Will Indulge Me

Feeling I am an outsider has been a thread throughout my life. Even today, in my eighties, having lived a long, productive life with many adventures and different social situations, it is not unusual for me to walk into a room and become overwhelmed with the sense that I don't belong.

I believe it all started when my birth father, George Brouwer, lay in a hospital, dying and asked his best friend, Harold, the Christmas Tree Harold, to take care of mom and me, knowing full well that Harold already had a thing for my mom. In fact, my birth father told her at some point, "Harold wants you, but he can only have you if I die." And soon after, he did.

Harold went off to fight in the Pacific Theater in World War II and came back as a highly decorated ball turret gunner, bad ass, and immediately asked my mom to marry him. And she agreed. In a thoughtful gesture, Harold and Hon made a courtesy call to the Brouwers to break the news that Harold and my mom were getting married. A squabble ensued between them. It was the 1940s and my mom hadn't been invited to the meeting.

It seemed to have been a name game. George Brouwer Sr., my paternal grandfather, whom I am told thought highly of himself, held his ground and argued that I was a Brouwer, his son's child, and he would do whatever it took to keep Harold from adopting me and changing my name. Result: Harold did marry my mom, became my father in all respects, but never officially adopted me. So, growing up, I was a Brouwer in a house of Petersons.

When my mom came to the school to meet my teachers at the start of the year or we would meet the mother of a classmate, I would nervously jump in front and explain that my mom's name was no longer Mrs. Brouwer with a *u*, it was now Mrs. Peterson with an *o*. For years I felt compelled to front run this situation. It was my obligation to handle that my birth father had died, and there was a new father in town.

Eventually, when my sister Korkye was born, Mom and Harold bought a new house and were planning to move out of Hon and Nanny's house, but I refused to go with them. The four adults had never thought to explain the situation to me; they simply convened a parental conclave and made the decision to leave me where I was, assuming all would work out eventually. First, it was choosing my own religion and then choosing where I wanted to live. I was only 6. And that was when my dream began:

Mom would be Hoovering in the living room of her new house, lost in the repetitiveness of pushing the wand of the vacuum back and forth, back and forth. She loved Hoovering. She called it "going to Florida." It was where she could lose herself as she cleaned her mental house as well as her physical one.

I would hear the doorbell, run into the living room, tug on my mom's dress, and wait for her to answer the bell, hiding behind her when she did. I always knew that on the other side of the threshold was an emaciated bald man wearing dirty-green overalls.

The bald man's right arm was missing, and he always asked the same question, "Is Judy here?"

Instinctively, I knew he was my birth father risen from the dead to take me away—possibly from having internalized some of the dogma from my early Easter Sunday attendance at the different Christian churches I had frequented. Who else do you know that has risen from the dead?

And, no doubt, I was disoriented by the upheaval of the new marriage, new house, new sister, which had lit a flame under my not-belonging issues. But leaving with this bald, one-armed man in dirty green overalls didn't seem such a wise cure for that. Eventually

I did move, but it took a while for me to remember where to go after school, and I often ended up in the wrong house.

When Arnie Geller knocked on my door, I went quickly and gladly. And with him in my life, the dreams of the one-armed bald man in the dirty green overalls faded away.

Adopting a child with Arnie felt so right; and in our family everyone would have the same last name. Adoption is a solemn oath between a husband, a wife, the child, and the world. You pledge that you will love and protect this astonishing wee human just as you promised to love and cherish each other under the chuppah. It was a forever and ever, amen, commitment. Our child would be a joyous addition to an already mixed marriage, an ultimate responsibility— one you would do anything to protect.

But before all that came to pass, we had to pack and move from LA to Cos Cob, Connecticut.

The Reluctant Stepford Wife

This time, no schlep in a U-Haul. MGM paid for a proper moving van. I remember when the van rolled up the driveway to our new home in Cos Cob. Arnie and I were sitting on the front steps, waiting. It was a Sunday afternoon on a perfect late-August day. Leaves had just begun to drop from the trees. And I was thinking, *We don't have a rake.*

Quickly the boxes were spread throughout the house, and we started to unpack, only to find that the professional movers in their twenty-foot, padded truck had manage to break my Nanny's crystal. It was smashed to smithereens. Arnie and I had driven it from Detroit to LA in a beat-up old U-Haul with no shocks, for God's sake, and it had arrived there intact. I started to sob.

It had nothing to do with Nanny's crystal, though that made me sad. It was the pressure and tension of the move, the change in locations, the pending adoption, and the frantic last-minute hunt for a house in Connecticut that had tripped my wires.

Arnie, without comment, stood up from the steps where he was sitting beside me, and disappeared into the house, and in his persuasive way, managed to get the president of the international moving company on a Sunday afternoon phone call and extracted an apology and compensation for our loss.

When Arnie came out, he sat by me on the stoop, and casually said, "I took care of it." And just like that, we began our adjustment to life on the East Coast.

In a frenzy, we ripped the 1950s wallpaper off the second bedroom walls as we went about preparing to turn it into a nursery. And Arnie began his fifty-two-minute commute on the New Haven Line to and from the city. I would drop him at the train in the morning, buy a *New York Times*, and drive to Long Island Sound to read it cover to cover. Reading the *Times* is a habit I still enjoy each morning. Though now I read it digitally and throw in an attempt at the crossword to keep my brain moving, not my furniture.

Living the wife-life of a commuter husband, truth be told, was difficult for me to adjust to. I feared I was slipping into the role of the Stepford wife and would soon have a martini in one hand and a golf club in the other.

LA had been so exciting and vibrant, Connecticut not so much. But it was all for the baby, I kept telling myself as I folded the day's *Times* and drove home to my white clapboard house in the woods where I continued the removal of the 1950s faded flowered wallpaper on the soon-to-be baby's nursery walls at 15 friggin' Carriage Road. Just for the record, I never said the F word or any permutation of it until I met Arnie. One day when we were still getting to know each other, he kept urging me to say it. "Just once, try it just once," he kept pushing. "Come on!"

I believe he was thinking, *Small town girl, too naive. Let's see if she'll do it.* So, I did, and it does come in handy once in a while. By the way, Arnie only rarely used it, at least not around me. Go figure.

Yes, I did grow up in a rather small town, but never in such a secluded wooded area. In Connecticut I became obsessed with bears. Black bears to be exact, the type that might be wandering in the heavily wooded area that surrounded our home. We knew that Connecticut had lots of trees—cedars, pines, spruce, hemlock; yes, similar to those in my father's coal yard at Christmas. But bears?

After nightfall in Cos Cob, waiting for Arnie to take the New Haven train home from the city, during which, he professed or confessed, he spent his time playing poker with the prostitutes also returning from their nightly jobs in the city, I would read. Sitting on the floor, behind a chair, back to the windows, knees drawn up like a bridge over a moat, hoping not to see or be seen by those critters—

the bears, not the hookers.

In August, a month before our soon-to-be daughter's birth, the Detroit lawyer, responsible for the details of the adoption, called to announce that Connecticut would not allow private adoptions. Bears, yes. Private adoptions, no?

We had been so confident that all the adoption papers were in order, ready to bring our newborn home to Connecticut from her birth in Detroit. The nursery was stripped of its old paper and repainted a buttercup yellow. A layette, which Arnie had taken a few hours from work to help me purchase, was now organized in the drawers of the new white dresser. I can see Arnie now in his blue blazer, leaning on the glass counter in the baby department at Bloomingdale's, briefcase by his side, helping me decide the color of onesies. He was all in.

Our creditworthiness, character references, educational backgrounds, letters of recommendation all extolled our competence to make a proper home for our child. We spent hours discussing names, settling finally on Samantha because Arnie liked the Samantha character on some detective television series, I have yet to remember which one. I hope someone reading this will know and tell me.

In all the craziness, we missed one crucial oversight—we never thought to check Connecticut's adoption laws. How could we have been so stupid? Arnie was the quintessential dot your i's and cross your t's guy. Me, I tend to do a lot on faith. But then, how could the lawyer have been so negligent?

The logical solution was a move to New York City, where private adoptions were allowed. It would be good. Arnie would no longer have to commute, and there would be no more playing cards with the hookers. And I would be in the city where I had always fantasized living. Our Connecticut decision, made in hasty ignorance, had reversed itself. Good ol' bashert had stepped in again.

Joyful about the exciting prospect before us, but manic about having to start all over with less than a month to do so, we didn't have time to repaper the Connecticut nursery; but the landlord decided it was an improvement and released us from the lease. In case you wondered.

Every day during this transition, I commuted with Arnie from Cos Cob to the city. Reaching Grand Central, Arnie would split off to his office at 810 Seventh Avenue and I would scour the city for an affordable two-bedroom apartment. At night we would train back to Connecticut where we switched into overdrive and continued to pack—again. I would be in New York, yes, but my longing to star on Broadway slipped farther down the list of my priorities—we were focused on living in New York with our daughter. She would be the star.

As you know from my reaction to the bears in Cos Cob, I am at the mercy of my environment, soaking it into my core—the visceral vibes it projects, the energy it exudes, the cultural opportunities it provides. I had visited New York twice in the 1960s and had fallen in love. At some point in our frenetic running around the city looking for apartments, Arnie and I discovered that we had both been in New York on the same day in the early 1960s and both had attended Johnny Carson's show on the same evening. I was with my ex-husband, and Arnie, if he described her correctly, had to have been with a long-legged Radio City Rockette, both of us oblivious to bashert mucking about in the background.

Finding a suitable and affordable apartment in a matter of days was frustrating and exhausting. And obviously, I was not too stable at the time anyway, considering all the crying in Cos Cob. One day during the search, I was standing on the corner of Fifty-First and First Avenue, looking at rental advertisements in the newspaper through a blur of tears, when a blonde lady with an equally blond boy in a stroller stopped and asked if she could help.

I described my situation and that I had seen an ad for an apartment in the area but couldn't figure out which building it was in. She said she believed there was a rental in her apartment building and pointed to a thirteen-story white brick building over her left shoulder.

And yes, there was, and yes, we took it: a two-bedroom rental on Beekman Place, on the east side of Manhattan near the river, a perfect location. I don't want to overuse the bashert thing, but by this time, wouldn't you agree that good ol' bashert was finally working for our benefit? Maybe making up for that last-minute business he pulled in LA.

Beekman Place is a charming oasis excluded from the hyperactivity of the city. Our ninth-floor apartment was at the back of the building and gave us a glistening nighttime cityscape of the Empire State Building. Or, as Samantha would call it when she first learned to talk, the "Umpire Mistake Building." It was a short twenty-four-minute crosstown walk or short bus ride to Seventh Avenue and Arnie's office. He took a cab.

Lucky us; our apartment came with free entertainment. Our bedroom shared a common wall with the bedroom in the apartment to our right. Multiple times a week the bachelor who lived there provided us with very loud and energetic entertainment. You would have thought Elvis lived there with all the screeching and hollering goin' on. But it had its rewards: The bachelor owned one of the finest restaurants in the city, and more than weekly we would find exquisite contrition cakes on our doormat. Ahh, New York, New York! It really is a helluva town!

The neighbor's sex life became less interesting when Samantha Rae Geller moved in. She was born on September 18, 1974—four years to the day that Arnie's Grandma Lena had passed away. Samantha was given the Hebrew name of Hannah Leba in Grandma Lena's memory. Hannah in Hebrew means God's gift. Leba in Hebrew means beloved. Samantha was a God-given, beloved gift to bring under the Geller family chuppah. Bashert.

Before we could actually bring her to Beekman Place, we had to fly to Detroit where she was born. Michigan's adoption laws required that she stay in a foster home until the adoption papers were in order. We flew from LaGuardia to Detroit Metropolitan Airport, rented a car, and drove immediately to the foster home. I began to tremble as we pulled up in front of the house and continued to tremble until she was placed in my arms—a tiny dark-haired beauty with long legs sticking out from the flimsy blanket they had wrapped around her. Arnie put his arm around me, and we stood side by side, staring at her in disbelief.

Our plan was to stay at Flossie and Bob's apartment for a few days so my parents could join us, and we could all get acquainted and acclimate. On the way there, I carried on a running dialogue telling Samantha about the members of both families she had entered and all their foibles, just as I had told Arnie about my family as we drove across Michigan to meet them that first time. Arnie was quiet, as usual, only glancing over occasionally to see how both of us were faring.

It wasn't until the day we were flying back to New York that Arnie's paternal instincts burst out in full force. The minute we got out of the car at the airport, he walked in front of me with Samantha in my arms until we got seated on the airplane—his right arm stretched out in front of us as if he were a Detroit Lions linebacker scanning for an offensive attack.

He kept saying to everyone we passed, "Watch out, lady with a baby! Watch out, here comes a lady with a baby."

It was unbelievably embarrassing and completely endearing at the same time. Bashert! Bashert! Bashert!

Welcome to Fear City

Welcome to Fear City screamed over a grotesque line drawing of a skull and crossbones on the pamphlet's cover. It was said to be a tourist guide; its real purpose was not to guide, but to terrorize the tourists visiting New York City. Inside was a list of all the horrors to be encountered if you didn't watch out: don't take the subway, stay in Midtown, don't be out after 6 p.m., try not to walk alone, have the doorman at your hotel or restaurant call a taxi, and the old chestnut, hold tightly to your handbag.

Arnie and I were aware that New York in the 1970s had a bad rap, but serene Beekman Place, the responsibilities of parenthood, and Arnie's new position at Polydor stood as a bulwark against the Visigoths and rumors running rampant through the city. Yes, the city had budget deficits and Mayor Beame, in an effort to control the budget, had threatened to tighten the city's belt by laying off 10,000 uniformed police officers. The city unions fought back with a bogus organization, the Council for Public Safety, and put out that fear city pamphlet. Its purpose? To scare the hell out of prospective tourists so they and their much-needed dollars would stay away.

We knew about the fear pamphlet but were too busy living our new life to focus on its message. We had our sweet baby, and the December 1975 edition of *Billboard* announced that Arnie, who had previously been director of artist relations, was to take over as national director of promotion for Polydor Records, responsible for coordinating and supervising all promotional activities for Polydor's roster of artists. One of his first assignments was to work with Columbia Studios in the promotion of the soundtrack from their new movie, the rock opera, *Tommy*. The movie was to be released in March in both the United Sates and the UK.

On January 19, 1975, while I was totally occupied with Samantha, now four months old, Arnie was in London, having flown there on a promotional tour with the cast: Elton John, Roger Daltrey, Ann-Margret, and others, along with the executives from Columbia Studios and Polydor Records to prepare for the opening.

Passing the time waiting for his nightly call, and needing fresh air, I decided to take Samantha for a walk over to Lexington Avenue near Sixtieth Street before nightfall to see what was new in Bloomindale's windows. I bundled her into her pink snowsuit, with its white faux-fur around her face to shield her from the cold, put her into her pram, and out we went. In retrospect, why in the hell, on a cold winter's night, when the sun was about to set, was I out on the New York streets with a four month old in a pram? An impulsive move, I guess. All I can say is, I had more guts than brains at that point, or cabin fever and the responsibilities of a new baby had atrophied my brain.

My attacker, a vagrant woman screaming like an Irish banshee, with a distorted face and matted dark hair, came running from the opposite direction screaming, "Bitch, bitch, bitch" into the frigid night air as she drew near and threw an open beer can directly at Samantha in her pram.

Strong-arming her as best I could with my left arm, while at the same time making an attempt at deflecting her flying beer can, I pushed Samantha's pram with my right arm and made a mad dash back to the security and warmth of Beekman Place and our apartment. I chastised myself all the way home for having such poor judgment.

When Arnie called from London that evening, Samantha had been fed and was fast asleep, none the worse for wear. I was still reliving the incident and smelling of beer, but held my story as Arnie had his own far worse tale to tell, and I was ecstatic to hear his voice. He was staying at London's Carlton Tower Hotel and earlier in the evening had taken the elevator from his room down to the hotel lobby for a dinner meeting. As he exited the elevator on the main floor, a car passing by the front of the hotel had stopped to strafe the building with a barrage of bullets that ricocheted around the lobby. Thank God the elevator doors had yet to close and Arnie had the presence of mind to step back in and push the up button into safety.

This was during the Troubles in Ireland and there was speculation that the attackers were an Irish Republican Army terrorist group on a fear campaign, targeting London's hotels in an attempt to discourage tourism in England, much the same as the ersatz Council on Public Safety was attempting to do in New York.

The New York Times published two articles on Sunday, January 19, 1975: The London terrorist story on page 13 titled: "2 London Hotels Are Hit by Shots—Machine Gun Fire Causes Injury to 7 Persons," and on page 48, one titled: "East Side Shop Manager Stabbed and Seriously Wounded Resisting Holdup."

The holdup had happened at 5:15 p.m. on Sixtieth Street near Lexington Avenue. According to *The Times*, "the manager, Harry Barr, was accosted . . . as he tried to place a bag containing the receipts in a bank's night-deposit slot." They said he was stabbed in the back, the stomach, and hands when he refused to give up the bag. It was exactly where I had been pushing Samantha in her pram before the Banshee of Lexington Avenue had her run at us. Samantha and I escaped the Banshee and had only missed the manager's stabbing by seconds, as Arnie had missed the machine gun fire by seconds.

Banshees, bullets, stabbings. The bashert message that night was the Gellers were meant to be alive. Thank God!

I joke with Samantha that she is the product of the mean streets of New York, visualizing *West Side Story* and rumbles in empty lots. Notwithstanding the vagrant banshee lady throwing beer incident, which she was too young to be aware of, most of Samantha's exposures in New York were normal childhood activities. She learned to walk and ride her tricycle on its sidewalks, played in the United

Nation Park's sandbox, and visited the animals at the Central Park Zoo, where later in her teens she would become a paid helper in the penguin area.

Well, maybe her childhood was not so normal. Frequently, when we took our morning walk up First Avenue—slowly, because Samantha was enamored by the fresh flowers stacked in the green plastic pots in front of the markets and insisted on sniffing every last one—the notoriously private Greta Garbo, on her own morning walk, would stop and have a chat with Samantha and smell the flowers along with her. I always thought Greta was instinctively drawn to Samantha because they had the same September 18 birthdate. I read somewhere that Garbo was a shy daydreamer who disliked school. Similar to Samantha as she grew older.

I still romanticize living in New York; the city continues to itch beneath my skin. Perhaps that's due to one of my acting coaches in college who told me he expected to see me on Broadway one day. It was a seed I have never been able to unplant. The closest I ever came to staking my claim on the Great White Way was the parking spot in front of Arnie's office at 810 Seventh Avenue, where I waited in the car to pick him up after work.

Arnie loved that office, as he had only to exit the building, make a quick turn left, and walk three minutes to Carnegie Deli at 854 Seventh Avenue. It had been in that location since 1937. Sadly, it is closed now. But when Arnie was a regular there, Carnegie was considered to have the best corned beef sandwich in NYC. He definitely concurred and would frequently meet there for lunch with Cousin Nat, who by then was president of Brunswick Records. The countermen would start slicing the corned beef as they walked in the door, already knowing Arnie's order, which never varied: a corned beef sandwich, thinly sliced, somewhat fatty, on rye, with American mustard. And the greeter would give each of them a white cloth napkin as they sat down, a privilege given only to regulars. Arnie loved that old New York atmosphere and celebrity treatment.

In December of 1975, Arnie, as Polydor's national promotions director, began to work with Gloria and Buddy Buie and their group the Atlanta Rhythm Section, a popular Southern Rock band.

Buddy was the originator of the Rhythm Section, and the writer and producer of all their songs. Gloria was the guiding force, in charge of daily business, the finances, the band's touring, and everything else.

I had never met Gloria and Buddy, though they were often in New York at the Polydor offices meeting with Arnie. During their multiple meetings, Buddy, Gloria, and Arnie had become friends, and Buddy began his campaign to lure Arnie to Atlanta to work with him on the Rhythm Section. Apparently, Arnie's inner entrepreneur had already been pushing him to leave Polydor. Buddy's proposal was the ideal way to exit the corporate world and return him to his entrepreneurial self.

This record executive's wife only learned about these discussions during a taxi ride up First Avenue when it was essentially a done deal. First Avenue was the conduit of our lives and now it was going to be our conduit right out of town.

Over My Dead Body

It was a New York City hot August day in 1977. The temperature was hovering somewhere in the high nineties with killer humidity. I remember the taxicab's windows were lowered for air circulation as Arnie and I made our way up First Avenue, even though Arnie always said we were on Third. It was sort of Hermione Gingold and Maurice Chevalier singing "I remember it well" in *Gigi* where Maurice sings: "You wore a gown of gold," and Hermione responds, "I was all in blue."

A stereotypical male-female exchange.

I know it was First Avenue because at the time we were passing the tall white marble-and-glass United Nations Secretariat building. Next to it was the UN playground, Samantha's playground, where she and I went practically every day, walking south against the traffic going north on First Avenue to get there.

On this particularly stifling August day, I remember commenting to Arnie that the multicolored national flags of the UN member nations were plastered against their poles in the windless summer heat.

It was then he turned to me and asked, "How would you feel about moving to Atlanta? The Buies have asked me to move there and help manage the Atlanta Rhythm Section." Apparently, Arnie and the Buies had been discussing this for some time—but not with me, obviously. I knew Arnie had been having meetings with Gloria and Buddy Buie, but he never discussed the particulars with me and I assumed it was just another artist group he was working with; that was his job.

"Over my dead body!" flew out of my mouth, along with, "You're kidding, right?"

Glancing at his face, I knew. He was not kidding. It had already been decided, and I had been deluded into thinking we were happily settled and not going anywhere. I was being sandbagged by Arnie as I had been as a child when my parents left me at my grandparents' house and moved away. Not wanting to give up, and trying not to cry, I still pushed the idea of staying in New York. Pleading my case, I ran through the life we had established in the city: "New York is our home. What about all the work we did on our apartment? I love our apartment."

Silence.

"Why did we bother removing every single damn carpet tack from the floors so they could be refinished and safe for Samantha to crawl on?"

Silence.

Winding up, I asked, "What about Dr. Meislen? Remember the time I couldn't get Samantha to wake up and called you at the office? And you told me to wrap her in a blanket and come to the front of the building, and you would be there in ten minutes to pick me up in a taxi and go with me to see Dr Meislen? Remember? And Dr. Meislen said: "Folks, folks, she's OK. She's just sleeping; she's tired."

Silence.

"How can we replace him?"

Dr. Aaron Meislen, a gentle and kind pediatrician, was practicing one mile south of us at New York University Hospital. He understood Samantha—and us, for that matter.

Arnie patiently listened, allowing me to carry on: "Who will I find in Atlanta to put up with that craziness, especially now that Samantha is having more problems with her breathing?" And, most likely whining at this point and trying to inject a little humor, I asked: "What about the Waxmans? Who will you call if you can't find me?"

Arnie had always tried to keep track of Samantha and me, especially after the banshee incident, which hadn't stopped me from getting mommy shut-in fever. Occasionally, wanting to be alone, I would break away from the other mothers and escape the building for a change of environment. If it wasn't to a different park or a toddler class of some sort, Samantha and I often ended up in a museum or at Bloomingdale's. On one of those days, as I pushed Samantha in her stroller in the Bloomingdale's children's department, I heard my name paged over the loudspeaker: "Mrs. Geller, Mrs. Judy Geller, if you are in the building, would you please go to the nearest cashier?"

Arnie had found me. How? He had asked Marcia Waxman. Marcia was well aware of my penchant to escape the apartment on a moment's notice, and she generally knew where I was headed.

Arnie and I met the Waxmans on Beekman Place when we first moved in. They lived in our building. Their son, Stephen, and Samantha played together in the UN Park while Marcia and I bonded over peanut butter and jelly sandwiches and fights in the sandbox. Our families celebrated many holidays and birthdays together and made trips to Disney World, Martha's Vineyard, you name it. In fact, Arnie and I joined New York's Temple Emanuel because of them—where, in later years, Samantha would be confirmed.

And not to put too fine a point on it, Marcia was the one who recommended Dr Meislen *and* she made the only brisket Arnie would eat.

Following is Marcia's brisket recipe, passed to her from her mother, Minnie Goodcuff, and Marcia passed it to me. Now that's a friend, giving up a recipe.

Minnie Goodcuff's Brisket

– 1 4-5 lb. first cut brisket

– 1 large onion, sliced

– 1 28-ounce can of tomatoes (if whole, crush)

– Several bay leaves

– 1 large lemon, zested

Sear meat on all sides; remove from pan.

Brown onions in remaining fat.

Add tomatoes.

Add hot water, using the now empty tomato can.

Add lemon zest.

Add bay leaves.

Return meat to pan, bring to simmer, then cover.

Cook for 1 ½ hours. Turn over.

Cook for additional hour and test for doneness; cool, and refrigerate.

Slice when cold.

Reheat in gravy.

———————

And speaking of food, I asked, "What about the Palm?"

Arnie and I had take-out meals from the Palm before take-out was a thing. They would package our dinner in a used cheesecake box. And talk about that cheesecake? I have no words. With some frequency, Arnie would stop by the Palm on his way home from Polydor and pick up a to-go of lobster and their to-die-for cheesecake, next stopping by the Waxmans' apartment to drop off a claw or two.

"For God's sake," I pushed, "on our kitchen wall we have one of the Palm's original menus—framed! Who else does that?"

Not only was the Palm's food superb, but Arnie loved the speakeasy atmosphere that had not changed from the restaurant's origins in 1926 when it was a hangout for newspaper people. *The New York Daily Mirror*, *The Daily News*, and *The Herald Tribune* were all within walking distance. The restaurant still had the look of the 1920s, when cigar-smoking newspapermen used it as a hangout. Often, when times were tough, they paid their tabs by drawing cartoons on the walls in lieu of cash—a tradition they have kept up to this day for their favorite customers as the restaurant branched out around the country. I always knew Arnie's caricature would be up on that wall one day.

Arnie not-so-jokingly decided that Samantha would be married there. In her bridal gown, she would pick her way down the steep, rickety stairs from the upstairs dining area to the main floor through the wafting smells of steaks and lobsters on the grill, to where her groom and the rabbi would be waiting under the chuppah next to the bar.

I was finally at home in a city I adored. But, no matter, it was a done deal, and all my pleading fell on deaf ears. It was my mind that had to adjust. And I tried, I really tried.

Not only was Arnie the love of my life, but he was also responsible for the support of the family, and his inner entrepreneurial itch was needing to be scratched. So, with reluctance, I started to pack—again—this time for Atlanta.

Just before we left, Arnie surprised us by hiring two horse-drawn hansom cabs from Central Park to clop across town to Beekman Place and pick up Samantha and me, her friends, their mothers, and Flossie and Bob, who were visiting for Samantha's third birthday, for a carriage ride around the city. I guess it was Arnie's way of saying, "Happy birthday" and "Goodbye."

Even though I knew it was an apologetic move on Arnie's part, it was a lovely generous one. As they say in the South, where we were headed, "Bless his heart."

PART V

Wandering in the Desert of Paran

At Least That's What the Torah Says

We left New York on the Southern Crescent overnight train to Atlanta. Samantha had an ear infection and Dr. Meislen had suggested that flying would not be a good idea. Naively, I tested the bashert concept by making a declaration to Arnie: "If we ever move back to New York, we must do it by train." In my head I had conjured up the idea that by doing so, we would be closing a metaphorical circle that would prevent us from ever leaving New York again. I don't recall Arnie's response. If he had one, it went something similar to: "OK, I'll remember that." All the while thinking, *This too shall pass.*

In Atlanta, we disembarked from the Southern Crescent at the Peachtree Southern Station located, you guess it, on Peachtree Road. The station house, a 1918 building the size of our New York apartment, was red brick Italian Renaissance, a white-columned design by Neel Reid, a lauded architect in the region. The area around the station was Peachtree Hills, known for some of the bloodiest battles of the Civil War. I hoped that by now they were through with all that.

We had left behind our apartment on Beekman Place, with its view of the "Umpire Mistake Building," to move into a quickly purchased, three-story, red brick house on a hill at the end of a cul-de-sac named Paran Valley. It was a secluded, dead-end road off a winding access road called Mount Paran. One of the neighbors in our new location had nicknamed the area The Parans and it stuck.

It was an emotionally difficult transition for me, and I have lost or repressed (which might be the better word) all the details of how it happened. I only vaguely remember the packing or the truck taking our belongings from Fifty-First Street. Nor do I remember the truck arriving on Paran Valley Road in Atlanta and how our belongings got up the steep slant of the hill and into our new home.

I was overcome with this unwanted change in our life—the isolation of living in a home in the suburbs and not in an apartment in New York with supportive friends to rely on, and the adjustment of having to drive to absolutely everything we needed to buy or do. I worried about the responsibility of keeping this larger house up and running, along with finding a new nursery school for Samantha and establishing a structure for her with new friends and activities. Plus, and most significantly, finding a new pediatrician and pulmonary specialist as her sick days had become more unnerving.

Overthinking (me!?) our situation, I recognized that Paran sounded biblical, especially Mount Paran. Lo and behold, in Genesis there are many biblical references to Paran. It was definitely a wilderness—*appropriate*, I thought—similar to the one traversed by biblical heavyweights like Abraham and Moses. And remember Sarah and Hagar whom I mentioned before? Well, let me finish that story.

Sarah was barren, unable to gift Abraham with a child, remember? She sent Hagar in as a pinch-hitter, to get to third base, so to speak. It all got messy when Hagar quickly became pregnant. Full of herself, literally, she became a tad uppity and looked down her nose on barren Sarah.

Sarah may have been infertile, but believe you me, that makes you touchy and tough. Thus, she was not having any of Hagar's mishigas. So, Sarah begged Abraham to take care of the situation.

To which he replied, "Your maid, your problem. Deal with it." (In the Torah, really?)

In the fullness of time, Hagar produced Abraham's son, Ishmael, meaning God will hear. And God did hear and told Abraham to shape up as he had not been as appreciative of Sarah as he should have been. Crawling back into Sarah's tent, Abraham cast Hagar and Ishmael out into the Desert of Paran, where previously the Israelites had wandered for forty years after their Exodus from Egypt.

When Abraham turned ninety-nine, God said to him: "Get Ishmael back here and bless him as he shall father twelve chieftains and be the maker of great nations; and Sarah will feel less guilty about all that kicking the baby and mother out into the desert business. Ishmael, your son, will be OK. OK?"

"Further, you, Abraham, shall have a son with Sarah and will be the father of many nations together with her."

At that, Abraham laughed, not being able to fathom how a man of ninety-nine would have the wherewithal to conceive a child. And Sarah laughed thinking how a woman of her age would be able to bring forth a child, or want to, with an old cocker like Abraham!

But it came to pass as it always does in the Torah that Sarah and Abraham produced a son whom they named Itzhak (Issac), Arnie's Hebrew name, by the way. Sarah lived to be 127 years. And all the men got circumcised. At least that's what the Torah says.

Don't Be Ugly Now, Ya Hear?

Easy to say, tough to do. We were now below the Mason-Dixon line, in the Deep South, submerged in a culture where an irritated mother would say to her acting-up child, "Don't be ugly now, you hear?" *Ugly* in old Southern speak is more than an adjective, it's an attitude. And I guess you could say my attitude was a wee bit ugly.

We had to adjust to a slower life in a Southern town, in a red brick house on a hill, in a suburb, not far from the famous original Peachtree Street, which was then one of the most elegant streets in Atlanta. It was lined with gracious mansions and flowering magnolia trees that are essentially gone now. The other Peachtrees, seventy-one by last count, must have been laid out willy-nilly on old Native American Indian trails—my ugly take on the situation.

The Peachtree Road of old—on which, I confess, I currently live, in a high rise not a house and have done so off and on for thirty years (I sometimes adjust)—was the road to everywhere back then, the social and physical lifeline of what was on its way to becoming a major metropolitan city. It had suffered terribly in the Civil War when over 3,000 of its private and public buildings were burnt to the ground and its population had sunk to under 10,000. Atlanta's reconstruction was aided by its central location and the four major railroads that connected it to all areas of the Deep South, and by its money crop: cotton.

When Arnie and I and three-year-old Samantha arrived, the population had reached 1,478,000, and we watched those numbers ticking up on a digital counting board a few miles south of us, yup, on Peachtree Road. Five minutes from that sign, farther south on Peachtree, stands the Temple, another red brick Southern Colonial building, designed in the 1930s, by architect Philip Shutze, an associate of Neel Reid. There will be more of Reid later.

The Temple, which we joined soon after our arrival, was established in 1867 by twenty-six German Jews. It was bombed in 1958 when white supremacists, aka the Confederate Underground, all fired up by Rabbi Jacob Rothschild's association with Martin Luther King, felt compelled to strategically place fifty sticks of dynamite under the Temple's north doors in an attempt to blow it away. It didn't work.

In fact, the Temple endures, and it was there Samantha intermittently attended religious school. Intermittently, because she was not always feeling well and missed classes. When she did attend, like father like daughter, she spent a good bit of time in the girls' bathroom, not kissing boys, but avoiding her teacher's expectations. School of any kind was problematic for her.

Atlanta at that time, still clinging to vestiges of its old Southern ways, had one of the most popular restaurants south of the Mason-Dixon line—Aunt Fanny's Cabin, a slave cabin from the 1880s, set deep in the muddy woods in an area called Smyrna. Arnie loved going there even though it was not the Palm. Its allure was their greasy-good fried chicken.

The entire staff was black. The patrons, white. The menu, written on chalk boards, was carried by young black boys on a rope around their necks. It took my breath away when we first went there. The waitresses served wearing plantation dresses, aprons, and head wraps, mammy style, straight out of *Gone with the Wind.* You were being transported back in time, only this was in the present, and I found it appalling and uncomfortable.

As we got to know our neighbors, the majority transplants from the North, more than one of them told us they were convinced we were an offshoot of the Mafia because Arnie drove a black Lincoln sedan with its windows blacked out. It would have been better if we had been connected as, shortly after we moved in, we awakened to a white cross planted on our front lawn. Someone should have informed them of my Italian family's legend (unsubstantiated) that one of our relatives had worked for Al Capone in Chicago. Though his specialty was not planting crosses but drowning people in bathtubs. Armed with that association, the cross-burners may have been too scared to plant one in the first place. Thank God the culprits never set the cross on fire.

Was the Confederate Underground, the torchers of the Temple, at it again? Or, perhaps, it was Atlanta's version of the *Welcome to Fear City* pamphlet.

It didn't make sense. There were several Jewish families living on our street and not one of them had ever been threatened by a white cross stuck into their front lawn. It never happened again and for some reason, we never alerted the police. Instead, we took the incident in stride, perhaps toughened having lived in NYC where crazy ladies attacked prams on the street with beer cans.

P.S. We never solved the mystery of the cross.

The Buie-Geller Organization (BGO)

Every day, Arnie left the Parans in his black Lincoln, with its tinted window cracked so he could flick his ashes into the wind as he drove across town to Doraville and the offices of the Buie-Geller Organization on the second floor over Studio One, a recording studio. Buddy owned the studio along with the charismatic, much loved Bill Lowery, prominent music publisher well known as the father of Atlanta music. Multiple hits by Lynyrd Skynyrd, Journey, .38 Special, and many others had been recorded at the studio, and the handshake-partnership between Arnie and Buddy would produce more.

The Gellers were in a different world in every respect. Arnie went from wearing a blue blazer and gray slacks to no blazer, blue jeans, and big ol' gold aviators. He kept the open collar shirt and the same beaten up attaché he had carried for years. I thought he looked very rock 'n' roll and sexy as hell. So attractive (kidding) that Governor George Busbee, Jimmy Carter's successor, appointed Arnie to be a member of the state's Music Industry Advisory Committee for his passion to stop record bootlegging, rampant at the time. Arnie's goal had always been to see that artists got full remuneration for their creations, and now he had a government official set on doing something about it. I have plaques and citations on the wall behind me commemorating Arnie's efforts.

Across the street from Studio One was a fast-food restaurant specializing in, you guessed it, Southern fried chicken. Since a corned beef sandwich was now an airplane ride away, it wasn't too long before fried chicken climbed the charts to the top of Arnie's approved food groups. All day long, the smell of frying chicken permeated the air over their offices.

When Arnie wanted to smoke, he did it on a small balcony off his office where chicken fumes were inhaled along with those spiraling from his cigarette. The word is that Arnie mostly went outside to smoke, but Buddy, avoiding the chicken fumes, flicked his ashes behind the couch in Arnie's office. What a team!

In the midst of all those fumes and flames, the Buie-Geller Organization flourished with Buddy's hitmaking, songwriting, and production; Arnie's innovative artist management and international promotion ability; and Gloria's oversight of everything. It was a productive period for Arnie, who loved working with the Buies and the Rhythm Section. We became fast friends with both Gloria and Buddy. Gloria and I are still friends, though both of our husbands have passed away. *The New York Times* wrote of Buddy in his obituary: "Mr. Buie was a textbook example of a figure behind the music without whom there would be no music."

During Arnie and Buddy's partnership, the Rhythm Section was at the top of their game. Their *Champagne Jam* album made the top 10 and a single from the album, "I'm Not Gonna Let It Bother Me Tonight" made it to the top 20. And another cut, "Imaginary Lover" made it to number 7. They played to sellout crowds wherever they went. I attended two of their concerts in Atlanta's Grant Field, one in 1978 and another in 1979. It was a sight to behold; the crowds went as far as the eye could see, all fired up to see their hometown boys so successful! The first trip we made back to New York was when they played in Central Park. My two world's were coming together.

Just prior to those successes, during the run-up to the 1976 presidential election, the band had been on the road, playing gigs to help raise funds for Georgia's Governor Carter, who was running against incumbent Gerald Ford for the presidency. President Carter, as we know, won the race and was on his way to the White House to be inaugurated on January 20, 1977.

Thanks to the Rhythm Section's fundraising efforts, the Buies and the Gellers were invited to the inauguration ceremony and to one of the inaugural balls. It was a thrill, even though it was an elbow-to-elbow experience, and we damn near froze to death during the ceremonies as the temperature hovered around 27 degrees. I think that the masochists who set that date way back when must have figured if the president could live through the weather in January, he could live through anything the office threw at him.

Later in the year, Chip Carter and family held a backyard barbecue to thank their volunteers, fundraisers, cabinet members, and their families—anyone who had helped win the election. We were invited along with the Buies. Arnie, always looking for a way to promote the band, finagled the White House to add fifty of the most prominent record promoters from around the country to their list of invitees. A move designed to make sure they would promote the Rhythm Section after the event. And it worked.

During the picnic, the Rhythm Section presented President Carter with a shiny maroon ARS touring jacket before they took the stage. When the president came on the stage in the jacket to introduce the Rhythm Section, he said, "My son, Chip, said I was too old for this, but Chip said if I let him use my backyard, I could come. I think I have a lot in common with the Atlanta Rhythm Section. I remember when they first started, critics and commentators said they didn't have a chance. They said the same thing about me." The crowd loved it.

The picnic tables were covered with the same red-and-white tablecloths Arnie and I had used in Farmington, Michigan, years before, but there was not an egg salad sandwich in sight. Traditional barbeque pits had been dug on the White House South Lawn and the picnic tables groaned with smoked pork, Brunswick stew, potato salad, rolls, sweet pickles, ribs, beans, and pecan pie. Mrs. Carter's menu.

During the festivities, she stopped by my picnic table and sat beside me, discussing our families and our husbands' responsibilities. We talked about her adjustment to living in the White House and about our daughters—Samantha and Amy—and she asked me all about Arnie, what he did, and how much he traveled. I was telling her about radio stations and arenas. I suspect she was thinking about Camp David, from which President Carter had recently returned after twelve days of secret negotiations with Egyptian President Anwar Sadat and Israeli Prime Minister Menachem Begin to establish a framework for a historic peace treaty between Israel and Egypt, which was signed in September 1978. They were the Camp David Peace Accords, which held and paved the way for the Abraham Accords that followed in 2020.

We were just two normal wives chatting at a family picnic, only she was First Lady and her backyard was behind the White House. She was very sweet and very smart and became instrumental in her husband's presidency.

When I was introduced to President Carter, he took my hand, smiled, and then turned his head to greet others in the crush around him, not releasing my hand as he spoke with them. I looked up to see Arnie craning his neck in the back of the crowd, trying to figure out what the holdup was. And just as you would expect, it was captured by yet another professional photographer Arnie had hired to memorialize the event for the Rhythm Section. That photo, along with the one in which I first met Arnie, sit side by side on my desk.

This handshake incident happened just after Carter's revealing interview in *Playboy* during which he told the interviewer: "I've looked on a lot of women with lust. I've committed adultery in my heart many times. This is something that God recognizes I will do—and I have done it—and God forgives me for it."

President Carter regretted that interview and I intend no disrespect by telling that story here—it is just a fun one to tell. I must admit I was looking good that day. Aren't we all at thirty-eight? From there, believe you me, all the "good" parts start slip-sliding away.

That said, the visit to the White House and shaking hands with the president, whom I admire greatly, was an extraordinary experience—one I will always cherish.

Mrs. Carter died in 2023 and President Carter in 2024. He was 100. His funeral was stately and moving, as were the eulogies by friends and family. The chronicling of his post-presidential achievements, with Rosalynn by his side, was one of great public service as they spread charity, health, and peace around the world. I am honored to have met them and to have held their hands.

I Love the Nightlife

—ALICIA BRIDGES AND SUSAN HUTCHISON, 1977

In the February 4, 1978, edition of *Record World Magazine*, a story ran, announcing the official formation of the Buie-Geller Organization, an international management company with its own proprietary label, BGO Records, and with not only the Rhythm Section in its roster, but seven other acts as well. Arnie and Buddy were up and running.

It was the most unlikely partnership one could imagine: the bonding of a famous laid-back Southern Baptist songwriter with Northern hard-driving Jewish record executive. Buddy bragged that Arnie was the first Jew he had ever met, and in turn, Buddy was Arnie's first encounter with a born and bred Southerner. An odd cultural match that turned out to be a terrific partnership and a lasting friendship made on a handshake. And with nary an argument between them.

"I Love the Nightlife"—well, Alicia Bridges did with her 1978 hit of the same name. Disco was raging in the 1970s when John Travolta was moving his tush-clutching white pants across a Brooklyn dance floor in *Saturday Night Fever.*

Alicia was signed to Lowery Music and was recording "I Love the Nightlife" at Studio One. Arnie and Buddy happened to walk into the studio when Alicia and Steve Buckingham, the producer, were going back and forth about whether the song was R&B or disco. Alicia was not fond of disco and wanted it to stay as R&B. Steve wanted to do a disco remix. Buddy's musical ear heard a disco sound, and Arnie's promotional ear heard a disco hit. They took over her management and signed her to BGO Records.

Believing wholeheartedly in the song, Arnie began an all-out campaign to get it on the charts and work it to the top. As with everything he did, if Arnie believed in you, he would do anything to make you successful. So, he brought the record to his former company, Polydor Records, an agreement was made, contracts were signed, and "I Love the Nightlife" was released in 1978 on BGO Records under Polydor's umbrella.

Arnie, determined that it be a hit, put in immense effort to expose Alicia to the widest audience possible, going on the road with her to make that happen. One of Alicia's first bookings was in a nightclub in Connecticut. Unbeknownst to Arnie, the club was owned by members of an organization—the one we had been accused of belonging to when we first moved to Atlanta. In the middle of the night, my phone rang. It was Arnie calling from a payphone on the New York side of the Connecticut-New York border. He and Alicia had just been led to that border in a sheriff's car, lights flashing, having been warned to never come to Connecticut again if they were at all concerned about their health and well-being.

The Connecticut Mafia, we learned later, were well organized and exceptionally violent at the time. The Gambino and Genovese families were heavily involved there in gambling and drugs. Something else we had not known when we had first moved there in 1974.

That night they roughed up the members of Alicia's crew and held Arnie at gunpoint in a back room of the club, threatening to kill him and destroy all the band's equipment if he didn't hand over all the night's proceeds.

I said all those things a normal wife does when her husband has been held at gunpoint by the mob: "Oh my God! Are you all right? How did you get away? Oh my God! Are you all right?"

Arnie, with his usual calming voice, said, "Yes, everyone's OK. I called a friend who knew a guy with a connection to the mob (again, not my famiglia), who called the county sheriff, who sent a squad car to escort us out of town. He warned me, if I cared about living, to never again come back to Connecticut."

And yes, Arnie left the proceeds behind. Wouldn't you?

Tough business, rock 'n' roll.

Did I mention I hated Connecticut? You couldn't adopt a baby, but you could get your head blown off by the mob. But I digress, again.

We all know that old adage "the show must go on," and due to Arnie's expertise and Alicia's talent, in 1978, BGO/Polydor Records had one of the biggest hits of the disco era, "I Love the Nightlife," which reached number five on the *Billboard*, *Cashbox*, and *Record World* charts and became a gold record with over one million sales.

In 1978, Alicia was nominated for a Grammy in the Best R&B Vocal Performance, Female category. Arnie pulled every string he had to get her to be the opening act at the Grammys' award show, a coveted television showcase for a new talent, one that could make or break a career.

The night of the Grammys, Arnie and I were in LA at the Shrine Auditorium, settling into our VIP seats, center aisle, second row, on the left, in full view of the cameras, dressed for prime time—Arnie handsome in his black tuxedo and me, not believing I was there, in an emerald-green floor-length caftan, a Saint Laurent number lent to me by Arnie's sister. (I had nothing that stylish in my closet.)

Arnie was shaking hands and chatting with people as they walked by, while I was totally enamored by all the famous faces in the room. Then someone from production walked down the steps from the stage, tapped Arnie on the shoulder, and whispered in his ear, "Alicia isn't here."

Arnie knew she was there, somewhere; he had just seen her backstage. It was Chuck Berry all over again. Arnie calmly kissed me on the cheek and left his seat to find Alicia pacing in the parking lot behind the theater in her purple spangly pantsuit, totally incapacitated by nerves. In what could only have been his most persuasive, Tupelo honey voice and comforting manner, he talked her back into the theater to her position center stage mere seconds before the Grammy Awards were to go live on TVs across the nation.

Had Alicia not come back, all the efforts and persuasive techniques Arnie had wielded on behalf of this relatively new talent would have been for naught, and her career could quite possibly have gone up in smoke. Instead, "I Love the Nightlife" reached number five on the hot 100 singles in 1978 and became one of the anthems of the disco era. The song was featured in multiple movies and on Broadway in *The Adventures of Pricilla, Queen of the Desert.*

I frequently hear it on my car radio and take it as a sign Arnie is still looking after me, and I say: "Arnie are you listening? That's your song, honey. That's your song."

• • •

Then along came Jerry and Gary, aka Buckner and Garcia, advertising and jingle writers, who had become mesmerized by a video game they discovered one night when having dinner in a restaurant called Shillings on the Square in Marietta, Georgia. Simply put, they played the game, got hooked, and wrote a hit single about their experience as gamers. That song was "Pac-Man Fever."

Buckner and Garcia took the song to the Buie-Geller Organization, and seeing its potential, Arnie and Buddy signed them to BGO Records and "Pac-Man Fever" was recorded in Studio One.

All in on the concept and wanting to better understand the new emerging gaming world before he promoted the song, Arnie took then seven-year-old Samantha on a tour of Atlanta's burgeoning game parlors where they both learned to play the game, and Arnie was convinced "Pac-Man Fever" would become a mega hit. Which it did. And I believe that learning to play that game was inspirational for Samantha and the precursor to her later-in-life extraordinary virtual drawings.

Arnie went to New York and shopped "Pac-Man Fever" around to all his contacts at the top labels but found no takers. The New York record labels had yet to understand the cultural juggernaut arcade games would become. Not to be deterred, Arnie and Buddy put it out on their BGO Records Label, where it was debuted on a local Atlanta radio station by a DJ named Jim Morrison.

The audience response was so enormous that according to Jerry Buckner in his book: *Pac-Man Fever: The Story Behind the Unlikely '80's Hit That Defined a Worldwide Craze*, Morrison's phone rang off the hook with requests, and he played it over and over.

On air Morrison said, "Arnie, you've got a smash record. You've got to get moving on this." (As if he hadn't been.) Meaning promotion, promotion, promotion, one of Arnie's strengths. An on-air endorsement such as that was unusual in the business and so were the immediate phone calls BGO received from major record companies wanting to put it out under their label.

Buckner and Garcia finally signed with Columbia Records and "Pac-Man Fever" was put out with the tagline under the title, "Produced by Buckner & Garcia for the Buie-Geller Organization." Pac-Man the game turned out to be "Pac-Man Fever" the mega hit.

Jerry tells this story about the time the Buie-Geller Organization held a party to celebrate the single going gold: "During the party, Arnie took Jerry and me into a bathroom, pulled out two envelopes with huge checks in each, and told us 'This is just a little taste of what's coming.' Before, we were taking soda bottles back to the convenience store for refund money so we could get to the studio." The whole situation was mind-boggling to them.

In his book, Jerry calls it "crazy fame." The BGO phones never stopped ringing as CBS, ABC, the *Today Show*, and *Good Morning America* kept calling for personal appearances. The song was played at the Rose Bowl, on *The Tonight Show*, *The Simpsons*, *South Park*, you name it. They knew it was a worldwide hit when Imelda Marcos, wife of the Philippines' dictator, Ferdinand, was quoted in an article saying, "'Pac-Man Fever' is my favorite song."

Can't you just see Imelda clicking her heels around the palace singing "I've got Pac-Man fever" in one of her 2,000 pairs of shoes?

I enjoy listening to Jerry's stories about that heady time when "Pac-Man Fever" was a worldwide sensation. My favorite of his stories is when Arnie arranged for Buckner and Garcia to make an appearance on *The Dick Clark Show*, and Arnie brought Samantha to the taping and asked Dick to let her dance on the program that day with the teenagers. Arnie always kept his priorities straight, and family was Arnie's priority. He knew Samantha would love doing it. (Yes, I have that video.)

Gary has passed away, but Jerry and I meet for lunch occasionally, shed a tear or two, and tell stories about Arnie, as we both terribly miss his presence in our lives. At our last lunch, we confessed to each other that we often reach for our phones to ask Arnie's opinion on something. At that lunch, Jerry told me Arnie had always counseled him, "Do the right thing." Arnie never gave up his Boston Blackie persona.

We all ended up with a full-size Pac-Man arcade machine in our homes. Ours was the most well-traveled, as it moved with us many times over the years.

But back then in The Parans, it was an exciting and busy time for Arnie. But it also was a time when Samantha was starting to have more and more asthma attacks and missing more and more school days.

There's an Elephant on My Chest

The asthma attacks hailed their arrival when a harsh raspy sound rose up from Samantha's lungs, her skin became translucent, the tissue under her eyes became gray, and her struggle to breathe became more labored. Once she said, gasping for breath, "Mommy, there's an elephant on my chest."

During one Christmas holiday, we were in Michigan for a family gathering, and Samantha had one of her asthma episodes that steam showers, hot tea, back percussion, and albuterol inhalations could not control. Arnie and I knew it was time for the hospital. The closest one was in Lansing—twenty-five miles away. After we bundled Samantha in her pink-footed pajamas and a heavy blanket, Arnie drove as fast as possible through a whirling Michigan blizzard, where the visibility was close to zero and the snow continued to pile up to the point where even the snowplows weren't able to keep ahead of the onslaught.

When we finally arrived at Lansing's Sparrow Hospital, the ER doctor quickly prescribed a shot of epinephrine to relax the lining of Samantha's air passages, causing them to dilate, allowing additional air to circulate into her bloodstream and through her struggling lungs so she could begin the breathing cycle again and her heart rate returned to normal.

Then something went horribly wrong. The nurse who administered the shot had mistakenly given Samantha an adult dose of epinephrine rather than a child's. Samantha's heart was beating so rapidly she had to be strapped to a gurney to keep her body steady while her heart struggled to return to its normal beats per minute. At five years old, Samantha was at risk for a heart attack.

Later we would learn that Samantha is a rapid metabolizer, breaking down medications more quickly than is normal. If that indeed was the case with the epinephrine shot, it had been a godsend, perhaps shortening the time Samantha had to suffer on the gurney. Whatever the case, we were grateful that she had come out of that gut-wrenching incident with little memory of the event.

I once asked her what she remembered about that experience, other than what we had told her over the years. Her answer was, "I vaguely remember the snow and that I was strapped down and felt as if my body was floating, and it kept getting bigger and smaller, bigger and smaller, bigger and smaller."

During the wait, Arnie and I stood at her bedside, holding her hand and speaking to her softly, "You'll be OK, you'll be OK, sweetheart. Mommy and Daddy are here."

Arnie left the room once or twice to stand in the snow in front of the hospital to take a few calming puffs on a cigarette and then return to stand by her bed or pace in the corridor: always steady, always calm. I, who thought I had learned to become calm in fraught situations, especially medical ones, lost all reasonable control as the hours ticked by.

When the reckless nurse tried to enter the room again, I erupted in rage as if she were the New York banshee approaching us on the street, "Get out of here. Now! I don't ever want to see your face again," I screamed.

Thank God, Samantha came through it as a champ, and I, mostly I, became even more neurotic. For Arnie and me it was interminable until the electrocardiogram's monitor indicated that her heartbeat had started to drift down into its proper rhythm. From then on, at the first sign of stress in her breathing, I would begin rushing around the house grabbling my dated journals with notes of every doctor's visit; a list of Samantha's medications; her favorite books; her stuffed rabbit, Valentine; fresh pajamas—whatever we might need in case she had to be admitted to the hospital.

Anxiously and incessantly, I would continue to ask her: "Are you OK? Is it time we go to the hospital?" until finally one day she said to me in her father's steady, soft style, but with exasperation, "I don't know, Mommy. I'm not a doctor."

My hard-earned coping skills of seeing that Samantha had a normal childhood, with birthday parties and playdates, that she kept up with her schoolwork and after-school activities, became harder as her asthma worsened and she got further behind. I was frayed by being always on alert for her next asthma episode, the next dash to the hospital, the next albuterol inhales and epinephrine shots. With that episode in Lansing, I had been pushed over the edge. Or as my grandmother Nanny would have said, I was off my rocker.

Knowing the specifics of Samantha's genetics may have given us a clue to her asthma, but they had not been made available at her adoption. We would never know if she had inherited the gene or if the asthma had developed from Atlanta's invasion of spring pollen, when even the healthy have trouble breathing as pollen clogs the air, falling on the city like green rain. And when it actually rained, the streets ran with a thick green guck, and the air became momentarily breathable, and then it started all over again. But what did any of that matter? Heredity or not, an emergency is an emergency.

For years I struggled to be a perfect mother—combat the weather, master all things domestic; of course, impossible. I felt unqualified and incompetent. I had failed at being the mother Samantha needed.

Over and over and over, Arnie and I would rush Samantha to the doctor's office or the ER, where each time she was given large doses of theophylline, the bronchodilator that treated her wheezing and helped keep her air passages open. And if that didn't work, she was given large doses of prednisone, which would lessen her coughing and decrease the inflammation in her lungs. Returning home, she would have albuterol inhales at regular intervals on her own portable nebulizer, which she decorated with stickers to jolly it up. It had become her sidekick and best friend.

We were cautioned not to let her eat food cooked on charcoal grills, which were brimming with carbon compounds that would reduce the efficacy of her daily dose of theophylline. And when medications and steam showers and hand-cupped percussion on her small back would not loosen the plugs of mucous in her lungs, wherever we were, she would be admitted to a hospital where she received larger doses of prednisone, which helped by reducing her lung inflammation but also caused her to gain weight, have sleep interruptions, and become more susceptible to infection.

Released from the hospital, her little face all puffy from the medication, she would spend days at home, missing school as she recuperated from both the disease and the medication used to control it. All the while, I became the quintessential nervous, intense, hovering mother trying to maintain Samantha's health and keep her on a school schedule, which was impossible.

Through it all, Samantha pressed on. She learned to swim, rode horses with Arnie, suffered through ballet class and French lessons (the latter two fell quickly away), and had sleepovers where a gaggle of girls would run around, play dress-up and scream . . . a lot. Normal activities.

For her seventh birthday, Samantha's wish was to have a Princess Penny event. Princess Penny was a vibrant young girl, dressed as a superhero who came to birthday parties to play games and entertain the birthday girl and her friends. Seeing photos of Samantha at that birthday party still crushes my heart. Her tiny face was pale, her eyes ringed with dark circles as she sat on the floor, legs crossed, body slumped over as if she were protecting her lungs, watching her guests participate without her in the Princess Penny festivities.

A few days before the party, as her breathing was gradually becoming more difficult, Arnie and I had consulted her asthma doctor about canceling the event. Knowing how not-normal Samantha's life was, his advice was not to stress or disappoint her by canceling. "If she has to leave midway through the party, then so be it," he said.

She had missed so much in her seven years—endless school days, after-school activities, being a flower girl with her cousins at her Aunt Jan's wedding—that neither Arnie nor I wanted her to miss something as important as her birthday party. Consequently, we agreed with the doctor. And consequently, Samantha did have to leave her birthday party early and did spend several days in Northside Hospital recovering. It was a balancing act.

Those were the years we traveled with peak flow meters to access her oxygen levels and her portable nebulizer in case we had to give her an albuterol treatment. We would fill the nebulizer's small green cup with 2.5 mg of albuterol sulfate inhalation solution, add 2.5 mL of sterile normal saline and turn on the nebulizer. Again and again, Samantha would sit in her father's lap or hunched over on the floor, staring at a TV screen, holding the green cup's mouthpiece between her lips, inhaling the solution until her chest loosened and her breathing became less labored. Over and over and over and over and over—I hovered, always waiting for an increase in her pulse rate (bad). Or for the color to come back into her face (good).

Arnie and I made every effort to make her childhood as normal as possible, but to what end? Her happiness? A well-rounded childhood? How were either of those possible as she continued to struggle with more asthma attacks and more absences from school? Eventually, all her activities dwindled away, and she spent more and more time sitting on the floor, nebulizer at the ready, staring at the television rather than a teacher at school.

It's possible that what I had is now called Post-Adoption Depression Syndrome (PADS). What I know for sure was the realities of parenthood and my fears for Samantha's health had overwhelmed me and my ability to cope had vanished.

I convinced myself that Atlanta was the reason for her health issues and moving back to New York was the cure.

It was an impulsive decision, made without consulting Arnie. I just called him at his office at the studio one day and said, "Samantha and I are moving back to New York."

He didn't say no, he didn't say yes; he just got into his car, drove home, and stood by as I crammed a jumble of Samantha's and my clothing into a FedEx box and sent them to a small corporate apartment we kept on West Fifty-Sixth Street in New York.

I rationalized my escapist behavior by saying we needed a better doctor. Our unflappable pediatrician, Dr. Aaron Meislen, who had followed Samantha from birth, was still practicing at New York Hospital. I knew he would be of help to Samantha and hopefully to me. And he made house calls.

Arnie drove us to the airport, and I can't remember our ever having discussed my erratic behavior or the reasons for it. Arnie was never one to tell anyone what to do; he would suggest, discuss, then step back and let whatever it was play out. He knew I was emotional and sometimes irrational and impulsive, and he knew that New York was a haven of sorts for me, so he followed his playbook and let me get on with it, knowing I wouldn't be completely alone as long as Dr. Meislen and the Waxmans were there as well.

I enrolled Samantha at the Hewitt School for girls from K-12 on Seventy-Seventh between Madison and Park Avenues. My days consisted of taking her to and from school on the bus, helping her with homework, and sitting on the rim of the ethereal dandelion fountain at the Bernstein Plaza on Sixth Avenue and Fifty-Fifth Street as she roller-skated around it with Stephen Waxman. We made frequent visits to Dr. Meislen, and he to us, at the apartment. I tried to carry on a normal life for Samantha. But how normal could it have been? We were back in New York, but we had left Arnie behind—something I deeply regret to this day.

Of course, Arnie and I spoke on the phone every day about Samantha's health, her school, what I was doing, what he was doing, and when he was coming to visit.

Until I researched these dates, I never realized that this was during the "Pac-Man Fever" days. Arnie must have been so torn between promoting the record and worrying about us. I was inconsiderate and irrational, wallowing in my own issues. I know now I should have had therapy. We both should have had therapy. Instead, we just carried on as if nothing had happened. And I don't believe we ever discussed it again.

Samantha's memories of that time are foggy, but she did tell me, "I was confused about why we were back in New York. And I remember there was a girl in my class from France named Raine. Remember her? I named my cat after her in later years. And when I looked out of my window at night, I could see the bright red 666 sign on the top of the building at 666 Fifth Avenue, which I thought was cool."

I am glad her memories are more positive than mine. My memory is that we were there for months and months, but now I am not so sure. It could have been only weeks; it remains a blur. I was in a mental crisis, I know that now, and selfishly, I never thought of the pressures Arnie was experiencing or how he felt about our leaving. When I told Samantha that I always wondered why her father didn't stop us from going, or at least discuss it, her response was, "Maybe he wanted some time alone for himself."

She has always been more sanguine about everything than I.

Bewildered by it all, Arnie's patience was unbounded, letting my craziness play out until visiting New York at Passover, when he quietly said, with no judgment, "Please come home."

We returned to Atlanta for maybe six months until we sold our red brick house on the hill. I called Dr. Meislen for the name of an asthma doctor in LA, and we moved from The Parans to California, this time to Malibu in time for the start of another school year.

PART VI

Round and Round We Go

Ya Got Trouble Right Here In River City

—MEREDITH WILSON, 1957

Well, it wasn't River City, but water was involved. It was Malibu on the Pacific Ocean. In 1973, Arnie and I had lived in that charming railroad apartment in Beverly Hills. This second time around we (likely me) decided we should live in Malibu where our friends Vicki and Marty Cooper lived on the Old Road directly on the beach. Both Vicki and Marty were in the music business, so Arnie would be among friends. Vicki was a record executive and Marty was the one who had written "A Little Bit Country, a Little Bit Rock 'n' roll," as I mentioned earlier.

Arnie and I found our own beachfront house a few doors north of theirs on Old Malibu Road and settled in. Samantha was enrolled in the Malibu elementary school, and I was thinking how healthy and calming it would be waking up each morning to the sound of the ocean!

Having felt comfortable in California when Arnie and I had moved there from Detroit early in our marriage, I thought—hoped—that living there again would be good for us all. When in doubt, moving seems to have been my go-to solution for all problems. Apparently, I flourished in the distraction of change. Like Goldilocks, I was in a search of a bed that felt just right.

A few weeks into the Malibu school year, I arrived to collect Samantha after school to find her sitting on a knoll near the pickup point, head protected in her pulled up knees, stoically trying not to cry. One of the eight-year-old boys in her class had seen her holding the miniature pink rubber ball she carried when she felt stressed or nervous and had grabbed it out of her hands.

When she got in the car, she told me: "He was bullying me. He grabbed my ball, and I fought back. So, he peed on my backpack."

"Good girl," I said. It was she who had every right to be pissed off, not him.

The new school had been a change of location, but attending any school remained difficult for Samantha. During her grade school years, she had tested in the gifted range, but she had missed so many days of school over the years, she continuously struggled to live up to that potential. Under those conditions, a theoretical physicist would have given up.

On her last testing, the psychologist admonished me with: "So why isn't she keeping up, Mrs. Geller? Look to your parenting, Mrs. Geller." Another push on my guilt buttons, revving up my insecurities as an adoptive mother—confirming I was not up to motherhood's responsibilities. I compensated by overreach and applied stricter after-school rules for her homework—causing more stress for both of us. At some point along this path, one of her teachers had said to me, "She's struggling now, but she's going to be one heck of an adult. She is so bright; she can do this."

"Try a tutor," school counselors said.

Maybe I'm a shitty parent.

"Samantha should stay with me for a month, and I'll straighten her out," my well-intentioned mother-in-law said.

She thinks I'm a shitty parent.

My mother and father didn't comment but sent her study cards for math and English.

Confirmed. I am a shitty parent.

The stress Samantha felt trying to meet everyone's expectations must have been enormous. To this day, I carry the guilt of causing that destructive period in her life with my need to make everything turn out as it should be. But now I ask myself: *Whose "should be"?*

This was before Attention Deficit Disorder (ADD) became a

recognized condition, before any of us understood the ramifications of the ADD diagnosis, and before Arnie and I completely understood that ADD is not environmental, it's genetic. The "look to your parenting" comment when having a child with asthma and ADD is only partially the solution. Parenting a child with ADD is a combination of love, patience, and structure. Adding Samantha's health issues made everything more complicated.

In 1980, when the psychiatric community agreed to list ADD in the third edition of their bible, *The Diagnostic and Statistical Manual of Mental Disorders*, AKA the DSM-3, it was finally codified as a genetic neurodevelopment disorder. Samantha was one of the afflicted, which, when mixed with the perils of being an asthmatic, made her life a challenge, if not a nightmare!

We hired tutors and sat beside her like human Ritalin pills as she did her homework. With the brilliance of hindsight, it's obvious that not only had her asthma caused multiple missed school days, but later studies indicated that upheaval also plays a part in the condition. Our moves, the different schools, different friends—Samantha was being clobbered by her undiagnosed ADD, exacerbated by our lifestyle.

When I read the description of ADD, I was devastated—it became crystal clear what Samantha had endured. Unfortunately, I, her mother, was a victim of the current general opinion, which at the time was: "Just keep pushing; keep her tush in the chair and she'll live up to her potential." I was mixing the "I don't want to do it" with "I want to do it, but concentrating for me is difficult."

Later, the DSM revised the diagnosis from ADD to ADHD by adding hyperactivity into the mix. Samantha had ADD, she didn't have hyperactivity. They must have met the kid in Malibu who peed on her backpack.

It was not until 2019, when research codified that ADHD was 74 percent inherited, that I was able to stop flagellating myself and scrape the bad parenting tattoo from my forehead. Discussing all this with Samantha during the writing of this book, she said: "I eventually found out it was hereditary. I would have had difficulties no matter how you parented."

I have apologized to her for my lack of understanding and for our many disruptive moves. Some were a business necessity; some were to assuage my incessant need to find an environment where I felt I belonged. Arnie, thank God, was intuitively a better parent for Samantha than I was. He encircled her within his calm demeanor. His unlimited patience toned down the edges of my overly aggressive pushing to make her succeed. He balanced her and gave her a terrific sense of humor. She was his Mundi, his pet name for her shortened from Samundra, which our pharmacist on First Avenue in NYC had mistakenly printed on her prescriptions when she was a child.

I had hoped California would be better. Arnie knew a few people in the record business, we had friends there, and my sister Jan lived just an hour and a half away in San Clemente. But sometimes life just doesn't work out as you had planned. Other elements can change the scenario completely. This time ol' friend bashert was about to take a negative turn.

I've Seen Fire and I've Seen Rain

—JAMES TAYLOR, 1970

When Samantha was a toddler, one of her favorite books was *Alexander and the Terrible, Horrible, No Good, Very Bad Day,* written by Judith Viorst in 1972. Obviously, Samantha could relate to Alexander, the boy in the story who wanted to move to Australia because his life was not going so well in the USA. How could that book not have appealed to her?

Who could predict that in the fall of 1982, Malibu would add apocalyptic to the lineup of Alexander-type, "no good, very bad days." Moving to Australia with Alexander might have been the right idea for all of us.

On October 10, the Santa Ana winds were blowing west from their namesake mountains, picking up the embers from small brush fires, hurling them at a wind speed of sixty miles per hour toward the Pacific Ocean. In awe, we watched the embers as they approached and became flames.

The fear was that these devil winds, El Niño, would jump the Pacific Coast highway and cross Old Malibu Road, a narrow line of macadam that separated a string of beach houses, ours being one of them, from the hills of fire behind us. Our houses were lined up cheek by jowl—our fronts facing the vast Pacific and our backsides on the Old Road, waiting to be picked off by the approaching flames like ducks in a shooting range.

Most of the houses on the road were built of wood and stood on pilings pounded for stability sixty feet deep into the sandy shores of the Pacific—similar to the bricole anchored in the lagoon on the approach to Venice.

As the air grew heavy and smoke and embers filled the air like a raging mob of fireflies attacking from the hills behind, we knew the drop in air pressure and the smoke-filled air would be detrimental to Samantha's lungs—as would the emotional turmoil of potentially seeing her house go up in flames.

Arnie arranged for her and a sitter to evacuate to a hotel high on a hill in Santa Monica, thirteen miles south of the fires. To this day Samantha remembers trying to cram her family of stuffed animals into her small red suitcase, when her father intervened, saying, "Let's go, honey. We don't have time for this! How about this: Take what you have already packed with you now, and let's put the rest in my car for safekeeping. I promise you nothing will happen to them in my car." Samantha reminded me that he had just become the owner of a vintage red Ferrari. The stuffed animals definitely would not have been in danger.

Arnie and I stayed behind, as did most of our neighbors on the Old Road, to water down our roofs as a twenty-foot-high wall of flames, pushed by sixty mile an hour winds, raced down from the burning hills, sending flying embers to land on our roofs. Neighbors stood shoulder to shoulder sending arcs of water looping up on their roofs like heavy rain, in the nervous hope our houses would be spared.

And thank God, the houses on the Old Road got a reprieve that night. But in the hills behind us, 75,000 acres were blackened, and according to the *Malibu Times*, in "Malibu Canyon Corridor, 44,000 acres, 15 homes in Paradise Cove destroyed and 100 Malibu homes in the hills were burned to the ground."

We tried again to settle in and live the casual beach life. Arnie's mom visited for all the holidays and birthdays, I walked the beach and played tennis badly, we went whale watching with my sister, discovered avocado and sprouts sandwiches, and Samantha took acting lessons. She turned out to be quite talented, and her coach suggested in the future we take her to a few auditions. She wasn't interested.

Arnie hated avocado sandwiches and rarely walked on the beach. And I, not wanting to accept the obvious, tried to overlook that the Malibu lifestyle was not going the way I had wished. That reckoning was soon to come.

Exit the Santa Anas, Enter Le Deluge

We welcomed in the new year with Vicki and Marty Cooper and their friends, all raising our champagne flutes in wishful solidarity that 1983 would be a better year. While clinking our stemware across the table, my enthusiasm for the concept caused me to do my clinking with a little too much bravado, causing one of Vicki's family heirloom flutes to shatter. The look on her face was an omen that the coming year might not be what we were hoping for. And so, it began.

The hills behind us were coming back from the fires and were again lush and colorful as carnations, ceanothus, and snowdrop began to sprout out of the blackened earth. I would drop Samantha off at school in the morning and drive through the hills and canyons just to revel in the calming beauty of the growth.

But peaceful was not in the cards. Enter another apocalyptic event when torrential rains and Noah-level floods did to our house, and to others on the Old Road, what the fires had not managed to achieve. January 28, 1983, at high tide, under the gravitational pull of a full moon, waves over seven feet high rolled in so fast and furiously under our house and all the others around us, that the water was forced through our floorboards, causing them to buckle and break open, and geysers to burst into our house.

Anything attached to our walls, or sitting freely on a flat surface, was dumped into the rushing water, turning our living room and master bedroom into a soggy mess of floating debris. When the tide receded, we were left with gaping holes between our floorboards; deposits of dirt and seaweed in our carpet, where mold spores began to sprout and mushrooms to grow, and our possessions in shambles.

I didn't look forward to the cleanup but was energized by the drama of it all.

And besides, we couldn't very well complain, as we had better luck with that incursion than most of our neighbors. Luckily, the back of our house was on higher ground, and we still had the kitchen, bedrooms, and the garage.

When the water began to recede, the beach went with it and multiple sections of devastated houses began to drift by, riding the waves as if they were giant surfboards. The house to our right listed on its pilings so badly toward ours that we could reach out and touch it. The front of one of the houses to our left disappeared into the sea, joining the parade of sundry other sections of Malibu houses as they floated by.

The Malibu government came to the rescue, releasing their more benign prisoners in orange jumpsuits to assist in moving people's belongings to higher ground. The prisoners sloshed in and out of our mess in their orange jumpsuits, stacking our possessions in a jumbled assortment in our garage. I became a woman with a mission, pointing here and there, trying to rescue the rescuable while checking on Samantha, who was now confined to her bedroom on the upper level.

Arnie, who never let chaos mess with his head, was unruffled and stood barefoot in the garage, in his navy bathrobe, cigarette between his lips, wearing a felt, dove-colored cowboy hat, calmly playing Pac-Man on our full-size arcade machine. To an outsider, he would have appeared more interested in having Pac-Man escape Inky, Blinky, Pinky, and Clyde than in attending to the wreckage behind him. But I knew he was ruminating on our current predicament. Knowing that I would be reticent to leave Malibu, he wasn't just playing Pac-Man, he was deciding how to present the idea of leaving to me.

We spent a few days driving the area, visiting open houses and looking at neighborhoods, tossing around the concept of moving to the hills above Malibu, where floods were not possible. But, on the other hand, fires were. This was the first time I was willing to take the risks and Arnie was not; our roles had reversed.

I had taken to the lifestyle, the drama, the living on the beach where you could hear the sound of the sea. It all worked for me. But not for Samantha, who told me she hated it. And not for Arnie, who had agreed to move there for me but ended up spending much of his time driving around thinking and looking at antique cars. He needed a set routine, an office, a desk, a quiet structure.

Arnie had had enough. I wondered at the time if it were me, he'd had enough of. He had made this move for me, but our relationship had been a little tense in the last few months. It wasn't something we discussed. I didn't wish to question him or argue, knowing that with Arnie I wouldn't win. He just retreated into his head and remained silent, weighing his options. Maybe he was thinking it would be a good time to . . . to do what? I had no idea. I wouldn't have minded a little yelling to clear the air. What I did know for sure was he needed normalcy. Malibu was definitely not normal.

We finally agreed to leave; this lifestyle was not desirable for our marriage nor for Samantha's health. Boys peeing on backpacks is one thing, but particulate matter in the air and mold spores in the carpeting are another thing completely. Arnie made the decision that for the time being we would move back to Atlanta, and he prepared to drive there the next day to find a place for us to live.

I asked if I could go with him. The drive across country in his vintage Ferrari would be fun. He said no, which he rarely ever did— usually finding a smoother way around whatever he wanted to avoid.

He left the next day. He could have flown. Actually, he did in some respects. Normally, it takes thirty-four-plus hours, with ten hours of driving each day. Arnie made it in twenty hours, including being pulled over by a police car in the Utah salt flats when he was going over 100 miles per hour. He was anxious to put the mishigas of Malibu behind him and move on.

Reaching Atlanta, he bought a house, flew back to LA, put Samantha and me on a plane to Atlanta, packed the rest of our belongings with the help of my sister Jan, and it was bye, bye Malibu.

Our Painful Gap Year

And what a unique house he found: the Nunnally House on a hill in an area called Buckhead. No water in sight, save for a goldfish pond in the garden behind the house. Not as dramatic as the Pacific Ocean, but the house was lovely and there were no Santa Ana winds in Atlanta, or boys who peed on book bags in the surrounding neighborhood—to my knowledge.

In 1923, the Nunnally House had been the country house of James Nunnally, owner of Nunnally Candy. He'd partnered with Coca-Cola in soda fountains, very successfully, and built this beautiful home. Arnie must have sensed that kinship when he first walked in the front door as *Coke*-Cola (Southern pronunciation) had always been his go-to beverage from early morning to late at night. When Coke dropped its old formula in 1985 and put out New Coke, Arnie was out there writing letters and making calls to the company to stop that nonsense. Changing the Coke formula to him was like making a hamburger out of tuna fish and still calling it a hamburger.

Atlanta's population had been growing rapidly. The gracious old Southern homes on large lots had become an Atlanta Realtor's dream and were being picked off right and left by developers. The money goal was to demolish one large house and replace it with multiple smaller houses on the same acreage. That was the plan for the Nunnally House, a Neel Reid, Beaux-Arts gem, sitting on seventeen acres of lush grounds. It had been bought and saved from the wrecking ball by an astute builder, whom Arnie knew. When Arnie found the house, I believe he thought of it not as our home, but more a real estate opportunity. A good call, as we were not there long.

The house was huge, but the builder who bought it, rather than demolishing it, had it divided in half for modern living. Arnie bought the left side of the Nunnally, which included the kitchen with an old fashioned butler's pantry, the library, the dining room, and whatever rooms corresponded above. Those areas were reconfigured into useable modern bedroom spaces, maintaining their Southern charm. What was left untouched were the exquisite plaster moldings, the wood-paneled walls, and a charming screened-in sleeping porch surrounded by magnolia trees, originally designed for those hot Georgia nights before air conditioning was a thing. Scarlett O'Hara would have loved this house.

The porch happened to be off Samantha's bedroom and became her playroom in the trees, along with a garden and an attic with secret nooks and crannies for her to explore. The idea of parceling out the land for eighty-two houses was to me a shanda, but it was a sign of the times, from which we profited, having had the experience of living there, so I shouldn't be judgmental.

The house soon became unimportant in the scheme of things when Arnie was diagnosed with prostate cancer, the reason for his father's death, and something Arnie had dreaded, knowing there was a possibility of his receiving the same diagnosis—prostate cancer is 60 percent genetic. And smoking didn't help his odds.

This was at the time doctors were arguing over what was the correct procedure to stop prostate cancer's progression. I can't remember what Arnie was working on then, but he continued doing it, and I did all the research on an appropriate approach to battling his cancer, trying to understand the efficacy of each suggested procedure before I presented it to him.

The first procedure was waiting to see if the cancer progressed (best for older patients). Another was nerve-sparing surgery, which frequently led to other complications such as impotency. The third was brachytherapy, a relatively new process where radioactive seeds were implanted in the prostate to kill the cancer cells. It had fewer side effects, was less damaging to surrounding tissues, and had a quicker recovery time. Arnie chose the latter.

The radiation treatments may have had fewer side effects, but they were debilitating and exhausting. Arnie would take a nap after each treatment and then return to work. No complaints. That is, until I was asked by his doctor to write a personal experience article for a new publication directed at prostate doctors, and I tried to be the Erma Bombeck of the disease. I wrote (what I thought was) a humorous line that the seeds implanted in my husband's prostate, though painful and debilitating, would be exciting for the TSA girls at airport security. That's when Arnie took me off the case.

Truth be told, I remember little of what we did during our time in the Nunnally house. Samantha had a birthday, Arnie had a birthday, I had a birthday. We celebrated the holidays season by season. And we held a party to raise money for some politician whose name I can't remember. But what else? You know how in movies they show time passing by ripping month after month from a calendar releasing each page off into space? That's how it felt living there. I can only remember two other incidents worth sharing.

Just after we moved in, the sky darkened to an ominous gray and a tornado ripped a portion of the roof from the smurf house across the way, snapping a tree in half, missing our house by inches. And I thought we had left the perils of Malibu behind. That same day, Samantha fell off a jungle gym at school, fractured her arm, and the teacher couldn't reach me on the phone (no cell phones back then) as I was at Atlanta's Design Center searching for ideas. I was redoing one of the neighbor's smurf houses, readying it for resale.

For the first time in her life, an employee at the school took Samantha to the hospital, where she had her arm put in a cast without her mom or dad. As with Arnie and the prostate article, she was not a happy camper. It's nice to be needed, isn't it?

The second incident happened when we invited a young student from Sweden to spend the holidays with us. To welcome her, I purchased a Scotch pine, thinking I would place it next to the fireplace and have her and Samantha decorate it with a nonreligious mix of popcorn and blue bows. All my Christmas paraphernalia had been disbursed to family. This would be my first sort-of holiday tree since my conversion umpteen years earlier. I told myself it was simply a benign way to celebrate the traditions of the season, and it would be pleasant for our guest.

So maybe I didn't do it for our guest, but for myself wanting to experience the season's traditions of pomp and glitter as I had growing up. What I did know was it had nothing to do with religion; I was happy with my Jewish life. But I must admit, as the years went by, Arnie and I had become a little lax in our rituals. We had begun to celebrate both the eight nights of Hanukah and to open Santa presents on Christmas morning—accommodating the material world and our different upbringings in a somewhat half-assed way.

Still, it felt as if I were breaking a sacred oath, especially when I had to ask Arnie for help with the tree. Its base had to be cut and leveled so it would fit into the tree stand I also had to purchase. Not being an axe user, I asked Arnie if he would find his axe—I don't know why he even had one, come to think of it. He was definitely not a lumberjack nor an axe murderer type.

Arnie, not being comfortable with using an axe either and thinking twice about why he was doing it, and not having handled a symbolic "Christmas" tree since that time in my father's coal yard, finally swung the axe at the tree—missing its trunk completely. We both watched as the axe head separated from its handle, did double flips in the air, landing just short of our toes.

Arnie looked at me and then, lifting his head to the sky, said, "God, give me a break, please. This wasn't my idea."

No, it was mine. And I swore I would never push my luck again.

The whole incident took place on the stoop, outside our front door, under the stone lintel carved with 1923, the year the house was completed. A dramatic scene, at least for the neighbors. Why we didn't go around the back to the garage for the tree chopping, beats me. Maybe it was another bashert. The house was telling us something, metaphorically pushing us out the front door.

Within a few months, we put the Nunnally house on the market; it sold to the first couple who came through the door. And we were packing again or went packing seems more appropriate. Arnie wanted to go back to the music business. Where? New York! Another upheaval for Samantha, but she knew the school, and Dr. Meislen was there along with the Waxmans, the Met, the Palm, and the theater. Be still my heart.

In what I hoped was a final good-bye to Atlanta, we donated Reid's original architectural house plans to the Atlanta History Center, where they safely reside now as an important element in Atlanta's history. And we were out of there in what a Southerner calls, "a hot minute."

Remember when I had made the declaration that if we ever left Atlanta for New York again, we must do it by train from Neel Reid's station to close a circle and boost our chances of never coming back? Good luck with that! We flew.

PART VII

Back to Our Future

New York, New York, Still a Helluva Town

We rented an apartment on East Eighty-Third Street. It was a tree-lined, short block between Fifth and Madison. It was a movie-perfect location, and I was ecstatic to be back.

The entrance to Eighty-Third from Fifth Avenue was guarded by two prewar buildings standing to the right and left like Roman centurions. To make the location even more appealing, if you turned left out of our apartment building, passed through the centurions, and crossed Fifth Avenue, there stood the Metropolitan Museum of Art. It was an institution that would soon nudge Malibu a little farther out into the Pacific Ocean, as wandering the galleries became more and more my meditative escape.

If you turned right out of our apartment building and walked half a block, you were at Madison Avenue. We soon joined the morning ritual of parents walking hand-in-hand with their children as they hustled them to the neighborhood schools. I loved those mornings in New York. I suppose I love mornings in general. Arnie was a night owl, perfect for his business choices.

For me, mornings in New York had the exhilaration of an important migration where people with purpose were on their way to substantial pursuits. The aroma of men's cologne, mingling with the fresh starch of their shirts as they passed us by, gave me a heady feeling. The spray of water catching the sunlight as super after super hosed off their building's miniature stake of New York sidewalk, was reminiscent of the misty air on a Malibu morning.

We re-enrolled Samantha in Hewitt on Seventy-Seventh Street off Madison, and Arnie would often join the parade as he dropped her there on the way to his new office on West Fifty-Fifth. His first project in New York was as executive producer on a TV movie called

O. Henry's Christmas, staring Eli Wallach and Anthony Quinn. One of the investors had known Arnie from the Polydor days and asked him if he wanted to produce the film. I believe that may have had a hand in his motivation to return to the city.

But Arnie seldom discussed the details of his business endeavors with me, as he usually spoke on the phone with his lifelong friend Joel, using him as a sounding board. When Arnie finally got home in the evening, he gave his full attention to our family. Arnie was a master of compartmentalizing the different aspects of his life. What I do remember is his telling me how much he enjoyed producing that movie and hanging out with the cast at Pete's Tavern in Grammercy Park where O. Henry had written *The Gift of The Magi*, the basis for the movie.

During that time, the US Treasury Department contacted Arnie to evaluate Elvis Presley's estate. I can't tell you the results of his evaluation, as there were NDAs all over the place. And, frankly, I don't know either. What I do know is Arnie's reputation of being a problem solver was pulling him in multiple directions.

Music eventually won out when Jerry Buckner asked for his help. Jerry Buckner and Gary Garcia, with Spielberg's permission, had written a tribute song, called "E.T., I Love You," for his new movie *E.T. the Extra-Terrestrial*. CBS Records, Buckner and Garcia's current label, was slow-rolling them about putting the song out in coordination with the movie's opening. Jerry called Arnie, no longer his manager, but his friend, to find out if he might be able to speed things up.

It seemed that Neil Diamond, also on CBS's label, had seen the movie, loved it, and had written his own tribute song called "Heartlight," which was being recorded with Quincy Jones as its producer at the exact same time. A tough twosome to fight.

Jerry said, "I never saw Arnie work so hard to get a song out. He called everyone he knew in New York and LA, but CBS stood firm. Arnie always wanted to help you, if he could; he was a fixer and usually could figure out a way to make things work out. But this was one of the few times in his career Arnie couldn't fix the problem."

Buckner and Garcia's song was not released until later in the year. CBS maintained they couldn't very well pit two of their acts against each other; but, again in my wifely/nonbusiness way of thinking, they could have done the right thing by putting the first song written and recorded out first. Arnie and I went to the *E. T.* movie to see how Neil Diamond's song worked in the film. Of course Arnie wasn't objective, and he hated both the song and the film and wouldn't talk about either for the longest time.

Why is this worth mentioning? *E. T.* was nominated for nine academy awards that year and won four of them: Best Sound, Best Film Editing, Best Visual Effects, Best Musical Score. Anything associated directly with the film, if put out concurrently, would have been a roaring success as well. There were a lot of people not to like. And a lot of publicity lost for Buckner and Garcia.

Cyndi Lauper's manager, David Wolff, was working in the same offices as Arnie. Cyndi had become a pop sensation with her song "Girls Just Wanna Have Fun," which had very quickly soared to number two on *Billboard Magazine's* Top 100. And in 1985, Cyndi won a Grammy for Best New Artist. One conversation (over a telex machine and not a water cooler), led to another, and David asked Arnie if he would like to join Cyndi's management team. Arnie accepted.

All over the world, teenage girls were strutting out in mesh gloves, neon-colored hair, and layers and layers of color-matching net skirts. Samantha and her friends were among them. Pulling into the underground VIP parking at Madison Square Garden in a black stretch limousine to meet the biggest pop artist of the era sent them over the moon and back. Arnie was a very popular dad.

One of Arnie's first international tours with Cyndi was to Asia.

The first stop was Nippon Budokan, a popular arena in Tokyo for touring British and American rock bands. Arnie invited Samantha and me to fly over with him to celebrate her twelfth birthday, then he would go on to finish the tour, and we would return home. We still traveled with all the asthma paraphernalia, but it turned out to be an amazingly memorable and trauma-free experience.

I am aware that no one wants to hear about someone else's travels or see their photos, so why am I going to carry on? Because it was so amazing to me that Arnie would take us along on such an important business trip. So, allow me this digression:

First stop, Hong Kong. I was unable to sleep the first night of our arrival and spent it staring out of the hotel window at the boats in the harbor and the colorful, ever-changing lights on the skyscrapers across the way. My only experience with anything Chinese, except the Americanized version of its food, had been in the movies, particularly when I experienced Rogers and Hammerstein's musical *Flower Drum Song* in which a young Hong Kongese girl, played by Nancy Kwan, moves to San Francisco and falls into a messy love situation. One of the songs in the movie, "I Enjoy Being a Girl," had stuck in my head. When we crossed the Hong Kong harbor on the famous green and white Star Ferry, I was that girl in the film. (The film was shot in San Francisco, so this is definitely a stretch.)

We walked the streets, rode the funicular to Victoria Peak, and bought blue-and-white antique china—though later we learned a few of the pieces were not antique—but which I still own and cherish. For our final night in Hong Kong, Arnie arranged a private boat tour on the South China Sea with a box dinner from the hotel and a gorgeous birthday cake for Samantha. The location, the soft air, the lights of the sampans floating on the sea, the . . . everything made it magical.

The next morning, we flew to Tokyo to see Cyndi in concert at Budokan, which was attended by thousands of screaming Japanese teens decked out in their pop-star Cyndi Lauper garb, jumping up and down like a sea of colorful lollipops.

Arnie continued to travel with Cyndi, and in 1989, when she released her *A Night To Remember* album, she embarked on another tour in Asia. Again, Arnie went with her. Tokyo and Budokan were on their itinerary, and again, Arnie invited Samantha and me to meet him in Japan for her birthday, her fifteenth. This time Samantha and I had to fly alone. Arnie was the type who, for our entire married life, carried all the necessary papers needed for a journey abroad: passports, tickets, inoculation papers, itineraries. I don't think it was because he didn't trust me; he just wanted everything to go smoothly. This time I had to put on my big-girl pants.

He booked Samantha's and my flight to Tokyo as a direct from JFK to Narita, Japan's major airport. Straight line, thirteen hours fifty-five minutes, no plane changes to contend with—until three-quarters of the way across the Pacific, when our plane was unexpectedly diverted to Kimpo Airport in South Korea. Samantha and I, along with the other 400 or so passengers, were asked to deplane as quickly as possible and were led in a silent parade to a locked detention area where we were held—for hours, which seemed like days—never being told why, no matter how many times or how many passengers asked.

Samantha stretched out on a hard plastic bench and slept. I paced, ruminating on the headlines from a year before when, at approximately the same time, Korean Air 007 had been shot out of the sky by an air-to-air missile, delivered by a Soviet fighter jet. Korean 007 had crashed into the Sea of Japan, killing all 269 on board. The Soviets claimed Korean 007 was a spy plane, when in actuality it was simply a plane, like ours, that had drifted off course toward Kimpo International Airport, where we were now being held in a locked room.

The room was windowless. I walked the perimeter over and over, commiserating with other passengers and worrying about Samantha, distressed that I couldn't speak to Arnie. We had never been out of touch, and I longed to hear his reassuring voice. I didn't have a cell phone at that time, though I believe Arnie, a true believer in the concept, may have. His first had been one of those brick phones in the console of his car. Driving, smoking, and talking on the phone were his heaven.

But back then at Kimpo Airport, locked in a room in a strange airport in a foreign country, I knew full well that even if I had a cell, and there were some sort of network intact, our watchers most likely would not have let me use it.

I consoled myself by assuming Arnie was monitoring our flight and working on a plan to rescue us. So many questions: Had there been a hostile plane stalking us? Were they searching our plane for bombs? Was it a mechanical failure? If they kept us for an extended period, would I have access to refills of Samantha's medication? And how would I reach Arnie? Our plane was not Korean Air 007, but I felt as if we were in a Bond film nonetheless and hoped that Arnie in full 007/Boston Blackie mode would bust through the door and rescue us.

We were held for several hours and finally escorted back to our plane in the same hurry-up manner, again with no explanation. Being held in a locked room, in a foreign country, with a fifteen-year-old, and not being told why, was nerve-wracking in the extreme. Arnie, of course, had been following the flight the whole time and calling JAL repeatedly, but he also could never get a straight answer from any of them.

We finally arrived—tired but safe—and Samantha has only a few memories from that part of the journey. She was more fixated on Arnie's promise to take her on a shopping trip for her birthday. Her priorities were video games and clothing. This was the period when the teens in Tokyo were leading the fashion world with weird getups mirroring their pop idols and characters from video games, which was sort of a punk rock, naughty schoolgirl look.

Cyndi had named this tour to Japan A Night to Remember; a name coined in 1955 by author Walter Lord as the title of his book based on the 1912 sinking of the Royal Mail Steamer *Titanic*. Little did we know that ship would become an integral part of our life.

Shall We Stay or Shall We Go?

Arnie left Cyndi's management after five years and was anxious to leave the clank and rattle of garbage cans and horn honks on New York's Upper East Side. He wanted, again, to go back to Atlanta.

Over the years, Arnie and I had multiple "shall we stay or shall we go" conversations over that issue; one ending with our living on Eighty-Third Street for several weeks, sharing our space with the odor of corrugated boxes stacked tall in every room, because we were unable to come to an amicable solution about where we were going. I admit now that I was the culprit, dragging my feet.

When I first visited New York, I knew this was where I belonged. And when I first met Arnie, I had a visceral feeling we belonged together. So, in reality, for me there should have been no choice; Arnie wanted out of the city, and we were leaving. We came to our senses when we both realized we didn't want to be that far away from Samantha, who was attending school in the Berkshires only a few hours' drive from the city. So, we stayed.

By now you know that I believe in the concept of bashert, of fate, of things that come about because they are meant to happen, much as Arnie and I were meant to meet on the day of my divorce. And I also believe it was a prescient move when Arnie and I agreed to stay in the city, but to leave the Upper East Side and move to an apartment at the southern tip of Manhattan Island in Battery Park City. It was as far from the turmoil of the Upper East Side as you could get and not scream for a life buoy—a quiet oasis for Arnie and still within the confines of Manhattan Island for me.

Battery Park was a new extension of the island, built upon three million cubic yards of soil and rock excavated during the building of the World Trade Center. The apartment Arnie and I chose was located at 200 Rector Place, in a building named Liberty Court: forty-two stories of new construction, high enough in the sky that street noises were muffled, and with a sweeping view of New York Harbor and the entire Lower Broadway and Battery area. Adjacent to our building was a calm, unsullied green space, which extended to a river walk along the Hudson under the gaze of the Statue of Liberty. Perfect for walking our dog. Yes, we had a dog. Daisy. A bichon frisé, Samantha's dog, guaranteed to be nonallergenic for her sake, but now essentially mine as Samantha was away at school.

Arnie took a small personal office in the area and came to appreciate the multiple compensations of being a resident of the Battery—space, quiet, peaceful strolls along the Hudson, and a five-minute walk to work. And I learned how to take the subway.

For the first time since our on-and-off living in the city, we had an eat-in kitchen with a window that framed Lady Liberty in all her welcoming, tarnished glory. Every morning, I would start my day by saying good morning to her as I prepared my coffee and then sat with her as I planned my day. And be still my New York heart—we had a balcony, albeit a postage stamp version of a balcony, reminiscent of the crow's nest on a ship. If you stepped out, you could see the tip of Manhattan Island jutting into the confluence of the East and Hudson Rivers and follow as the boats navigated the narrows on their approach to New York Harbor and the Verrazzano Bridge.

The Battery is where New York was born. In 1524, Giovanni da Verrazzano, an Italian, and thus I claim him as my kinsman (though I put the neighborhood pizza maker in that category, as well), sailed into the harbor and described it as "a very agreeable site located between two hills between which flowed to the sea a very great river." In May of 1626, another of my lineage on the Dutch side, Peter Minuit, stood on that agreeable site and bartered with the Indian Lenape to purchase the island named Manhatta for sixty guilders.

And just to put a finer point on things, in 1866, my Italian great-grandfather and great-grandmother (the Ventos) entered the country through Castle Gardens, a round fort-like building located in the Battery, which was the main immigration point before Ellis Island came into play. Last but not least, the first paved street in the Battery was called Brouwer Street, my maiden name. Just saying, just saying.

During the late 1800s and early 1900s, the area was awash with steamship offices where travelers could book passage to multiple ports around the globe. The White Star Line, owners of the *Titanic*, had their offices at 9 Broadway. As knowledge of the *Titanic's* loss began to reach the White Star offices, some say 40,000 concerned citizens, anxious family members, and eager newspapermen looking for a scoop, converged and jostled for positions in front of 9 Broadway as they waited for the latest dispatches of the sinking.

And from those offices the news of *Titanic's* sinking was first disseminated to the world by the new Marconi apparatus thanks to Guglielmo Marconi (Italian), the inventor of the telegraph.

A five-minute walk from 9 Broadway was another maritime building, the twenty-story Whitehall Building at 17 Battery, a 1904 precursor to the World Trade Center buildings, which would soon have a dramatic impact on our lives.

Arnie and I knew little to nothing about this historic neighborhood or about *Titanic* itself when we moved to Battery Park. Back then, 9 Broadway was no longer the offices of the White Star Line; it was a Radio Shack, an ignominious end to a horrific maritime event. We were simply trying to find a serene location suitable for us both.

It wasn't long after we settled in when Arnie said casually one morning, as he was halfway out the door, "Oh, I forgot to tell you, I'm driving to Connecticut today; I have a meeting with a man named George Tulloch about *Titanic*.

To which I cavalierly responded, "Didn't that ship sink?"

Iceberg Right Ahead!

"Isn't that an iceberg on the horizon, Captain?"
"Yes, Madam."
"What if we get in a collision with it?"
"The iceberg, Madam, will move right along as though nothing had
happened."
—CARL SANDBURG, *THE PEOPLE, YES*, 1936

Carl Sandburg was correct: The iceberg moved right along to its own melting demise; leaving death, destruction, and controversy in its wake. A disaster that was awakened on September 1, 1985, seventy-three years after its sinking, when the *Titanic* was discovered in the North Atlantic by a team of French-American undersea explorers. *The New York Times*, my paper of record, had printed the story on its front page, but below the fold on the lower-left side, so let's blame them for my missing that discovery. But that discovery was one that would change Arnie's and my life forever and assured that I would never miss a *Titanic* headline/story/article/movie/documentary/book again.

If you're one of the few who are not familiar with the particulars of *Titanic's* story, here's a recap.

At 11:40 p.m. on April 14, 1912, the largest, most luxurious moving object ever built collided with an iceberg in the North Atlantic Ocean. The moving object—Royal Mail Ship *Titanic*— was left with irreparable damage to its forward starboard side. Rivets popped, the one-inch steel cladding separated at its seams, and it was estimated that seven tons of seawater per second began to push through those breaches. Somewhat similar to the water that had burst through our floorboards in Malibu, but more dramatic and deadly.

"We are putting passengers off in small boats. Women and children in boats. Cannot last much longer. Losing power," tapped Jack Phillips, the Marconi operator. "Come at once. We have struck a berg. It's a CQD, old man."

By 2:20 a.m., April 15, 1912, three hours after the collision, a final agonizing death roar emanated from deep in the bowels of *Titanic* as she reared up, looking like a giant mythical sea creature, took her final bow, and plunged to the ocean floor—12,500 feet, 3810 meters, two-and-one-half vertical miles below the surface of the North Atlantic. Breaking in two as she went.

On April 16, 1912, *The New York Times*'s announcement of the sinking was more aggressive than that of its recovery seventy-three years later:

Titanic sinks four hours after hitting iceberg; 866 rescued by carpathia, probably 1250 perish; Ismay safe; mrs. Astor maybe. Noted names missing.

As the death toll mounted, affluent relatives of the first-class passengers began making plans to raise the ship. Vincent Astor, the twenty-year-old scion of John Jacob Astor, one of the richest men in the world (a sophisticated Elon Musk), naively proposed the ship be blasted open with dynamite in hopes his father's body would be shaken loose and float to the surface. Astor's body was ultimately found by the funeral ship, the *Mackay-Bennett*, sent to the disaster area by the White Star Line to collect as many bodies as possible, and Vincent Astor was able to give his father a proper burial. There were multiple other strange and impossible ideas to resurrect the ship over the years, such as filling it with Vaseline to make it buoyant or with thousands of Ping-Pong balls to do the same: float it to the surface.

None of these ideas were doable with the depth of the sunken ship and 1912 technology. More to the point, unbeknownst to Vincent

Astor and the rest of the world, first, the ship had to be located.

The ship's coordinates telegraphed by the harried Marconi operators at the time of the sinking had been incorrect. *Titanic* lay at rest 400 miles off the coast of Newfoundland, yes, but thirteen miles from where the world believed it to be. Eventually, as with most historical events, *Titanic* was pushed off the world's front pages as World War I loomed on the horizon.

Titanic was alone, left to become the holy grail of shipwrecks for oceanographers, deep sea archeologists, and adventurers with dreams of icebergs, dollar signs, and fame dancing like Christmas sugar plumbs in their heads. Enter wealthy Texas oilman Jack Grimm, who had already attempted to find the ship in the summers of 1980, 1981, and 1983 by donating $330,000 to Columbia University's Lamont-Doherty Geological Observatory for the use of their wide-sweep sonar equipment. Grimm was not successful.

Titanic only caught the world's attention again (though not mine, obviously) when, on September 1, 1985, a combined international team of the French Research Institute for Exploitation of the Sea (IFREMER), led by oceanographer Captain Jean-Louis Michel, and the United States Navy, led by Captain Robert Ballard, had the technology, the funding, and, most importantly, the burning determination to find *Titanic*, which they did by scouring the assumed area with deep water sonar and Argo, a video camera.

For seventy-three years, *Titanic* had rested in her unknown location off the coast of Newfoundland, where it began its demise by disintegration. Hungry mollusks were eating away at the exotic woods, and bacteria in the seawater, named *Halomonas titanicae*, were having a feast on the ironclad hull. Once satiated, these daemons of the deep were spitting out undigested lacy strips of that iron (aka rusticles), which now dripped down the sides of the ship's hull similar to rust-colored tinsel on a Radio City Hall Christmas tree.

Underwater video, taken by Argo's camera during that first joint expedition in 1985, revealed *Titanic's* bow resting elegantly upright in all her majestic beauty. The stern had broken away, plunging in a violent spiraling motion to the seabed, landing a third of a mile away from the bow, whipping off large pieces of her steel cladding and scattering her innards over an area of 1.1 nautical miles north to south and 2.9 nautical miles east to west around the ship. Between the bow and the stern was a vast field covered with artifacts from the ship; a snapshot in time of a journey in 1912.

The two halves now rested a third of a mile apart. Among large fragments of her hull was a seventeen-ton piece from the starboard side. Known now as the Big Piece, it was brought to the surface in 1998 by RMS *Titanic*, Inc. It was the largest piece of any ship ever to be lifted from that depth. Interestingly, it was lifted by an idea somewhat similar to one first posited in 1912: large lift bags, filled with diesel fuel that was lighter than water, were attached to the Big Piece by lifting lines, which pulled it to the surface by hoisting chains that were operated by a winch attached to the back of the support ship *Abeille Supporter*.

But I am getting ahead of my story. In 1985, camera lights revealed unopened wine bottles and delicate pieces of china in the debris field and giant boilers resting on the seabed while davits and bollards remained attached to the deck.

Later, in 1986, these areas would be explored again by Robert Ballard on another American-French team; their mission was to photograph the ship for posterity. Images from that dive show much more of the debris fields—copper cooking pots, leather luggage, a man's boots, champagne bottles with corks intact, and, then the leading lady—a cream-colored porcelain bisque doll's head, her empty eyes peering out from the gray ooze, startling the crew as she came into view. It was opening night.

The previously unknown coordinates of *Titanic's* position in the North Atlantic would soon become public knowledge when Colonel

Ballard published them in a book and now, despite how complicated and expensive it would be to visit the wreck, any adventurer or government with voluminous amounts of money, access to research vessels, agile submersibles, side scan sonar, and underwater cameras, could locate the wreck and potentially loot the site. What to do? How to do it? Who to do it?

Let the games begin.

The conservationists thought the artifacts in the debris field should be recovered and conserved as a cultural heritage and a memorial to the dead. Headlines abasing that position screamed "Grave robbers, have you no respect for history?" Others, protectionists, wanted the ship left as it was found. Ballard, initially wanting to recover some objects, later testified before the United States Congress in support of legislation that would protect *Titanic* as a maritime memorial to honor those who had lost their lives that frigid night in 1912.

The result was the RMS Titanic Maritime Memorial Act, passed and signed into law by President Ronald Regan in October of 1986, designating the ship:

> *an international maritime memorial and to provide reasonable research exploration, and, if appropriate, salvage activities with respect to the shipwreck, provided the ship itself was not disturbed.*

Only the United States and Canada signed on, so it was essentially a law with no teeth. *Titanic* was up for grabs.

A Guy Who Knew a Guy

As *Titanic*'s discovery was dominating headlines in 1985, Arnie had been on the road with Cyndi, dealing with the business aspects of her tours—*Titanic* was not on his radar. Nor mine. I was involved with Samantha, of course. These were her runaway days from her language school in San Miguel de Allende, Mexico, which she pulled off with no passport or money—but with a guy and his skateboard. True! They hitched a ride with a trucker who fed them and managed to get them past customs at the crossing between Mexico and the US. You can't make this stuff up.

During that time, I was collaborating with a friend on a never-to-be-published novel, which now rests deep in my storeroom under piles of books and memorabilia as if it were an artifact from the *Titanic* to be discovered one day by my ancestors during a deep dive into the flotsam and jetsam of my life. My coauthor and I were told by an editor that it was a mid-list book, so we let it go. Now how I wish for a mid-list book.

After its discovery, *Titanic* was all the rage, and many speculators, not knowing anything about the location or depth of the ship and the difficulty in bringing anything from its debris field to the surface, were willing to bet their money on the value of the ship's artifacts, as evidenced by an article published on April 16, 1987, in *London's Daily Express* with the title, "Fortune is sunk into the Titanic."

An auctioneer yesterday bid £70,000 [$189,188.56 today] for the Titanic's steering gear . . . without even knowing whether the ship's artifacts could be recovered. Among the other poignant reminders of the Titanic auctioned for a total of £107,000 yesterday [$289,188.22 *today] at London's Park Lane hotel was a silver plated visiting card pilfered by a steward.*

Titanic fever was everywhere.

At this point Ballard was proselytizing in lectures that *Titanic's* artifacts and the ship itself could be seen through his photographs and underwater footage, and others could wait to see them in situ when private submersibles were available. Enticing but aggravating.

That was similar to telling interested private citizens in 1922, when Howard Carter opened King Tutankhamun's tomb, if they wanted to see those treasures, they should travel to Egypt, take their own shovel—and dig. Difficult for most, but possible for those with money. The pyramids had been a popular tourist attraction for the wealthy and adventurous for as long as one can remember, shovels or not. As a matter of fact, Colonel John Jacob Astor, his pregnant nineteen-year-old bride, Madeleine Astor née Force, and the famous Molly Brown were all returning home on *Titanic* having spent some of their holiday in Egypt. But the pyramids were on terra firma, *Titanic* was not!

Ballard in the mid-1980s may have been partially correct, as having a private submersible with the capability to reach those depths was not likely. However, the French government did own a submersible; *Nautile*, which could. And in conjunction with Titanic Ventures Limited Partnership (TVLP), they had already been to the sunken ship in an expedition in July of 1987. Under the command of Pierre-Henri (PH) Nargeolet, they had retrieved 1,800 artifacts, (hereafter known as the '87 artifacts), from *Titanic's* debris field. This expedition set the precedent for all future expeditions and years of litigation.

How it began: Taurus International, a facilitator of sorts, assembled the alphabetical consortium of TVLP (the money) and IFREMER (the maritime experience, equipment, and manpower).

Having played a crucial role in the 1985 discovery dive and having visited the site again in 1986 with Bob Ballard, who wanted to document the ship with additional photographs and footage, IFREMER had been considering mounting their own expedition, so they were primed and ready to go when TVLP came calling.

To complete the list of acronyms was EDF, Électricité de France, an arm of the French government with a belief in the preservation of the world's patrimony. EDF's interest was not entirely altruistic. They had developed a new method of preserving metals using electrolytic reduction and came to the table with an offer to conserve *Titanic's* '87 artifacts if they could exhibit those artifacts in small exhibitions in Europe to demonstrate their new state-of-the-art conservation methods.

Another of the French government's stipulations was any recovered artifact must be conserved, maintained, and, if there were others to follow, they must be kept as a collection. TVLP agreed with the stipulations, which changed the trajectory of the *Titanic's* artifacts forever.

No one could predict that one agreement between a French government agency (EDF) and a private American company (TVLP) would bring forth an international uproar, a tsunami of lawsuits from governments and jealous adventurers with money, and from *Titanic* aficionados, the last living survivors of the wreck, relatives of the deceased, and Lloyd's of London—who as original insurers of *Titanic*, having already paid on claims presented to them in 1912, believed they too had an additional claim to any recovered artifacts. A claim subsequently denied by the US courts.

That not-so-minor business aside, TVLP's 1987 expedition had been a successful mission and the 1,800 recovered artifacts were shipped, as promised, to EDF for conservation, and after were presented in Sweden and in France in immensely popular exhibitions.[1]

When George Tulloch first reached out to Arnie through an interesting chain of inquiry in which one guy knew another guy who had a lawyer who knew a man named Arnie Geller, he was looking for a person with Arnie's business acumen and entertainment industry credentials to bring *Titanic*'s story beyond Sweden and France to a wider world—to make *Titanic* a star.

At that first meeting, Arnie found George to be a gregarious, talkative, easy-to-like public-facing guy, who was not afraid of taking risks. Arnie was an idea man, a planner, and a numbers guy who preferred to stay in the background doing whatever it took to make things happen by pulling out his contacts and persuasive language skills. Remember, he persuaded me to marry him after only four months into our relationship. So, obviously, he was not opposed to risk-taking either. And his interest had been piqued by George's enthusiasm and dedication to the *Titanic*.

Not unlike Arnie's resolve to complete the puzzle in my apartment at the start of our relationship, I am certain by the end of this first meeting with George, Arnie was already in his head working on ideas for a plan, knowing he would have to build a company explicitly for those purposes. For him it was another puzzle to conquer, even though, ironically, he was not especially fond of boats, which at that point was not relevant; it was the challenge that excited Arnie.

What could not be clear at the time was how many years of legal challenges, negative press, and incessant grousing of governments, worldwide maritime museums, and avid *Titanic* enthusiasts would

---

1 The artifacts were ultimately delivered to LP3 conservation laboratory in Semur-en-Auxois, France, where they were kept under the protective eye of conservator Stéphane Pennec. He had been on the 1987 dive, was familiar with EDF's new process, having studied there, was a specialist in metal conservation, and had worked with multiple other cultural institutions worldwide on projects of this magnitude.

be endured to pull it off. EDF may have paid for the initial conservation of the '87 artifacts; but after that, any recovered artifacts would have to be conserved by private money to maintain them in the proper condition.

It was to that meeting with TVLP where Arnie was headed that morning in our apartment in Battery Park and I had asked, "Didn't that ship sink?" And it was that morning *Titanic* became Arnie's challenge and passion, and he began his eighteen-year dedication to keeping all things *Titanic* "afloat." (Couldn't resist.)

Fore and Aft

Immediately, George invited Arnie to join their team, and they went to Europe to see a selection of the '87 artifacts in exhibition to give Arnie an idea of what lay ahead.

After seeing the enthusiasm of the waiting lines at the small-scale exhibitions in Sweden and later in France, it became clear that the best plan for the protection of the artifacts would be to let the artifacts themselves generate the funds needed for their care and feeding. They are the tangible items that would bring the enticing unknowns and cinematic drama of *Titanic's* epic tale of heroism, social inequality, greed, and tragedy to the world.

As his wife, let me tell you, Arnie was energized, zoned in, determined—ready for such a complicated endeavor where controversy hovered over the ship as the seagulls in Venice hovered over my tramezzini. When he returned home from Connecticut that day, it was as if he had traveled from a universe where people used phrases like "pressing a record," "working it up the pop or R&B charts," or finding the "next gig," to an alternative universe where the vocabulary was laced with "fore and aft, port side, hard-a-starboard, reciprocating engines," and of course, "Iceberg right ahead!"

Iceberg Right Ahead!

It was September 1992, TVLP had taken offices in the historic Whitehall Building in lower Manhattan, a short walk from our apartment in Battery Park. In fact, we could see the building from our windows and I would follow Arnie walking to work carrying his lucky briefcase. Their office windows appropriately faced New York harbor through which its 1912 occupants would have watched the largest moving object ever built make its triumphal march up the Hudson to its docking slip at Pier 59. A journey, of course, the doomed liner never completed. Instead, it sailed into maritime history by sinking, changing the lives of thousands of people, and ushering in rules and regulations in the maritime world that exist to this day.

TVLP was in the throes of planning both an exhibition of the artifacts and their next research and recovery expedition for April 1993, when they were confronted by the first of many "icebergs" coming their way. Arnie called from his new office to tell me that Marex Titanic, a salvage company from Memphis, was on-site in the North Atlantic anchored over *Titanic*'s coordinates—a scant few hours away from making their own first dive for artifacts. The concern in Arnie's voice was palpable.

Marex Titanic, Inc., led by Jack Grimm, an adventurer who, as mentioned previously, had already made three attempts to find the ship and plenty of claims that he had, felt confident that his crew could retrieve their own cache of artifacts from the sunken ship. They had filed a petition (surreptitiously) in Norfolk with the United States District Court, Eastern District of Virginia in August of 1992, to be awarded salvor in possession of *Titanic*'s artifacts—something TVLP had not done.

It was Grimm's contention that TVLP had not protected their salvor in possession rights to the artifacts, having not returned to the wreck site since their 1987 research and recovery expedition. TVLP quickly moved for a preliminary injunction against Marex Titanic in the same court to stop Grimm from proceeding with his expedition.

TVLP was also concerned that Marex Titanic was not using a French vessel for their expedition, making them free of any French government stipulations to keep the artifacts in a collection, nor were they mandated to search for proof of any claims of ownership or government restrictions for each and every artifact they retrieved, which TVLP was mandated to do. Any artifacts Marex recovered could be sold at auction or possibly used in competing exhibitions.

Salvage law dating back to the 1700s states, among other stipulations, the first person to bring up an object from a sunken ship is considered to be the salvor in possession, if the property salvaged is in extreme danger. From TVLP's point of view, *Titanic's* artifacts were indeed in extreme danger from their prolonged time under the sea and from Jack Grimm and Marex.

Though they had alerted the court of their recovery expedition to the wreck in 1987 and, I am told, they had brought a wine decanter into court to prove that fact—and, additionally, each and every '87 artifact had a certificate of authenticity signed by *Nadir's* captain and had been protected on the expedition under lock and key by expedition leader PH Nargeolet; TVLP had never officially applied for the actual salvor in possession award.

On September 29, 1992, while Marex hovered over the site in the North Atlantic, the two contenders, TVLP and Marex Titanic, met in Norfolk, before Judge J. Calvitt Clarke, Jr. in the United States Federal Court in the Eastern District of Virginia, to plead their cases as to which claimant should become *Titanic's* salvor of record.

This was the turning point in *Titanic's* future.

Marex, led by oil tycoon Grimm, came to court with a fragment of *Titanic's* hull and a glass vial, claiming they had been given to him by PH Nargeolet on the 1987 expedition. When PH Nargeolet was called to the stand, he testified under oath that Grimm had never been on the 1987 expedition, nor had he given Grimm anything.

TVLP argued that they had not returned to the site due to putting their energies and money into preserving the '87 artifacts and developing new exhibitions; and were in the throes of planning another research and recovery expedition in 1993.

After several days of testimony, resulting in 425 pages of transcript, Judge Clarke, taking into consideration that Marex had come to the court with unclean hands, having learned that the glass vial and the fragment from the hull had been taken from a previous photographic expedition (one that had been prohibited from recovering any artifacts), and acknowledging all that TVLP had accomplished thus far—their care of the artifacts, their plans for another dive in 1993, their exhibitions—ruled that TVLP would be salvor in possession of any artifacts recovered from the ship.

This did not include the 1,800 retrieved in 1987, as they were under French jurisdiction, but ostensibly all those yet to be recovered as long as TVLP maintained their salvor status.

Salvor in possession did not mean ownership; it had conditions. The collection must be kept intact; must be conserved according to international law; made available to the world for educational, historical, and cultural purposes; and to the scientific community for study, interpretation, and verification.

It was a ruling essential for the protection of the ship and her artifacts and would guarantee that they would remain in a collection to tell the *Titanic's* story to the world.

Jack Grimm had to sail away, leaving TVLP with an award that was argued over, challenged, overturned for procedural purposes, reaffirmed, and under constant scrutiny for years to come. The largest downside was that TVLP must continue to finance the whole shebang.

I have press photos taken on the first day of that hearing when Arnie and George, all suited up for the big game, walked with determination into the US District Court for the Eastern District of Virginia, Norfolk Division, to appear in US District Judge J. Calvitt Clarke, Jr.'s courtroom, flanked by their attorneys. Arnie was carrying his lucky, travel-worn briefcase, antithetical to his gray double-breasted persona, for sure. But he wouldn't leave home without it.

Inside his briefcase, along with his legal pads, Bic pens, contracts, and other businessman paraphernalia, he carried a Barbie doll's high-heeled bright-yellow shoe. We never knew how or when Barbie's shoe got there. Samantha, the obvious suspect, never admitted culpability. No matter: From then on, Arnie never left home without that wee talisman in his briefcase. In court that day, with the soul of *Titanic* at risk, let's attest to the fact that Barbie's shoe helped in its salvation.

Having done the biggest task in her life, Barbie's shoe now rests on her laurels in Samantha's collection of her father's memorabilia, among his gold records, his Bar Mitzvah yarmulke, tallis, and the congratulatory telegrams of that event. And every birthday card Samantha and I ever gave him.

From that point on, Arnie's focus was on the artifacts and the security of the ship that had carried them. I have reread all the case law over the years, engendered by the multiple times Arnie went to court to protect RMST's salvor award, and it was exhausting. I marveled at his dedication and fortitude as he lived day after day after day with all the rancor *Titanic* engendered and still had the energy to build a company and call me every evening to ask, "What are our plans for dinner?"

BOOM!

It was February 26, 1993. It was a cold gray day. We were still living in Battery Park on the forty-second floor of that high rise with its wonderful views.

TVLP, soon to become RMST[2], was in the throes of planning their July 1993 dive with IFREMER, when something horrific went boom!

At seventeen minutes past noon, a block north of Arnie's office and a block east of our apartment, the terrorist Ramzi Yousef and his band of coldblooded cohorts detonated a bomb in the parking garage of the World Trade Center's North Tower. Six people were killed and thousands were injured on that cold winter's day when the bombing opened a 100-foot crater "several stories deep and several higher," according to the FBI's history site, which continues with this prescient statement: "Middle Eastern terrorism had arrived on American soil with a bang."

The explosion produced an unnerving boom that ricocheted through the canyons of skyscrapers in the Battery—breaking windows, cracking plaster, emptying shelves, and causing all the buildings in the immediate area, including ours, to tremble and sway.

Immediately, our landline rang; it was Arnie calling from his office. "Did you hear that? Are you OK?" he asked.

"Yes. Are you OK? Whatever it was caused our building to sway. Do you think it might have been a gas explosion?" I asked.

"I don't know," Arnie replied, "It could have been a train accident

---

2 On May 4, 1993, TVLP was rebranded as RMS Titanic, Inc. and the French Office of Maritime Affairs of the Ministry of Equipment, Transportation, and Tourism gave RMST full title to the 1987 artifacts still housed at LP3 conservation lab in Semur en Auxois.

in the tunnels beneath the Trade Center. Maybe a bomb. Whatever it was, please don't leave the building until we know more. And stay away from the subway!"

Assuring him (fingers crossed), that I would not leave the building or take the subway (which would have been impossible as it was in ruins), I scooped up Daisy, forgetting her lead and my coat, and we rushed as close to the bombing site as possible—until a tight blue line of New York's finest stopped me at the Westside Highway confirming it had, indeed, been a bomb.

Across the highway, devastation reigned. The acrid smell and airborne debris from the cars and ashes aflame in the Trade Center's garage were being carried by the wind over lower Manhattan, causing a blanket of snowflakes floating like gray ash, to settle on everything, including Daisy's white fur and me. We didn't stay outside long, and I never told Arnie we went, but what we, and the world, soon learned was that bombing proved to be the clarion call, pointing the way for an unsettled era for the nation. Serenity was no more.

PART VIII

Oh, the Places You'll Go

Yellow Submarine

—THE BEATLES, 1966

Arnie and I were standing on the deck of the French research ship *Nadir*, one of the largest and most advanced research vessels in the world and the support ship for the submersible *Nautile*. We were anchored in the North Atlantic two and a half miles above the location where *Titanic* had plunged to her early demise in 1912. The long-awaited Research and Recovery Expedition of 1993 had begun.

Arnie and George were co-expedition leaders, and I was on board as Arnie had asked me to coordinate all the necessary papers and tickets for the historians, press, scientists, investors, and others who had been invited to participate. We had flown into Halifax, where I met them for the first time over dinner, a group of many talents and countries. One member of the group looked at me skeptically and asked, "And what are you doing here?"

Stunning myself, perhaps emboldened by Arnie's faith in me, as I am not usually quick with a quip, I said, "Sleeping with the director," which broke the ice.

The next morning, our group was flown to the barren and isolated French islands of St. Pierre and Miquelon to board the fishing trawler *Gölette* for a two-day trip to join *Nadir* for the expedition in the North Atlantic. We left St. Pierre with the trawler's three whistles loudly wishing us well, after which I spent the two travel days in my cabin vomiting. Turns out, I had been given the "best cabin" by Captain Jean-Luc Derouet. Its location was situated directly aft of where the fish were cleaned at sea, making them ready for sale when the trawler was on its regular duty. Between the fish smell and the rolling sea, I didn't see any of my new friends again until we spied

Nadir waiting for us on the horizon 500 feet away in six-foot swells.

Down *Gölette's* rope ladder and into a waiting rubber raft, a Zodiac, we were transported to the *Nadir*, where we each had to wait to board until the sea dipped to the level of *Nadir's* tailgate and then, one by one, we could step hurriedly from the Zodiac to the support vessel. When it was my turn, Arnie was standing on the stern, waiting for me in his yellow slicker with a look of concern on his face, knowing that I can't swim. Which, in hindsight, with the anger of those waves, I may not have survived even if I could.

Quietly, he said, "Hi, honey," and we hugged each other with excitement and relief.

All involved in the expedition wore those slickers with an oval patch on the left breast depicting the *Titanic,* and embroidered with Research & Recovery Expedition 1993, and below that, the words RMS Titanic, Inc. and IFREMER. The canary yellow slickers were replicating the color of *Nautile,* the small titanium submersible hanging in *Nadir's* garage. It was on that day I first met two essential people in *Titanic's* world: Commander PH Nargeolet, dive master, and Stéphane Pennec, archeologist and artifact conservator.

The next day dawned sunny, the high waves had subsided, but the air was awash with a heavy presence. Before the first dive, our new onboard team and *Nadir's* entire crew participated in a solemn prayer service. We stood in silence as two commemorative wreaths were tossed into the sea in respect for the death of more than 1,500 passengers and crew that night in April 1912.

The anticipation of the day's launch of submersible *Nautile* was palpable. Hanging in the air were the lingering heart-wrenching goodbyes, hasty prayers, and final screams as families parted and the frigid sea took the breath of life from one *Titanic* passenger after another.

The *Nadir,* now on its second research and recovery expedition to the wreck site, was under the same mandate as on the 1987 dive:

to survey the decaying ship and its condition, and to photograph, catalog, and recover from her debris field any personal artifact or tangible remains of *Titanic* suitable for scientific analysis and the telling of her story.

Midships, swaying on her launching crane, hung *Nautile*, a titanium embodiment of the Beatles' Yellow Submarine, with all the latest technology needed to accomplish that mission and to bring any collected artifacts to the light of day for the first time since lookout Frederick Fleet said, "Iceberg, right ahead."

Similar to Russian nesting dolls, *Nadir*, the mother ship, housed *Nautile*, the submersible, and *Nautile* housed Robin, the robotic probe whose job it was to enter small areas unavailable to the bigger submersible and to send real-time images through a cable to *Nadir* waiting above.

We stood in awe as PH Nargeolet gave the word and *Nautile*, hanging twenty feet in the air attached to a crane by lift lines, was rolled in her cradle to the aft platform. There, one of the seamen in a black wetsuit, called a cowboy, straddled the dome of the seventeen-ton submersible until it touched the sea. Then checking with the crew inside the submersible that all was well, PH gave *Nadir's* captain a thumbs up, and a cowboy unclipped *Nautile* from its lift lines, releasing her to the sea and her journey.

Arnie and I stretched our torsos over *Nadir's* rail as far as we safely could, mesmerized as the little yellow submersible sank lower and lower beneath the surface, leaving only a slight ripple as she disappeared on her 12,500 feet (eight to twelve hour) pilgrimage to the North Atlantic seabed. The three men onboard the submersible, a pilot, copilot, and an observer, were on a mission.

Eight hours later, as *Nautile* was about to reemerge, Arnie sent me out into the Atlantic in a Zodiac, with two cowboys and a journalist, to be there as the bright yellow dome broke the surface. When it did, there was a large three-legged copper water heater that had been attached to its side on the seabed by underwater articulating arms. It had to be removed from those arms so it could be lifted to the deck of *Nadir*. When it was unclipped, I was overwhelmed when one of the cowboys handed it to me, making me one of the first people to touch it in the seventy-three years since it last stood on a sideboard in one of *Titanic*'s dining rooms, providing hot water for the passengers' tea. Touching it sent an exhilarating jolt through my body and my mind spinning back to the anguish that caused it to be in the sea. The tragedy was no longer a newspaper article, it was real.

As the day's retrieved artifacts were lifted from the sea to the deck, they were deposited in a foam-lined collection box and carried to the onboard conservation laboratory where conservator Stéphane Pennec photographed and cataloged them, separated each by material, brushed them with a soft brush, gently rinsed off their salt water, and submerged them in fresh water to begin their stabilization into the atmosphere of the present time.

Arnie and I stood on the deck as the collection boxes were being offloaded from *Nautile* when he noticed a layer of velvety-gray mud remaining in the bottom of one of the boxes. Carefully, he reached into the mud to be sure nothing had been overlooked, nodding to me that it was OK to help.

Using my hands as a tool, I gathered a scoop of the soft, mysterious ooze that had been ground into velvet by the undersea currents. Arnie, in fun, smeared a dab of the mud on my cheek; it was cold and soothing—reminiscent of a luxurious substance that would be found in an upscale spa and not on a research vessel in the North Atlantic. We let the ooze slip and slide through our fingers as we searched for any possibly missed fragment of *Titanic* as the more dazzling pieces had been lifted to safety. As the last bits of seabed filtered away, two tiny treasures revealed themselves—a woman's faceted jet bead and a child's marble. Arnie handed them both to me.

These minuscule remembrances, plucked from the vast ocean floor, spoke to us as none of the larger artifacts had. How astonishing that in seventy-three years they had not been carried away or buried with the drifting currents. What woman and child had last touched these small bits of a life? Had they survived? Was the woman married? Did the child kiss his or her father goodbye, never to see him again? Had the owners been mother and son? Mother and daughter? What had become of them? So many questions generated by objects no larger than a green garden pea.

We will never know the exact identity of the lady whose necklace contained the jet bead or of the child who last played with the marble. No matter—they have become our symbols of every woman and child who made that maiden voyage into the world's collective consciousness and who suffered dreadfully for having done so.

I was lucky to be invited on three expeditions: the first one on the *Nadir* in 1993 with the submarine *Nautile,* the second in 2000 with the Russians on their research vessel, the *Keldysh,* and their two submersibles *Mir I and Mir II.* The last in 2004 with Oceaneering when remotely operated vehicles (ROVs), provided by Phoenix International Inc., were used to retrieve the appropriate artifacts during round-the-clock undersea explorations. At each and every expedition, prayers were said in remembrance of those who had perished.

And the French had the best food—hands down!

Arnie had entered a fascinating new world of not only expeditions, but one of history, science, litigation, exhibitions, and travel. I am grateful he had included me on this complicated, exhausting, emotionally perilous journey of a lifetime.[3]

---

3 This chapter is a revised version of a chapter from my book *Women and Children First*, published in 1996, by W.W. Norton & Company.

A Night To Remember

I left the 1993 expedition early, making the short journey on another Zodiac back to smelly *La Gölette*; however, by this time I had my sea legs. All my compatriots were on board, and all were now friends. We spent the journey back to St. Pierre telling stories—lawyers, scientists, authors, businessmen, and historians, speaking French, Norwegian, German, and English—replicating animal noises in their native languages. Listening to someone say the French or German version of *quack, quack* is hysterical, especially after quite a few glasses of French wine.

Arnie stayed onboard *Nadir* with the artifacts as they completed their journey to the United States. Among them were the jet bead and the marble, which had captivated both Arnie's and my thoughts. They had posed so many questions that I decided to write a book that centered on those women and children whose lives had been forever changed by that voyage.

When I told Arnie my idea for a book, ever the marketing man, his immediate suggestion was, "Why not name it *Women and Children First?*"—Captain Smith's command as *Titanic* was sinking. Perfect! But first I had to understand more fully the tragedy of the sinking and the grip it would have on the world thereafter. What better source than Walter Lord, who had written the quintessential book on the ship, *A Night to Remember.*

Stanley Walker wrote a review of the book in 1955 for the *New York Herald Tribune*, and he describes it best: "[It is] a kind of literary pointillism, the arrangement of contrasting bits of fact and emotion in such a fashion that a vividly real impression of an event is conveyed to the reader."

I couldn't agree more. As Lord's reviewer had stated, it was indeed these contrasting bits of fact and emotion after the sinking, and the technical questions yet to be answered, that has kept the interest in *Titanic* alive to this day.

Arnie did his magic and arranged for me to meet with Walter, who fortunately was living in an apartment on the Upper East Side of New York, a subway ride away. He was suffering from Parkinson's disease, but still a gentleman, he met me at the door in his wheelchair and graciously shared how he had researched his book and its sequel *The Night Lives On*. He regaled me with stories of the sixty interviews he had with survivors that had enriched his story. The two stories I related to most were those of Ida Straus and Edith Russell. Perhaps because one was devoted to her husband and the other a woman traveling alone who had grit and a dramatic flair I admired.

Ida and her husband, Isidor, were returning to New York, having been on holiday in Europe. He was the founder of Macy's Department Store and they were an extremely philanthropic couple. It was said of them that "no worthy charity appealed to them in vain." When the time came for the lifeboats to be filled and lowered, Ida was seated, and Isidor, due to his age, was urged to enter with her. But hearing it was women and children first, Isidor climbed back to the deck and Ida followed. They stood hand in hand as they waited for *Titanic* to founder. It was reported that Ida said: "We have lived together for many years; where you go, I go."

Isidor's body was recovered. Ida's body was not. On their monument in Woodlawn Cemetery in the Bronx, where Isidor rests alone, the memorial inscription reads: "Many waters cannot quench love. Neither can the floods drown it." Song of Solomon 8:7.

At one point in the afternoon, Lord, with much effort and grace, wheeled over to a glass cabinet to get Maxixe, a black and white paper-mâché pig who, when you wound his tail, played a popular song from *Titanic*'s era, "The Maxixe." The pig belonged to *Titanic* passenger Edith Russell, whom Lord had met on the set of the movie *A Night to Remember*, when both had been advisors to the director.

In 1912, Edith was a self-sufficient fashion consultant traveling in *Titanic*'s first class on her way back from Paris with little piggy Maxixe by her side. This toy had been a gift from her mother after Edith had survived a devastating car accident that had taken the life of her fiancé, a German industrialist. From that time on Edith swore Maxixe was her lucky charm and would not travel without this nine-inch, black-and-white, papier-mâché critter.

Walter told me that, though Edith was aware *Titanic* had collided with an iceberg, she was reticent to leave the warmth of the ship. As many others did, she took her sweet time packing and locking every one of her nineteen trunks and suitcases before handing her cabin key to a steward with instructions to see that her luggage arrived safely in New York. There are other variations of her story, but essentially, swaddling pudgy Maxixe in a towel, Edith finally ascended to the boat deck where a startled Bruce Ismay, managing director of the White Star Line, stunned to see her still on board, yelled: "What are you still doing on this ship?" as he hustled her down the stairs to A Deck where Lifeboat 11, already in descent, had momentarily stopped to pick up additional passengers in the last, desperate escape from the dying ship.

Edith, dressed in a woolen hobble skirt, only eighteen inches in circumference, a light broadtail coat, silk stockings, silk embroidered velvet slippers (very chic even by today's standards), and no under-wear, may I add, was not quite appropriately dressed for swinging her leg up and over the railing into a lifeboat. Frustrated with her reticence, a sailor grabbed Maxixe from her arms, yelling, "Well if you won't go, I will toss your baby in instead." And he did just that.

Immediately coming to Edith's rescue, two male passengers

clasped their hands, made a sling with their arms, and scooping Edith up, swung her unceremoniously over the ship's railing to join Maxixe lying in the bottom of the lifeboat. His nose was smashed, his legs broken, and his talented tail askew. But he had indeed been her lucky charm.

Edith and Maxixe, both a little the worse for wear, did their duty by entertaining the children in Lifeboat 11 on that infamous, devastating night until the following morning when they were rescued by RMS *Carpathia*. Edith was one of the 705 passengers who survived. If you count Maxixe, that makes 706. Edith was quoted as saying: "I have had every disaster but bubonic plague and a husband."

She continued her trans-Atlantic journeys as a fashion consultant, a World War I correspondent, and an advisor on multiple *Titanic* projects. Maxixe always by her side.

When she died in 1977, Edith bequeathed him to Walter Lord for safekeeping. Before his passing, Lord bequeathed Maxixe and Edith's velvet slippers to the National Maritime Museum in Greenwich England, along with 60 other pieces of *Titanic* memorabilia.

I choose to think that having held the little piggy who went to sea, along with having Lord's advice, my *Titanic* book was allowed to survive in the vast sea of *Titanic* books existing today.

Had Cyndi reached up into the ether of everything and pulled the name *A Night to Remember* down into the 1980s pop culture by accident? Or maybe it was predetermined, another meant-to-be that Arnie would spend eighteen years of his life deeply and emotionally invested in that ship. I never had the opportunity to ask Cyndi how or why she had chosen that name. However, it doesn't matter. It was bashert.

Great Britain's National Maritime Museum to the Rescue

Even though the small exhibitions in Sweden and France had drawn enormous crowds, the criticism of removing the artifacts from the debris field continued to fester. The expeditions drew outrage from governments, historians, marine archeologists, academics, *Titanic* afficionados, *Titanic* membership societies, and worldwide maritime museums—all initially agreeing with Ballard and the preservationists to let sleeping artifacts lie. Their hue and cry was that a commercial company could not handle the artifacts in a "proper" underwater archeological or academic manner. And as always, that the site was a graveyard, and quite possibly there could be bodies within the ship's hull.

(Let me clear that up: If passengers were not rescued by the *Carpathia,* they died from hypothermia in the frigid twenty-eight-degree (-2 Celsius) water. Their bodies were either gathered by the funeral ship *Mackay-Bennett* or would have drifted away with the currents and their bones would have decomposed in the seawater. By the time *Titanic* was discovered in 1987, if there had been any poor souls trapped in the bowels of the ship, their bones would also have decomposed in the seawater. Excruciatingly sad, but true.)

All that naysaying fell away when the world's most prestigious maritime museum—Great Britain's National Maritime Museum in Greenwich, England—came to RMS Titanic, Inc's rescue. Thanks to Director Richard Ormond CBE and Deputy Director, Dr. Roger Knight, plus Director of Exhibitions Stephen Deuchar, and their belief in RMST's intentions and capabilities, they hosted the first major *Titanic* exhibition, a prelude to RMST's own exhibition in production for a worldwide tour.

The National Maritime Museum's exhibition, *The Wreck of the*

Titanic, opened in October 1994 to unprecedented crowds. Before it closed one year later, more than 860,000 visitors had cued for hours under the museum's stately colonnade, waiting to see *Titanic's* artifacts. It was the largest attendance for the museum since its opening in 1937.

During the exhibition's development, I traveled back and forth between New York and Greenwich to assist with the merchandising of the gift shop—an important last stop in any exhibition for its bottom line. One of the most popular items in the shop was a third-class white pottery mug emblazoned with the White Star Line's iconic red flag. Arnie and I found the pottery factory where the mug had been originally produced in 1912, still up and running near Stratford-upon-Avon. And they still had the original mold.

Other less-authentic versions remain for sale in antique stores. Alert: If you see that mug anywhere besides an exhibition, it is most likely the copy Arnie and I had made for the Maritime Museum's gift shop. Also, for that shop, we assembled the largest collection of *Titanic* books to that date. The books were piled high on three long tables and sold remarkably well. *Titanic* remains an evergreen subject, attested to by the now hundreds, if not thousands, of books written on the subject. Just ask Amazon, they have over 300 pages of them.

My *Titanic* book was not published until 1999, too late to be on one of those tables; however, James Cameron's movie *Titanic* was still in the headlines and our exhibitions were going strong; both creating an excellent condition for a new book. But at first, it was a little touch and go as to its being published at all, as I decided to negotiate the book contract myself.

I am not the most astute person in business, and Arnie, who was a master negotiator, kept asking, "Do you want me to help?" And I kept saying, "No."

As a first-time writer, I was afraid that Arnie would be too tough and negotiate me right out of a deal, which, of course, he would never have done. Never once did he criticize me about the deal I made. I know he was hurt and a little pissed. And I know it was a thoughtless thing to do. But I did dedicate the book to him as it would never have seen the light of day were it not for his believing in me.

In the same year my book was published, Arnie had become the president of RMS Titanic, Inc. Aware I was nervous about the publicity tours that had been scheduled for the book, Arnie took time from the office to accompany me on several of my tours.

He was by my side, guiding me through the radio interviews, the bookstore appearances, the slide presentations, and the questions from the enthusiastic fans who attended. And for added value, he also operated the slide projector and jokingly told me to introduce him as the AV man.

I wish to believe he enjoyed my tour more than he enjoyed Cyndi's. Though on her promotional tours she had thousands of adoring fans and on most of mine, I had Arnie and maybe twenty or thirty enthusiastic book readers. Nonetheless, Arnie did what all professional managers do: coordinated with the publisher; approved the venues, hotels, and the transportation; and made me feel like a star.

Remember when I said Arnie loved women? He always had a special place in his heart for older women, most likely based on his early respect and care for both his mother and Grandma Lena and later my mother. And remember he had married an older woman. With *Titanic*, he added another favorite to his list, Millvina Dean. It was during that exhibition at the National Maritime when Arnie first bonded with Millvina, one of *Titanic*'s last survivors.

Melvina, only two months old at the time of the sinking, had become a star when the ship was discovered in 1985, and she continued to hold the world's attention with her special sense of humor that tickled Arnie. At *Titanic* events, she would hold court, regaling the crowd with stories about the vessel she had memorized over the years from extensive reading and other survivors. Her favorite bon mot was a never corroborated story that John Jacob Astor was heard to say as the ship was sinking, "I always like ice in my drink, but this is ridiculous!" Melvina was always quick to tell the crowds that she liked ice in her drinks as well.

Shortly before Millvina passed, Arnie and I made a special trip to visit her in her care home in Ashurst, England. Yes, I was there, and brought her a lovely nightgown, but her attention was all on Arnie. They had always kept in touch. She called him her "boy toy" and he called her his "sweetheart."

On May 31, 2009, newspapers around the world announced that Millvina had passed away. The British newspaper, the *Telegraph* reported: "Miss Dean's ashes were to be scattered from a small launch on the water of berth 43/44 at Southampton Docks from where the *Titanic* departed 97 years before." And which, coincidently, was the ninety-eighth anniversary of the launch of *Titanic*'s hull. OK, I won't say bashert.

Titanic: The Artifact Exhibition

After the success of the *Wreck of the Titanic* exhibition in Greenwich in 1994, where only a small selection of the ship's artifacts were first displayed to the public, a more contemporary version of that exhibition called *Titanic: The Artifact Exhibition*, began a global tour. During Arnie's tenure, there were seven *Titanic* exhibitions touring the world, seen by more than thirty-five million people in thirty countries. It became the most attended traveling exhibition in the world, and it continues to travel today. The exhibitions tell *Titanic*'s story, from its launch to its demise, by immersing the visitor into the experience through the artifacts.

When you enter the exhibition, you receive your boarding pass, inscribed with the name of a passenger who had made that journey, and you are plunged into *Titanic* and a 1912 world. When *Titanic* was launched, it was a pivotal period in history with the waning of class inequality and the beginning of the industrial age. On her decks sauntered the rich, the beautiful, and the ugly: a movie star, a mistress, and a card shark onboard to fleece that wealthy lot. Second class sheltered a French citizen taking his two sons to America to hide them from their mother, whom he had divorced. And on *Titanic*'s lower deck were immigrants seeking a better life in America, the land of opportunity at the start of the industrial world. The ship, thought to be unsinkable, sailed with 2,224 passengers and crew on board—with only enough lifeboats for 1,178 of them. When it sank, it was the greatest loss of life in maritime history.

All these stories become real when the exhibition visitors see the bronze bell that rang three times to warn of the iceberg right ahead, the steering wheel and telegraph in a replica of the wheelhouse, a wrench from the boiler room where you hear engines pounding, dishes from the dining rooms resting on tablecloths, and luggage in recreations of the staterooms. And yes, a replica of the iceberg on which you can place your hand and feel the cold of that -2 degree frigid night when the tragedy happened.

As the exhibitions toured the world, RMST made additional recovery and scientific missions to the wreck site in 1994, 1996, 1998, 2000, and in 2004, culminating in the recovery of more than 5,500 artifacts from *Titanic's* debris field. And Arnie continued to maintain RMST's position as salvor in possession of those artifacts, periodically going before the court to deliver status reports as to their condition. During those years, Arnie repeatedly petitioned the court to have the salvage in possession award converted to actual owner-ship or title to the artifacts. To no avail.

In 2001, Arnie felt it necessary and less costly to consolidate the artifacts in one location. The first 1,800 from the 1987 dive, now outrightly owned by the company, plus those from following dives, were still in Semur-en-Auxois under Stéphane Pennec's care at LP3, or in conservation laboratories and exhibitions around the world. They needed a home, a permanent location for their safety and control of their future.

Arnie asked me to go to LP3, along with Samantha, now an artist who had grown up with the importance and fragility of *Titanic's* arti-facts, and with Allie, who had joined the company in the production department and had become an integral part of the organization, to pack the artifacts for shipping to their new location.

I do not possess any psychometric ability, though I still hold Arnie's cell phone in my hands occasionally, trying to feel his pres-ence; but in LP3's laboratory with hundreds of *Titanic's* artifacts laid before me, I felt that same heavy sadness in the air as I had on that first dive in 1993. This time I crossed my fingers and hoped on their second Atlantic journey, these artifacts would arrive safely to their new location.

Where were the artifacts being sent? Yes, Atlanta. Arnie had moved RMS Titanic, Inc. there and had opened new offices and a conservation laboratory in an undisclosed and secure location for additional protection of the artifacts.

Waiting in Atlanta for the artifacts to arrive was Stacey Savatsky, with a Master of Library Science Degree and an MA in museum studies, whom Arnie had hired as executive director of collections. She was in charge of the new 11,000-square-foot laboratory fitted with climate-controlled areas for the more fragile artifacts, work-spaces for their ongoing conservation, and areas where they could be photographed, conditioned, and momentarily rested, or packed and crated for transfer to other exhibitions.

All this was recorded in a database where each artifact was meas-ured, photographed, and its condition documented. And whenever they were moved to an exhibition in a new location, that was recorded as well. The laboratory also had a library with a media center where thousands of slides, books and 900 hours of dive footage were cata-loged for posterity

Take that, naysayers, grousers, and maritime museums around the world who had originally said a private company was not up to the task of properly caring for *Titanic*'s artifacts. And that's not the only protocols Stacey put in place to protect the artifacts.

On their travels to and from exhibitions, the artifacts could only be handled by Stacey or her team as they are packed, unpacked, and installed in specially designed, often climate-controlled, museum cases. At every location, RMST's crew of carpenters and electricians created replicas of locations on the ship where the appropriate arti-facts were placed to enhance the reality of the visitor's experience. It was the first immersive exhibition in which the artifacts were not only in museum cases, but in recreated areas of the ship itself. Public or private museums, with their consistent lack of funding, could never have afforded such endeavors.

After the artifact's initial stabilization on board the expedition vessel, they generally go to this secret laboratory in Atlanta or to outside laboratories that specialize in a particular material's conservation. The Big Piece is a good example of that: EverGreene Architectural Arts was responsible for its conservation along with Stéphane Pennec at LPS in France. As Joseph Sembrat, who spearheaded the *Titanic* project, on the EverGreene website, writes:

> *Eventually, a cleaning procedure was devised that involved the removal of loose corrosion and the rusticles using a 3,000-psi water-jet system followed by drying with propane torches and then picking residual corrosion products and accretions off by hand using scalpels and dental tools. To help passivate the rust a 5% tannic acid solution was applied to the surface and the entire piece was then hot waxed with a specially formulated microcrystalline wax. The bronze elements required minimal treatment and the original paint residue was left intact.*

The artifacts are of extreme importance as a historical representation of an era, but how and where they were found in the ship's debris field was equally important for the advancement of marine forensics. *Titanic* is as important to marine archaeology as are the archeological remains of ancient civilizations, similar to the objects found in the pyramids of Giza or the terracotta warriors unearthed from the emperor's tomb in Xi'an, China. Exploration and understanding of the past can be applied to improve and enlighten our present and our future.

When in 2006, PH Nargeolet, an explorer, and Ken Vrana, a scientist and undersea explorer, presented Arnie with a project for underwater mapping of both the *Titanic* and its rescue ship, the *Carpathia*, Arnie readily sanctioned their proposal. He understood that the RMS *Titanic* shipwreck site is an archeological site of historic importance.

To quote Vrana: "Arnie Geller deserves special recognition for launching and supporting the *Titanic* Mapping Project, which resulted in the only peer-reviewed scientific article on the RMS Titanic shipwreck site using an archaeological framework…"[4]

On April 10, 2007, the ninety-fifth anniversary of RMS *Titanic's* sailing on her maiden voyage, Premier Exhibitions, Inc. (now the parent company of RMS Titanic, Inc.), rang the closing bell at NASDAQ as a publicly traded company, whose main objective was to maintain the protection of *Titanic's* artifacts, the patrimony of an era. I was there that day, standing behind Arnie on the balcony at NASDAQ, with others from the company. It was validation for Arnie's years and efforts made in the interest of saving *Titanic's* artifacts and building the company that cared for them

And as long as I'm discussing Arnie's role in the importance of *Titanic's* history, I must tell you of a paper written in 2012, by graduate Matthew E. Zekala for the *Lewis & Clark Law Review*, titled: "Liability and Salvage: Titanic Jurisprudence in United States Federal Court."

In his introduction, Zekala thanks his mother for introducing him to the ship by giving him a copy of Walter Lord's *A Night to Remember* when he was eleven and mentions a piece of coal from the debris field given to him by his sister in later years. Coal from the ship is allowed to be sold to offset the expense of preserving the artifacts where funds are always needed.

According to Zekala, ultimately, RMST would spend "$9 million and 500 hours in salvaging and preserving the artifacts for the benefit of all mankind." Zekala also discusses in length the litigiousness Arnie faced for years on *Titanic's* behalf and gives a compelling argument

---

4 See Marine Technology Society Journal Vol 46, November/December 2012 for more information on the mapping project.

for RMST's artifact retrieval:

> *Given the choice between allowing every historical and cultural artifact from the wreck to be destroyed or carefully recovering and preserving as much as possible for future generations, the latter option seems a more dignified and respectful way to honor the memory of those who were lost in the sinking. Allowing an historic shipwreck to continue to deteriorate without attempting viable salvage is not a preservation plan—it is an irresponsible lapse in responsibility to future generations. Human history must be preserved by those in a position to preserve it. The resolution in RMST is just and equitable and should serve as a model for future salvage of historic shipwrecks.*

Exactly Arnie's philosophy and operating principle.

Social Importance

Premier Exhibitions, Inc., with RMST as a subsidiary, was doing well. However, Arnie continued to search for additional traveling exhibitions to add to Premier's roster. He was looking for something remarkable, similar to *Titanic*—an exhibition that would attract visitors with its educational value and uniqueness, would help defray the costs of the artifacts' upkeep—and which could be produced in multiples. Another of Arnie's ideas that took over the burgeoning traveling exhibitions concept: multiples of the same exhibition presented in different world locations at the same time. Easy with *Titanic* and its 5,500 artifacts that could be split up and still tell the same story. Arnie knew there had to be others.

One Arnie particularly liked for its social importance was *Dialogue in the Dark*, with its message of social inclusion. It was a concept developed by social entrepreneur Dr. Andreas Heinecke who, among his many goals, strives "to raise awareness about people with disadvantages while fostering greater inclusion and respect for their contributions to society."

Arnie thought *Dialogue in the Dark* was inventive and thought-provoking and took our team to Hamburg to visit Heinecke's operations. There we experienced firsthand what it meant to be visually impaired in a sighted world.

We walked through an entire exhibition in complete darkness, following the voice of a visually impaired guide. I did the whole exercise holding on to the back of Arnie's belt. (That's a metaphor if I ever heard one.) It was an exhibition built around our daily activities. Walking to the bus stop, buying groceries, making coffee in the morning, all became unbelievably difficult and unnerving. We emerged into the light with a significantly better insight into the challenges for those who live around us in darkness and, without hesitation, Arnie added it to Premier's roster.

When we opened that exhibition in Atlanta, Arnie insisted that only the visually impaired were hired to work as guides. It was an extraordinary employment opportunity for them and an even more compelling experience for the visitors.

Soon after that, another even more compelling exhibition popped up; you could say this one was revolutionary.

Dem Bones, Dem Bones

The *Titanic* had a complex anatomy designed by an army of architects sitting in a large sunny room in Belfast working at their drafting tables. I had studied their drawings, read more than I care to remember of books on the subject, had written my own book on the ship's passengers, authored the catalogs that accompanied the artifact exhibitions, and believed I understood the ship's structure and functions. For me that structure was easier to learn than that of the new exhibition soon to confront me.

It was an idea that ticked all the boxes—however, Arnie thought long and hard as it was even more cutting edge and controversial than *Titanic*. It was a publicist's dream—educational, unique, and ultimately, Arnie couldn't resist an exhibition that featured scientifically preserved human bodies.

As the years went by, every time Arnie started a new endeavor and thought I would be an asset, he would ask if I wanted to be involved. So yes, I relished being involved, but I took a double take when he told me he was interested in an exhibition that used real human bodies to teach anatomy to the general public. He was going to China to investigate its possibilities and asked, "Do you want to come along?"

At the beginning of our marriage, we had worked side by side on multiple projects. We could have been the poster couple for opposites attract. Arnie had no neuroticism, little anxiety, and was confident in his decisions. I was more than a little neurotic and exponentially less confident. His belief in me gave me the confidence to step out and use my talents to the fullest. So, I said yes.

No matter how many boxes the exhibition ticked, Arnie felt, in the company's best interest, we must make a reconnaissance trip to

China's Dalian Medical University, where the body specimens were prepared. Dalian University is one of the oldest and largest medical universities in China, maybe in the world. The university is approved by NMC, WHO, UNESCO, and other major accrediting groups to provide a worldwide recognized MBBS degree, which is similar to an MD degree in the United States. But Arnie wanted to see for himself.

So off we went to China to observe their dissection laboratory where they utilized a process called Plastination to preserve the human specimens[5] as educational tools to be used by doctors and universities around the world, and which would be the basis of our exhibition.

The process to create these specimens is: remove all the fluids and fat from a specimen, make the necessary dissections, and replace the missing fluids and fat with silicone polymers to make the finished specimens more . . . user-friendly, shall we say. Not as easy or short as it sounds. Their value is described in an abstract in the NIH online site titled: "Silicone Plastinated Pathology Specimens and their Teaching Potential" by TP Dawson, RS James, and GT Williams:

> *The resulting specimens are dry, odorless, durable, life-like, non-hazardous, maintenance-free, and do not deteriorate with time. . . . Plastinated specimens are a useful adjunct to the teaching of pathology, anatomy, radiology, and surgery, and are particularly suited to use in small groups. They are much preferred to conventional "pots" (real human organs) by both students and teachers owing to their accessibility, superior illustrative powers, and comparative ease of interpretation.*

So, as I said, there we were—in China.

---

5 All the specimens were certified unclaimed bodies destined for medical use.

Stretched before us were specimens (I refuse to call them cadavers. It's demeaning.) laid out in neat rows on 73x24x36-inch stainless steel dissection tables, a version of the drafting tables used by the architects of *Titanic* in 1912. The atmosphere was quiet, the air smelled acrid, similar to a mix of vinegar and burnt matches, and fans whirred overhead to keep it circulating out the bank of opened windows. The odor was coming from formalin—a combination of formaldehyde and alcohol used to preserve the specimens. I lingered at the laboratory doors, trying to get my physical and mental bearings, asking myself again: *Why am I here exactly? I'm a theater major, an actress, but maybe not so much anymore.*

Believing in Arnie was the why. And this sure was dramatic!

Intense young anatomy students, all kitted out in goggles, gloves, and those white lab coats, were focusing their concentration on the specimen unveiled before them, too deep in their endeavors to pay attention as we circled their tables. Quietly, methodically, and I would say with respect and reverence, they dissected individual organs or complete bodily systems: a nervous system, a reproductive system, a respiratory system, and so forth. The human body has eleven of them.

The only system I was familiar with was, of course, the skeletal system, which hung in every high school science room or tree on Halloween when I was young. They scared the bejesus out of me then but seemed benign now compared to the other specimens in this lab.

Taking in all this science and creating an exhibition that explained the function and location of each and every part of the human anatomy—one that must be accessible for ages twelve and above—and must be presented in a respectful, beautiful, nonthreatening manner was an overwhelming task.

How could we possibly do justice to the marvel of the human body? Knowing the lyrics to "Dem bones, dem bones, dem dry bones, I hear the word of the Lord" wouldn't cut it. For some reason I always got tripped up trying to remember which of those dem bones was connected to which in that scenario.

With this bodies exhibition, there could be no tripping up. It was challenging, mesmerizing, overwhelming, awe-inspiring, humbling, and we had to get everything right!

As we continued our walk, I recognized a few organs: a heart here, the female and male reproductive systems there, and looming ahead, an entire digestive system, all twenty-nine feet of it, coiled from thorax to anus like a python taking a nap. I was getting involved at that point and thinking: *Who knew our intestines were that long? We must put that on a didactic in the exhibition. Everyone should know why it sometimes takes us so long to poop. That "stuff" has a long way to go.*

By far the most mesmerizing of all the specimens was a full body, dissected to reveal every vein in its body in all its intricate glory. In the Plastination process, each and every vein had been injected with a red silicone substance, making it shimmer as if it were a giant ruby, as breathtaking as any masterpiece in any museum in the world. It lay on the table glowing from head to toe, a specimen that would become the centerpiece for our new exhibition, which we would call *Bodies: The Exhibition*. What else could you call it? Though, occasionally, our office would get a call asking if our exhibition was a strip show and could they bring their children?

Eventually, the viscera of the human body became as familiar to me as the intricacies of *Titanic* and not unsettling at all. Our bodies are a wonder, and the exhibition must be written to reflect that, which fell to me and a cohort, along with designing the exhibition.

For good measure, Arnie brought in Dr. Roy Glover, associate professor emeritus, from the University of Michigan Department of Cell & Developmental Biology, to advise us and make certain everything we wrote—specimen label copy, didactics, catalogs—was absolutely correct.

Among the other specimens we viewed that day was a pair of

smoker's lungs all blackened and charred as if they had been held over an open flame. Whomever they belonged to must have smoked for his entire life and had died a painful death. This specimen was always presented in our exhibitions as a confrontational takeaway warning.

I have no idea of the number of smokers who ultimately visited one of our thirteen *Bodies* exhibitions as they toured the world, but I watched many of them standing by the display case of the diseased lungs, vowing to their families they would never smoke again. To help them along, we provided a thirty-six-inch-tall Plexi container with a slot in the top where they could toss their cigarettes away on the spot. At the close of every exhibition day, the container was usually filled to the brim, hopefully with more than good intentions.

Another gallery, the most beautiful and compelling for me, was the fetal gallery. Also, it was by far the most controversial. This gallery was separated from the rest of the exhibition, and people could choose to enter or not. Its walls were a warm red and the only lighting in the gallery was soft, directed to a single row of specimens, each in its own womblike protective case. They were fetuses, their arteries infused with the same red silicone as the larger body specimens we had seen in China. The specimens were lined up to demonstrate the miracle growth of a fetus from conception to birth. It was breathtaking.

I will never forget the night, during one of our exhibitions in Korea, when just minutes before closing, a very pregnant woman rushed in with a small girl by the hand. Through an interpreter, she thanked me for staying open longer, explaining she wanted her daughter to see how she had looked in her womb. In every traveling exhibition, we presented the didactics in English and in the host country's language. Thus, I had the experience of following along as the mother read every label in Korean to her small, spellbound daughter. It is a vivid memory, making my learning of anatomy and the work involved in the development of the exhibition all the more meaningful.

The exhibition was meant to be educational, done in the most respectful manner. During the developmental period, we had contacted religious institutions of every persuasion to confront any ill will or opposition, but not one of any denomination or persuasion made an effort to stop us. Still there was controversy: We were picketed by Falun Gong, a Chinese religious cult who protested our use of Chinese specimens, claiming our exhibition was a desecration of the human body. Of course we didn't agree, but their picketing made the news and, ultimately, turned out to be valuable publicity.

There was only one occurrence that did affect the company and Arnie personally when he was invited to appear on ABC's 20/20 to discuss the exhibition and was sandbagged with the accusation that the bodies in our exhibitions were murdered Chinese prisoners. With no explanation as to where the information originated, ABC's Brian Ross accused Arnie on live television of knowingly using them in the exhibition.

Sitting home, glued to my TV, I could see by the look in Arnie's eyes and the expression on his face that he was not only stunned, but angry to have been sandbagged that way.

True to form, he kept his usual composure and replied that Premier had never used bodies of executed prisoners, reiterating, "All our specimens come from a Chinese government-approved medical university."

Arnie always thought any publicity was good publicity; but in this case, it was a nasty personal attack on his integrity as well as on the company he had so carefully built. I felt his anger and dismay coming through the screen, and my heart ached for him. Arnie held his head high and, of course, took ABC to court for their accusations.

It wasn't until two years later that the truth came out: A Chinese medical technician named Sun Deqiang testified in a Florida lawsuit that he had worked for one of Premier's rivals in the exhibition business and had given the false story to 20/20 on the request of his employer, who had paid him to cast aspersions on Premier's integrity.

Under the duress of lawsuits filed in China and the United States, which told the whole story, ABC printed a retraction on ABC online (of course, not on the more visible 20/20 primetime show) never quite admitting they were wrong but blaming it on their source. Their statement read:

> *Sun testified he decided to recant his statements to ABC News to "protect himself" from possible legal consequences and to protect "the reputation of China" from human rights critics. He added that, as a Buddhist, "I had to confess myself, and finally tell the truth."*

Sun also testified in court to that effect and additionally sent a handwritten apology to Arnie, addressing him as "Uncle," a Chinese honorific. ABC sent Arnie an official apology letter as well. And in later years ABC parted ways with Brian Ross for his faulty reporting on another matter.

• • •

When Arnie first said the company had rented the old food hall space in a large warehouse building at South Street Seaport in lower Manhattan, all I could think of was the day we sat at a table in that warehouse with Samantha and told her about the birds and the bees. Also revealing to her that I had been married before. She didn't miss a beat, looked at her father and with his own delivery said, "So, Dad, you married a used car, huh?"

Now that entire second floor food hall had to be gutted, and Arnie tasked our team with redesigning the entire space, all 30,000 square feet of it, to make room for not only the exhibition, but also for the total infrastructure: bathrooms, ticket offices, business offices, up to and including fixing the escalators. Just before we opened the doors that first day of November 2006, I was on my hands and knees cleaning the treads in those escalators, determined that everything was ready for its closeup—it was New York after all, my town. It had to be perfect.

There was a little backlash there, as one of the board members found me on my knees cleaning those escalator treads on opening day and confronted Arnie with why his wife was doing that. Arnie's response, "You try to stop her."

Having accepted the concept, I had been in from the get-go: choosing the specimens best to tell the story, writing the didactics and catalogs, and designing the exhibition. Pushy, huh? However, I wasn't alone; there was a team working along with me. As with the *Titanic* exhibitions, where there were scholars with historical and technical knowledge of the ship, with *Bodies* there were medical professionals to scrutinize the texts.

Arnie was consulted for his approval along the way; but trusting us, spent most of his attention running the company. On any business day he and I seldom crossed paths, only meeting for dinner.

All that said, our *Bodies* opening in New York City at South Street Seaport was a rewarding experience for both Premier Exhibitions and the Seaport, which was brought back to life with the infusion of hundreds of new visitors.

Yes, I was committed, and it was exhausting work. But it was all worth it when an article in *The New York Times*, written by the then president of the United Federation of Teachers, said of the exhibition: "As an educator, I'm pleased to see that this exhibition does exactly what the best museums do for students . . . inspire a sense of awe, wonder and excitement that actually makes learning fun."

Oh, The Places You'll Go!

—DR. SEUSS, 1990

As the years went by, and *Titanic* and *Bodies* continued to travel the world, Arnie was anxious to establish a permanent space in the United States for both exhibitions. "Why not Las Vegas?" he asked me after some brainstorming.

"I don't think so," I said. "People go to Vegas to see bodies, yes; but of another kind." What did I know?

Arnie knew Vegas had a steady flow of new visitors. *Titanic*, particularly, was a popular subject and an educational one, and it would be a great family experience—there were not too many of those in Vegas. And the artifacts could stay longer in one place, safe from the perils of frequent moving.

We took a reconnaissance visit to Vegas to tour the iconic Tropicana Hotel and its convention venue behind the casino. It was the first time I had been back since my shiksa days and the encounter with comedian Rickles, and I was not that same person. Life with Arnie had seen to that. The "Trop's" venue area was 122,000 square feet of emptiness, the size of two football fields. "Think big or go home," was always Arnie's motto. So, we thought big.

I camped out in a hotel room for a month to supervise the *Bodies* part of the dual installation. As I left for work each morning before seven o'clock and made the long walk through the booze-infused gaming area, walking beneath the Tropicana's magnificent Art Deco domed glass ceiling, I enjoyed the theatricality of it all. Coming toward me from the opposite direction were the ladies of the evening on their way home after work. At first, they looked at me askance—like, "Girl, where did you come from?" But soon I became a regular, and we would nod at each other as we passed. I enjoyed being a regular.

Surrounded by all the lights and the glitter and the sound of the few people still playing the slots, I felt I was back in show business, reveling in the theatricality of it all—when Frank Sinatra played there with his Rat Pack and mobsters played the gaming tables. Who wouldn't think that was fun!

Both exhibitions were successful and stayed at the Trop for two years until Arnie decided to move them to the Luxor, which was a new space and provided the opportunity he continued to want for a permanent location. He knew the Tropicana would eventually close as it was one of the oldest on the strip and in much need of remodeling.

On April 2, 2024, the Trop did close. Its glass ceiling was dismantled and packed away. The property where it stood for sixty-seven years had been sold to Bally's Las Vegas, whose intent was to build a baseball park on the site to house their newly purchased Oakland Athletics baseball team, moving from Oakland to the Strip. The Trop had to be demolished. The implosion was scheduled for October 9, 2024. Allie sent me a video clip of it happening.

It was at night in a dramatic Vegas way with brilliant-white fireworks as the opening act, lighting up the night sky as they spelled out "Thank You" and "Tropicana 1957 to 2024" to the saluting crowds. The demolition started with a number of small explosions coming from inside the building and then floor by floor each crumbled upon the other, sending the smoke and dust of many memories rising into the night sky to drift away. And I was sad.

It may have been many years since we had moved our exhibitions to the Luxor, but for me it was another tangible link to Arnie's and my past evaporating into memories and the upper regions beyond the clouds. This is beginning to happen more and more as I age. One of the reasons I write this memoir is to relive those times.

Moving the exhibitions to the Luxor was a drama of its own.

An entire IMAX theater, plus an ersatz King Tut exhibition, had to be demolished and the entire second floor rebuilt before both the *Titanic* and *Bodies* exhibitions could be installed.

Allie, now VP of exhibitions, moved to Vegas for a year with a necessary budget of ten million dollars to make that happen. She became well known at Las Vegas City Hall as she went through the agony and cajoling of all the city's bureaucrats to satisfy their rules and permissions; Vegas has some of the toughest in the country. Rule of thumb: fireproof everything.

Her biggest challenge was not the government, but that space on the second floor of the Luxor, which was to be the home of *Titanic's* Big Piece, all twenty by twenty-six feet of it, with a weight of seventeen tons. My father was in the coal business, so I know what that meant: This was going to be a weighty theatrical event when the Big Piece was moved.

The Luxor is a pressure-built glass structure in the shape of a pyramid. The only opening big enough to bring the Big Piece into the hotel/casino was through the front entrance. But it couldn't be swept in like Liberace in a fur coat (for people of my age). The Big Piece had to be walked in slowly and carefully. Literally, inch by inch, with as little fanfare as possible. The press had their cameras ready in case (or hoping) something went awry.

Tenacity reigned. A plan had been conceived. Arnie and I were there the day it was executed. We were standing on a balcony, in our hard hats, overlooking the whole event, following hard-to-miss Allie in her pink hard hat, two-way radio in hand, directing the delicate moving procedure below, while Stacey stood guard by the Big Piece for the entire ten hours it took to make it happen. Two formidable women handling one of the biggest historical artifacts ever retrieved from the ocean floor.

With architects and engineers, Allie and Stacey had figured out every angle and possible problem that might arise. The Big Piece had been rigged to a custom dolly allowing it to *just* clear the front door with not a little maneuvering. It was then pushed through the lobby onto a specially built truss system and lifted by a series of pullies to the second floor, directly over the casino below, vacated for obvious reasons.

During the process, Arnie leaned over and whispered, "Can you imagine the aggravation and uproar if seventeen tons of metal were to crash through to the casino floor?"

It may have been good publicity, but I knew Arnie was thinking what would happen to the company, if . . . Nonetheless, he remained implacable. We were in Vegas, and his money was on his crew and the two women in charge.

Finally, the Big Piece was rolled into its place on the second floor of the Luxor, as the jewel of *Titanic: The Artifact Exhibition*. When you stand before it, its glass portholes still intact, reflecting the show lights back at you, it seems alive—an eerie and powerful reminder of the aftermath of *Titanic's* sinking and the effect it has had on the maritime world's regulations: Ships must now maintain twenty-four-hour radio contact to monitor distress signals, a sufficient number of lifeboats must be on board every ship to cover every soul on the vessel, and an international ice patrol continually monitors the iceberg danger in the North Atlantic, to name a few.

For me, the Big Piece is a metaphor for Arnie's and my life with RMS *Titanic*, the ship and the company. It is a manifestation of the exciting and the exhausting: the building of a company, the creation of exhibitions, the traveling, the learning, the constant sourcing of funds, and, for me, the faith Arnie placed in me as he fought the numerous legal battles to maintain the salvor in possession rights to the ship and for the protection of its 5,500 artifacts to keep them from being sold off to scatter the globe. Many are due kudos for their participation in those years and have memories of their experiences, but no memories could be more intimate than ours.

Talk Less, Smile More

—LIN-MANUEL MIRANDA, 2015

Though Arnie appeared calm to others and tried to appear so to me as well, I could sense the pressure he carried. He loved what he was creating, but his obligation to the artifacts, the government's oversight, and to his shareholders to turn a profit, had become tiring. Stacey, who has become my close friend, told me that Arnie's mandate to her as executive director of collections was always, "Artifacts first." And I felt my mandate was to make him take care of himself for a change.

There is a song in the Broadway musical, *Hamilton*, when Aaron Burr sings to Alexander Hamilton: "Talk less, smile more." I became the nasty Aaron Burr to Arnie's Hamilton. I didn't shoot Arnie, but sometimes I thought it might be a good idea, at least in the foot, to slow him down.

Perhaps only visible to me, his body began to outwardly reflect his internal burdens as his shoulders slumped and his weight increased from the stressful cortisol pumping into his bloodstream—and he smiled less.

In 2009, Arnie finally, without my urging, retired from the company he had given his all to. If he had stayed a little longer, he would have been there to enjoy when, on August 15, 2011, the United States Federal Court in the Eastern District of Virginia finally granted RMS Titanic, Inc. full title to the artifacts, providing they adhere to the stipulations of keeping the collection intact and maintained by international conservation standards. That would never have come to pass without Arnie's years of dedication to the cause.

Titanic, The Artifact Exhibition continues to tour the world and a version of it remains with *Bodies: The Exhibition* on the second floor gallery of the Luxor in Las Vegas.

PART IX

IT'S TIME, MS. JUDY

The Jaws of Life

March 27, 2016, Easter Sunday, late afternoon, is another date along with July 27, 1969, that will remain in my visual and visceral memory for the rest of my life. I have played that memory over and over in my mind, trying to sort it out.

Arnie was broadsided by a fast-moving white SUV, driven by an impetuous young man who had gotten in the left turn lane by mistake and was stuck behind another SUV directly opposite Arnie waiting to make own his left turn into our building's driveway. The kid, without looking, swerved around the car in front of him and smack into Arnie in his vintage Mercedes by then in the middle of his turn. No match for the weight of SUV or the force of the collision, Arnie in his small coupe was catapulted sideways across the intersection into a steel utility pole with such force that on contact, the pole was pushed off its cement base and was leaning precariously.

Knowing he was culpable, the antsy kid jumped out of his car, left the door open, motor running, and fled. Our building's security cameras showed him dash around our building, jump over a retaining wall, and disappear.

On the moment of impact, Arnie was thrown around the tight confines of his coupe, banging his head and body so violently that he blacked out when his car struck the steel pole, crushing his car door into his left thigh, leaving an indentation that went through to his bone.

With his incredible force of will, Arnie rallied long enough to call me and in a sheepish voice said, "Hi, honey. I had a little accident. Would you please come down to the street?"

And blacked out again.

Firefighters extracted him from the wreck with a hydraulic rescue tool—the jaws of life. I was vaguely aware of that rescue apparatus, having heard its name on the evening news. When described by reporters at an accident scene, I would silently do the pooh, pooh, pooh thing, glad it wasn't us. This time the pooh, pooh, pooh guys were working elsewhere, and it was us.

By the time I went down thirty-five floors and ran to the road, Atlanta's firefighters were ripping the roof off Arnie's car and preparing to lift him in a sling to a waiting ambulance. He went in and out of consciousness, waking intermittently to call "Honey? Judy?" to assure himself I was nearby. I was there anxiously waiting as they maneuvered him into an ambulance, where he give me a sheepish grin, as if he was sorry to have caused any trouble.

The ambulance driver hastily beckoned me to jump into the front seat beside him and we sped away to Grady Hospital's Level I Trauma Center, where Arnie's clothes were cut from his body, and he was strapped to a gurney at his forehead and chest and taken straightaway to be X-rayed. His clothes were left in a puddle on the floor, still covered with shards of glass glaring in the sharp overhead lighting.

The ER doctor said the indentation in Arnie's femur would probably be permanent, but thank God, no bones had been broken. What he did emphasize were the opaque spots on Arnie's right lung, and said, "They are highly suspicious due to their size, shape, and location, and they need immediate attention."

In the mid-1980s, when we were still living in New York, Arnie also had several suspicious nodules on his right lung, discovered when a chest X-ray was taken during his annual physical. *Could these be the same spots from before? Had they grown? They were benign, right? And hadn't he stopped smoking completely after that?*

In New York, he had gone through a needle biopsy, with no anesthesia may I add. It was painful, but Arnie had endured it without a complaint as the doctor, multiple times, stuck long needles between Arnie's ribs, through his back into his lungs, until he could extract tissue from each nodule for examination. Those nodules had been benign.

Leaving New York Hospital that day in gratitude for his reprieve, Arnie had hurried ahead of me, the tails of his navy overcoat flying behind as he pushed through the revolving doors of the hospital, pitched his opened pack of Pall Malls into the first garbage bin he found, never to smoke again! He didn't use nasal sprays, medication, anything—he just made up his mind and quit. Embracing that diagnosis, we moved on with our busy, peripatetic life. And now?

It had been years since that experience in New York, during which Arnie had stoically weathered that biopsy and later the prostate cancer in silence and with courage, his never-let-them-see-you-sweat demeanor in full force. During those experiences, he would chat with patients in various hospital waiting rooms, going out of his way to listen, especially to the elderly, commiserating with them on their medical woes, and more than once assisting them to their transportation waiting outside, or calling them a taxi or a Lyft.

Then, though exhausted from the treatments, he would return to his office to continue putting his attention to his business responsibilities—never complaining or explaining to anyone what he was going through. I referred to those days as his Mahatma Gandhi phase.

With this new development, we were both in denial, trying to convince ourselves that the recent nodules on his right lung had to be those discovered in New York years before, during a routine physical, which had been benign—until his Atlanta internist emphatically insisted that Arnie have another lung biopsy.

Dr. Y at NYU's Langone Medical Center popped up immediately in both our minds. He was a diagnostic radiologist with a special focus on lung cancer, and he had performed Arnie's first biopsy thirty years previously—the negative biopsy. Having Dr. Y do this second biopsy would be the lucky charm we needed to ensure these spots would also be noncancerous. *Long fine life. Long fine life. Long fine life.* My wishful thinking lurched into full gear.

After the procedure—which uncharacteristically, Arnie found significantly more painful than the one years before, Dr. Y didn't hurry to move on to his next patient, as doctors are wont to do. Instead, he engaged us by asking questions on how living in Atlanta was and what we had been involved with since we last met: Cyndi, *Titanic*, travel, Malibu, prostate cancer, yada, yada, yada. And we waited as the seagulls circled.

It dawned on me later that Dr. Y was making a kind gesture by stalling until the results of the biopsy were posted on his screen. He wanted to show us those results when they arrived because he knew what they'd say. When they appeared, he turned his monitor toward us and we knew as well—wishful thinking had met its match. The previous spots on Arnie's right lung had metastasized. Arnie had stage 4 lung cancer.

His reaction was silent anger. And I began hearing a loud and aggressive seven note refrain—*dah-dah-dah-dah-dah-dah-dahh*—in my head. We asked Dr. Y for a surgeon in the city he would recommend; his suggestion was Dr. X at Mount Sinai Hospital and arranged for us to meet with him that very day. Arnie's lung surgery was scheduled for June 21, 2016.

Waiting in Atlanta for that date on the calendar, we began to second guess our choice and consulted with Memorial Sloan Kettering in New York for second and third opinions. All agreed with the first diagnosis, and all suggested the same surgeon to do the surgery—Dr. Y's recommendation—a respected, highly sought-after doctor with an impeccable reputation. We went ahead with the surgery at Mount Sinai as planned.

In the waiting room after the surgery, Dr. X, George Clooney handsome, in his blue scrubs, stood in front of me and said brightly, "We had to remove a significant portion of Arnie's right upper lobe and half of his right middle lobe as well. His cancer had progressed further than we thought. But we got it all."

Repeating it to Arnie later, "Dr. Clooney" added, "No radiation or chemo is needed. Go live your life. See me in three months." *Long fine life. Long fine life. Long fine life?*

I was fixated on knowing if this was the accepted protocol at the time. "Go live your life. See me in three months," seemed overly cavalier.

We asked once more about a follow-up with radiation or chemo, and once more, Dr. Clooney said, "No need. We got it all."

I had a sense that I was hearing BS and thought Arnie had as well.

We consulted with another surgeon in Atlanta who confirmed it is not uncommon to use this protocol, if the surgeon was sure he had removed all the cancer. And, of course, I scoured the know-it-all internet and found, yes, this protocol was not unusual. According to the American Cancer Society: "If you are in otherwise good health, treatments such as surgery, chemotherapy (chemo), targeted therapy, immunotherapy, and radiation therapy may help you live longer and make you feel better by relieving symptoms, even though they aren't likely to cure you."

Arnie spent seven agonizing days in Mount Sinai Hospital giving his complete being to fight the morphine administered for his pain after the surgery. I knew he was playing multiple hands of poker in his head as he struggled to cope with morphine withdrawal, asking me repeatedly, "When are they letting me out of this place? Please ask the nurse when I can go home."

He wanted to control it on his own, to be in charge; while I fixated on what the American Cancer Society had written: "even though they aren't likely to cure you."

Go Live Your Life

When Arnie was finally released, we stepped from the Fifth Avenue doors of Mount Sinai, hailed a taxi, and took a forty-three-block zigzag ride along Central Park and then across town from Mount Sinai on Fifth Avenue and Ninety-Eighth to the corner of Third Avenue and Fifty-Fifth Street to PJ Clarke's for a cheeseburger and fries. Arnie's idea of go live your life.

PJ Clarke's has stood on the corner of Third and Fifty-Fifth since its inception in 1884. It is a bar and burger joint that hasn't changed since Nat King Cole had dubbed it the "Cadillac of Burgers." Buddy Holly wrote a love song to his future wife there. Frank Sinatra penned some of the lyrics to "It's a Quarter to Three" in one of the booths, and Arnie Geller had been eating cheeseburgers at a corner table there since the late 1960s when he was dating Rockettes and working on advertising for the Ford Motor Company.

Arnie's various black cars, with their opaque windows, had become a lunchtime fixture on that corner. Once, a man in a hurry to get to his house in the suburbs and mistaking Arnie for a limo driver, knocked on his window and asked, "How much to Westchester?"

That line became a running joke between us. Often when Arnie came to pick me up in front of wherever we were living, I would rap on his window and ask, "How much to Westchester?" And he would always chuckle and wave me in.

From then on, "How much to Westchester?" became a stand in for when will things get back to normal? Will our life be the same? Would Arnie be in the driver's seat again? In the office every day?

I have a photo of Arnie that day (of course I do) sitting at PJ Clarke's at his favorite table. He's smiling and waiting for his ump-teenth burger—cheese only, fries hot from the fryer, Heinz ketchup on the side—at ease and positive as usual. Ready to conquer what faced him next.

We spent two months in New York, in a rented apartment, while Arnie slowly came back from his surgery by walking first one block, then two, and then around the block as he built up stamina: his lungs adjusting to a new way of functioning at half-mast. During that time, we met with other specialists who assured us that Dr. Clooney's protocols of not following up with radiation and or chemo were universal—if the surgeon was confident that he had removed it all.

Had this option figured in ego? I asked myself as *dah-dah-dah-dah-dah-dah-dahhh* repeated over and over behind all my thoughts.

At the end of two months, Arnie was cleared to fly, and we began the back-and-forth commutes between New York and Atlanta, adhering to the three-month schedule. At the end of the first three months, X-rays—all good. At the end of the second three months, X-rays—again, all good. After the third three months, Dr. Clooney said, "Let's take a few extra X-rays for another look. I will call you as soon as I get the results."

Waiting for Dr. Clooney's call, Arnie, as he always did, turned inward, focusing his mind on next steps, controlling his emotions, displaying his normal, calm self on the outside. I continued to ruminate on our choices, filled with guilt that I had not pushed harder for follow-up treatments. But as Samantha had said to me that one day, "Mommy, I'm not a doctor. I don't know."

And I didn't know what to do for Arnie either; but whatever, we would be fighting it together.

At last, the call came and the "go live your life" guy was now cavalierly saying, "Your cancer has returned. But don't worry, I have patients still living ten years having had the same surgery. One plays baseball every week."

Was that meant to make us feel better? Top surgeon. Don't worry. False hope. Baseball? Are you kidding me?

And then he suggested meeting with Dr. Ramalingam, an oncologist in Atlanta at Emory University's Winship Cancer Center. Arnie's only comment was softly and to himself: "I thought I had more time."

And I thought, *What happened to long fine life?*

Long Fine Life

Idon't know if a violent car accident can be considered good luck. But I do believe that without that accident and the discovery of the cancer, Arnie and I would not have had the additional three years together. It had been a wakeup call—another bashert.

Searching for symbolic meanings in our life and adopting wishful thinking had obsessed me more and more as Arnie's cancer progressed. Have only green lights on the way to chemo? All will be OK. If Arnie sleeps through the night with less pain, tomorrow he may want to eat. If the extra-painful nuclear radiation treatment he just had lessens the pain in his spine, maybe he would enjoy a visit from a friend. Get bitten by a seagull? By now you know the answer to that: You bleed. Somethings are inevitable.

The American Psychological Association defines wishful thinking as "a thought process in which one interprets a fact as reality according to what one wishes or desires it to be." My desire, my wishful thinking, was that we would embrace every effort to exceed the ten years mentioned by the lung surgeon so Arnie could live a *longer* fine life.

All those mind games never overpowered the fear of what lay ahead for us, nor could they put a stop to that seven-note refrain playing incessantly in my mind since his accident. *Dah-dah-dah-dah-dah dah-dahhh* went up and down the scale, over and over and over again.

My internist said it was stress. And it would eventually go away. When?

Not being able to let the idea go that I had done something wrong, I pored again over the research and found much the same result: If a surgeon is confident he has "gotten it all," often follow-up radiation or chemo treatment is not prescribed. Our surgeon had been confident, but now he was telling us to see Dr. Ramalingam at the Winship Cancer Institute of Emory University.

Life is more than wishful thinking; it's a crapshoot where a risky choice has the potential to change your life immediately and forever. If Arnie had never been a smoker, if he had eaten something green, if I had only pushed harder about immediate chemo or radiation after his surgery, or if he had been driving a sturdier car when he made that left turn, maybe none of this would exist. *Stop, just stop!*

Arnie more than once had said to me when I ruminated over one thing or another, "Shoulda, coulda, woulda. Let it go." Not sure I ever will.

The Right Combination

—SEIKO MATSUDA, 1990

Dr. Suresh Ramalingam was a professor at Emory University, the executive director of their Winship Cancer Institute, and an internationally renowned oncologist specializing in lung cancer. Arnie became his patient on July 25, 2016.

We both relaxed when, during Arnie's first appointment, Dr. Ram gave us hope for the first time. He told us we were in luck as the new immunological drug, Keytruda, had been approved in October 2015, six months before Arnie's accident. It uses the patient's own immune system to fight the invading cancer cells. A new protocol of Keytruda, combined with Carboplatin, a chemotherapy drug, had been shown to prolong a cancer patient's life. Dr. Ram never said how long, and I didn't want to know. Having that doomsday countdown in my head would not be productive and would only exacerbate that damn *dah-dah* noise that had again taken residence there.

Strangely, what also popped into my messy mind was a song called "The Right Combination," a duet sung by Donny Wahlberg and Seiko Matsuda, a well-known Japanese singer Arnie had managed way back when. I prayed this drug protocol was another right combination for Arnie.

The time between Arnie's diagnosis, his surgery, and the return of the cancer had been a time of uncertainty, fear, and despair. At least we were in a system now and had a plan. Immediately, we were swept into the Winship Cancer Institute's rhythm of monthly blood workups in the lab, followed by a consultation with Dr. Ram to discuss the results of those blood draws, then on to the infusion wing for weighing in, temperature taking, a B12 shot, followed finally by his separate infusions of Keytruda and Carboplatin. And where Arnie again slid into his Mahatma Gandhi mode, joking with the lab techs and the nurses, and continuing to chat up fellow patients—always focusing the spotlight away from himself.

My focus was on Arnie, taking notes in my notebook as I had done with Samantha's illness. Notes about every doctor's visit, medication, infusion, temperature—everything.

Arnie continued going to the office, working on an interesting new exhibition concept with me, having brunch with Samantha every Sunday, and talking on the phone with friends. And once a month we would drive to Emory's Winship Cancer hospital for his infusions. We both began to dread that drive and often rode in silence until we pulled up to the hospital's doors.

Gradually, the hours Arnie spent at his desk became less productive. One day when he hadn't returned from lunch after two hours, I panicked and started calling his cell over and over; finally, I went to the parking lot to see if his car was there. It was, and he was sleeping, slumped over the steering wheel as if exhaustion had unexpectedly overwhelmed him.

I read that along with exhaustion, while having a go at the cancer, Keytruda had the potential to wreak havoc with one or more of the patient's vital organs. Let's take a few side effects from each column of organs listed on Keytruda's website:

Lungs—chest pain

Liver—severe nausea or vomiting

Kidney—blood in your urine

Skin—painful sores or ulcers in your mouth and nose

Intestines—issues with mood or behavior

. . . and so, it continued.

The television commercials for Keytruda explain that to you, if you can manage to read the fleeting declaimers below the happy-faced people on a Keytruda protocol. They're living out their lives, baking cakes, and playing cards with family—running a company, not so much.

On the Carboplatin website it also lists a string of side effects, the first being unusual tiredness or weakness. Arnie's chemo exhaustion had set in.

More diligent than ever, and scared, I made the mistake of trying to improve Arnie's diet by monitoring his sugar and beef intake, which only made him more miserable. Baked chicken and banana muffins made with wheat flour and no sugar were not going to fly when, for more than seventy years, his palate was used to Dunkin' Donuts and cheeseburgers. I was in deep denial—hung up on diet as part of the cure. I had blotted out Dr. Ram's innuendo when we had originally discussed diet: *It won't matter in the long run.* Ram had been subtle in his approach, saying things such as: "Let's hold off on that for right now," or "Let's wait for the next bloodwork and see if his kidneys are functioning better." I was too late.

After Arnie's infusion on August 31, 2018, two years into the process, Dr. Ram suggested we take a hiatus. Arnie's latest blood tests indicated that the infusions had begun to encroach on both his kidneys and his liver.

Dr. Ram's exact words to Arnie were, "If you want to travel, now would be a good time. We will suspend your treatments for a month to allow your body to rest."

Both Arnie and I assumed this was one of the required breaks, and we would start up with infusions again in a month. If either of us had focused on the true meaning of, "If you want to travel, now would be a good time," we never mentioned it to each other. This was not hope; this was a warning.

For two supposedly intelligent people, we were not analyzing anything at that moment, at least with each other. Arnie never broached the subject and neither had I. I was terrified, truth be told, that it would upset him if I did. I knew Arnie well enough to know that as a realist, he was making plans and would eventually bring it up.

And in an oblique way, one day he did, when he asked that we go through his small jewelry box where he kept special mementos: a small Torah scroll from his grandfather's desk drawer, his father's Purple Heart, a pair of cufflinks that were a gift for his Bar Mitzvah, a tarnished metal heart given to him as a teenager by a girl he was dating. And a gold bullet I had given him when his first record went gold. He told me stories about each one, never telling me why he was doing it then. He didn't have to. I knew.

So, I held back, accepting that this was Arnie's way and always had been. Never complain, never explain. The closest we ever came to letting our guard down was one day, out of the blue, he asked, "Well, is this all there is?"

And, scared, I replied with something inane, "I don't know, but whatever it is, you and I will face it together, as we always have."

I am plagued to this day by our never having the strength to engage in a deeper discussion of what lay ahead, both not wanting to upset the other. So much left unsaid.

Arnie was never reticent to take on a fight, nor was it new for him to live through the indignities and unsettling emotions of battling cancer. As with his prostate cancer, he never once complained about the pain or invasive treatments or their consequences. With this cancer, he followed the medical advice, barely questioning or objecting. For all intents and purposes, it felt to me as if he had stopped fighting.

PART IX

It's Time, Ms. Judy

Back to La Serenissima

We decided to take that trip to Venice, one of Arnie's favorite cities on the planet; he was enamored by its quiet and haunting beauty. We had been going there since 1973, our first trip abroad. This time, our late planning made it impossible to book seats next to each other, and we ended up on opposite sides of the cabin.

Our forever ritual before every takeoff was cheek to cheek kisses done three times, and a final quick lip kiss to assure that the trip would be a safe one. The only time we ever did air kisses was when one of us was traveling alone and then we had to do the kisses by telephone, and later by text.

Sadly, on this flight to Venice, it had to be air kisses manipulated by stretching our necks over multiple rows of passengers seated between us. Was this an omen, or was this my mind flipping into overdrive, I asked myself as we exchanged our air kisses and settled into our separated seats for the journey.

Arnie immediately went to sleep, and I attempted to do the same across the way. Airplanes have always been the best place for me to relax, to fuel up for the next crisis. This time I could not sleep nor calm my mind. The state-of-the-art headphones blocked out the ambient noise but could not override the constant atonal melody playing in my mind. Now *dah-dah-dah-dah-dah-dah-dahhh* was accompanied by the mantra *Long fine life. Long fine life. Long fine life.*

Notwithstanding the separate seating on the plane, the lost luggage on arrival in Venice, and the seagull attack on the fondamenta, our visit was pleasant and low-key. Our outings were based on the amount of strength Arnie could muster that day. He slept late, occasionally spoke on the phone, took his time over the bridges, and began to eat less and less—not even the chocolate cornetti enticed him.

I wandered alone through my favorite museums but was occupied with Arnie's illness rather than the exquisite art surrounding me. The anguish leaping off Tintoretto's paintings on the walls at the Scuola Grande di San Rocco could not compete with the anguish in my heart.

Late afternoons we took short strolls, tried a gelato here and there (cioccolato for Arnie, limone for me), tasted some of the best *cicchetti* at the *bacaro* across the way, and lingered by the Grand Canal to watch the never-ending stream of life in Venice passing us by.

One late afternoon, we stopped to sit on a canal-side bench to allow Arnie to rest. All that day he had been more pensive than usual and when we sat down, he looked at me in the strangest way. His face was soft, his eyes were clear, and he had the smallest smile at the corner of his lips. It was as if he had thought it all through and had made his peace with what was ahead.

On our last evening, we went to a small trattoria where we were seated quite close to two couples who had just arrived in La Serenissima. We exchanged polite nods to each other as we sat down and turned to our menus. Then the foursome began talking about their plans for the next few days. They were in Venice to see an exhibition at the Palazzo Ducale of Indian jewelry—*Treasures of the Mughals and the Maharajas: The Al Thani Collection*—and mentioned a few other museums they wanted to see. Of course, we overheard it all.

Perhaps they were jewelers. I don't know. Losing interest, I started to focus on Arnie (who was not eating, just slowly pushing his food around his plate) and my dinner until they mentioned *Titanic: The Artifact Exhibition*, followed by a discussion about the jewels that must have been left on the ship when it sank—considering all the wealthy passengers on board.

I couldn't believe what I was hearing—in this place, at this time. I looked at Arnie and tilted my head in their direction and mouthed, "Should I tell them?"

He drew his eyebrows into a frown and shook his head in an emphatic no!

Maybe he was too tired to get into it all, or maybe I was correct; he had made peace and wanted to move on.

On our return to Atlanta, Dr. Ram suggested additional nuclear radiation to lessen the extreme pain in Arnie's spine, which he had never once mentioned on our holiday. But it had been hard to miss how slowly he walked and how difficult climbing up and down Venice's bridges had become for him.

The nuclear radiation was excruciating to endure and provided no relief.

Then on April 23, 2019, Dr. Ramalingam sat in front of Arnie, put his hands on Arnie's knees, looked him in the eyes, and said, "I'm sorry; there's nothing more we can do," or words to that effect. I can't remember exactly how he phrased it as the rush of blood to my head blocked out my comprehension. The only things I remember hearing Dr. Ram say were, "palliative care" and "hospice," to which I naively blurted out, "Isn't that a little aggressive?"

All I thought was, *Isn't that for people who have only a few months to live?*

We left the exam room buried deep in our own thoughts: Arnie preceding me down the corridor, leaving me to trail behind as he had that day when he raced ahead of me out of the New York Hospital to throw his cigarettes away after his first lung biopsy, determined to never smoke again. Now there was nothing left to throw away, and it would not have mattered anyway.

I so wanted to take his comforting hand, to feel his touch, but he had retreated again into his protective shell of stoic silence. Arnie had always said he wanted to live longer than his father so he could accomplish his goals. He had eclipsed his father by two years at this point; however, Arnie's fertile mind had left many of his goals unfinished. Now time was no longer on his side.

We did see a palliative physician who suggested alternative procedures like acupuncture and cannabis for Arnie's pain. He signed a prescription allowing us to get a government permit to purchase what Georgia allowed at that time: a tincture of cannabis, but with less than 5 percent THC—the part of the component that calms you and gets you high. The good part, some would say. Even though Arnie had been in the record business for many years where it was an everyday occurrence, he had never tried cannabis himself, having seen its misuse, and, I believe, not wanting to let something foreign control his mind. This time, he agreed to give it a go. But the strength of this government allotment was not strong enough to do any good, and we stopped.

For Arnie's entire adult life, it was cigarettes *yes*, cannabis *no*. Why couldn't it have been the other way around?

One Last Steak

You matter because of who you are. You matter to the last moment of your life, and we will do all we can, not only to help you die peacefully, but also to live until you die.

—DAME CICELY SAUNDERS, FOUNDER OF THE FIRST MODERN HOSPICE

In 1997, the Palm Restaurant had finally opened a branch in Atlanta, and loyalist Arnie became one of their regular customers. I believe it may have been for his sixtieth birthday, in 2002, when I had his caricature put on their wall of regulars to acknowledge his many years of loyalty to the brand in New York, Atlanta, LA, Orlando, DC, and wherever else they had set up their grills.

On May 15, 2019, we sat in a booth in the main room. It was mid-afternoon and the restaurant was empty. Arnie was smiling. He was in his happy place. So many steaks, so many years, so many special occasions. This occasion was that Allie, now living in Chicago, had flown in to see Arnie her uncle, not Arnie her boss. She wanted to spend time with him, knowing how unwell he was.

It was Arnie who suggested we go to the Palm, as both of them loved the chocolate cake. As always, he did the ordering of rare steak, plus lobster with a half and half platter—onion rings on one side and hash browns on the other. He did his usual joking with the staff, inquired about their families, and appeared to be having a nice time. But I could see that he was flushed and barely touching his food, only taking a small forkful here and there.

That evening Arnie fell. Like *Titanic's* rusticles eating away at its hull, Arnie's lungs and bones had been compromised by cancer cells and further damaged by his impact with the power pole. He struggled to get up, and I was not strong enough to assist. Against his wishes, the paramedics were called. When they arrived laden with all their rescue paraphernalia, they insisted Arnie be taken to the hospital. Arnie insisted he was OK, though even with their assistance, it was difficult for him to stand. Per Dr. Ram's instructions, I asked them to put him in our bed and make him as comfortable as they could.

A heated argument erupted. The leader of the paramedics insisted that the hospital was imperative—protocols, legal, legal, legal—and she finally called her superior for support. I held my ground, and ultimately, she had no choice but to give in, making me sign a document stating that I had resisted their aid, and they would not be responsible for what came next.

Only life would be responsible for what came next.

I'm not sure I could have been so resistant if I hadn't been forewarned by Dr. Ram, who said, "If and when you are ever put into a similar situation, Arnie must not go to the hospital." Dr. Ram had impressed on me that Emory Cancer had done all that could be done.

"Don't put him through anything else. Spare him the requisite procedures demanded by hospital protocols and their attorneys."

Arnie didn't need any more hospital blood draws, X-rays, temperature checks, medication adjustments. He needed hospice.

"Call hospice; they'll know what to do."

That forewarning provided me with the strength to go on. Having surreptitiously investigated various hospice services in town since I had been given Dr. Ram's advice, I was prepared with a number but not prepared to use it. I remember thinking, *If I make this call, it will be the beginning of the end.* This was Arnie, strong Arnie, in control Arnie. I was afraid to take away that control, not wanting to override his decision or his pride. I was not prepared to be in control, but knew I had to make the call.

I was trembling so much I had difficulty engaging with the numbers on my cell. It would be the first serious life judgment I had ever made without Arnie's counsel—save the one fifty years ago to marry him in the first place. It was the realization that the end of his life was in my hands and in the "hands" of inevitability, if you prefer. It wasn't fair; we were not ready. There was so much left to say. To do. So many phone calls to have.

Managing the end of life for someone you love and have loved for fifty years, night and day, week in and week out, in sickness and in health, is a soul-crushing responsibility. But I knew I had no choice. The next day hospice placed a hospital bed to the right of our marriage bed. We were still in the same room, still together. But the emotional distance between us was devasting.

Arnie, in hospice, rallied and wanted to know definitely what was wrong with his leg; why he couldn't walk. The head hospice nurse had told him his femur was broken; but he insisted his leg be X-rayed—even though I told him that both Dr. Ram and the hospice people agreed that he could not stand surgery or the rigors of a stay in the hospital to fix it if it were. Arnie insisted, still trying to see for himself, to weigh the pros and cons of the decision.

Hospice brought a portable X-ray machine to our apartment and confirmed to Arnie that his femur was indeed broken. Because of our *Bodies* exhibition days, I now knew the importance of a femur: It is the longest and the strongest bone in the body, the one that should have supported his weight. Arnie would not be walking again.

From then on, he began to settle into the hospice routine, at least physically. Again, I couldn't figure out what was going on in his mind. Occasionally, he would stare at me in complete silence, as he had in Venice—with that soft, elusive facial expression—as I sat by his bed, nattering away.

Every hour of every day of his hospice, I doubted myself. I rechecked the medical instructions, spoke with his doctors, made sure the hospice nurses knew that he didn't want his phone removed from his tray and to leave the TV remotes placed beside it, *damn it!*

Those small gestures were the last control he had as the pain medication began to take hold.

Near the end, the night nurse said to me, "If he passes when you're asleep, I'm not going to wake you."

After the months of uncertainty and stress and fear, I grabbed her by the arms and, nose to her nose, made it perfectly clear that I was going to be there when he passed. And, "Who the *fuck* do you think you are?" Arnie would have had a laugh about that.

During Arnie's time in hospice, we celebrated our forty-ninth wedding anniversary, but he barely acknowledged the cards and orchid plant the nurses brought us. By then he had begun eating less and less, until less and less became nothing. He only wanted a few people to visit, insisting we have their favorite drinks and candy in the house when they did.

At one point he felt well enough to reminisce with Jerry about how much fun the "Pac-Man Fever" years had been, and he attempted again to smoke pot. Jerry had found a stronger version to aid with his increasing pain. Arnie, with a cheeky grin, said, "Maybe I should have tried this sooner." And took another hit.

Occasionally, he discussed the exhibition he and I had been working on for years. But I knew that discussion was more for me than for him; his mind wasn't in it anymore. One of his last phone calls was to a business associate telling him that he would no longer be able to work on a project we all had been developing, but he was leaving it to me and to him to finish. I am sure he did it to protect me, knowing I would need something to do when he was gone. We never talked about where he was going and why. And we didn't know when.

His greatest joy was having Samantha visit. And when Allie flew in from Chicago, they played cards, and Arnie, still a numbers guy, beat her. He continued to remind me to close the office, sell his car, there were important papers in the safe—and for a short moment in time, he was still Arnie: a gentleman, still calm, elegant, and in control. Appearing content in the inevitability.

Proud man that he was, Arnie eventually stopped seeing visitors and quit holding his phone. He had called me virtually every day of our life together, even if we were only rooms apart. And he had kept it up in hospice. And then he stopped.

The only person he wanted to see was Samantha. And only if she asked him questions would he respond in a soft weak voice, repeating stories we knew but wanted to hear him tell again. Stories of how great-grandfather Nathan sounded in his Russian accent when he got his w's and v's mixed up, and about his college days when he sponsored blonde twins for homecoming queen, and he could only drive his car backward. He told us about his time in the Catskills when he worked as a waiter to pay his college tuition, slipped on a broken glass, and slashed his palm open, then went on to serve the dinner that night and drinks in the bar where he had heard Don Rickles entertain.

He reminisced about the movie he made in Central Park with Anthony Quinn, which Samantha knew about and I had forgotten. He reminisced about our first expedition to the *Titanic* in 1993, when, after I left the expedition, the hurricanes in the North Atlantic were so strong that all aboard *Nadir* had to tie themselves to their bunks to ride it out. Worrying at home, I stupidly kept calling to see if he was OK. So, he, who always took my calls no matter what, had to unstrap himself from his bunk and climb two decks in the hurricane-strength winds up to the bridge to assure me he was.

And the time he was run out of town at gunpoint by the mob in Connecticut, and the flight home from Paris when his mother had unexpectedly passed away, and the stewardess, not knowing Arnie was grieving, asked him to stay awake for the whole nine hour thirty-five minute flight with a champagne bottle in his hand as a weapon because the two men in front of him were highly suspicious . . . until the storytelling tapered off, and he completely disengaged from the outside world. I called Dr. Ram, asking if there was anything else I could do, and he gently said, "That's normal; his body is preparing to die."

July 19, 2019

I had been sitting by Arnie's bedside all day, holding his hand, half-listening to the nurse's aide chatter in the background. Arnie never had wrinkles; now his skin looked even more translucent and serene. His hands were soft and cool, his eyes were closed. He looked comfortable; his breathing was even. He had lost so much weight that he looked as he had the day we met—tall, slim, handsome—only now his hair was a silvery gray.

He was peacefully napping, after which we would go out for dinner and have the Chinese-or-pizza discussion at the end of the driveway.

The head nurse had told me not to go too far away that day—a euphemism for what? Get ready, this is the day! Who can get ready for that? You may know it in your gut, but there is always hope. Arnie was always positive; I was not—I tried to be positive now.

She had left one of her associates in charge and a schedule for Arnie's medication, but she had not told us when to stop. Only later did I realize we would know—when to stop would become obvious. It was that "when" I dreaded.

Still diligently looking at the schedule—we were five minutes away from another dose. Reluctantly, I slipped my hand from his and hurried to the kitchen to remove his pills from the pill organizer. Today's pills were in the Friday slot.

Then I heard the nurse's aide cry out from our bedroom, "It's time, Ms. Judy! It's time!"

Dropping the pills, I raced down the hall. I knew *when* had arrived. Arnie's forehead was now covered with tiny beads of perspiration. I quickly dabbed at them with a soft cloth. He wasn't gone, I knew he wasn't gone; I felt his presence in the room. His body was still warm; he couldn't be gone. I swear I saw him breathe. I had only stepped out for a minute—the expression on his face hadn't changed. I knew in my head it was over—but my heart wasn't ready to accept that. Kissing his forehead over and over, I whispered, "Don't leave me, please don't leave me, I love you, I love you. Please don't leave me!"

I remember I had read somewhere that you should never say, "Don't leave me," to a dying person, as it's hard enough for the dying to break away. I couldn't help myself, overcome with grief and guilt that I hadn't been in the room. Only later did I understand exactly what Arnie had done. He had simply and quietly passed away when I was out of the room. As everything else he had done, it was with a calm dignity and on his own terms—protecting me in the process.

A deep quiet descended on the room.

Over the three months he'd been in hospice, I had told him what a wonderful life we had lived. We both knew he was dying, but neither of us had ever said it out loud, at least not to each other. On one of his visits, Jerry Buckner told me that Arnie had said he was worried about me. That was all I knew of his thoughts. Never was there a discussion of how much he would be missed in this world. How Samantha would survive without his daily phone calls, his counsel, his I-will-make-everything-OK hugs. How would I carry on without the protection of his love and his counsel, without his hand to hold?

He was born on a Friday and died on a Friday. It was July 19, 2019, and Arnie, true to how he lived, had drifted away in his quiet manner, leaving me in gut-wrenching grief from which I thought I would never recover.

Leaning closer, I gave him three kisses, three times for a safe journey, and one last on his lips to send him off to make this last journey without me.

As he had said in his wry way to Gloria Buie, the day she visited him in hospice, "I guess I'll try something new."

Quoth The Raven, "Nevermore"

—EDGAR ALLAN POE, 1845

Waiting with me for the pall bearers from Weinstein's Funeral Home was Samantha, her husband, and Stacey, who had come immediately when I called her, which I don't remember doing. I was calm. Something strange had overtaken me, and I was looking at everything from a distance, dazed in a fog of denial.

Arnie was still in the room, and I kept looking at him lying there, waiting for him to open his eyes. It wasn't real. It couldn't be real. I couldn't take it in. I stood at the end of his bed grasping his foot, unable to let go. We toasted him with a glass of wine, then each of us said something we loved about him and cried.

Finally, two serious Orthodox Jews arrived, looking like ravens in their black, wide-brimmed hats, black suits, with black ties slashing through the white of their shirts. Over and over, I asked them not to leave Arnie alone when they got to the funeral home. "Please don't. Please don't. I don't want him to be alone." And they assured me they would not.

When they transferred Arnie to the gurney and began to move him toward the door, Samantha and her husband followed behind and went with him as he was taken down the thirty-five floors to the hearse. I didn't have the stamina to go with them, to see the hearse doors close, to see him driven away.

After that I don't remember a thing about that night, or the next morning, or much of the following month. I had slipped into another world, separated from reality; until, finally, I summoned the strength to plan a memorial service with everything done correctly so Arnie would be honored and proud.

One Last Visit to the Palm

We held an intimate family and close friends–only service at the Palm Restaurant on Peachtree Road in Atlanta. To the left, when you entered the room, we passed Arnie's caricature on the wall: young, smiling, his head of hair still dark, and wearing his favorite gold-rimmed aviator glasses.

A female cantor led the service. She had visited Arnie during hospice and had reminisced with him about his life and had wrapped him in his tallis as we looked at photos of him wearing it at his Bar Mitzvah. In one, he was standing with his family and Rabbi Tulman, who had taught him his maftir—none of them knowing then what a long fine life Arnie had ahead of him.

Eulogies were given by Allie, Jerry Buckner, and Ben Buie, the son of Gloria and Buddy, who worked for and had become close to Arnie. They all mentioned that Arnie was their teacher, their mentor, and their friend, and he would be terribly, terribly missed.

If Arnie were watching the service, I'm sure he would have found the refreshment choice at the end of the service amusing—we were at the Palm, so naturally we served his favorite chocolate cake with prosecco as a tribute.

Later in the day, we followed this service with a celebration of his life, at home. The tables were laden with his favorites: miniature cheeseburgers, hot dogs, ice cream with chocolate sauce, Topo Chico, and hundreds of multicolored candies displayed in tall glass jardinieres. In the background a soundtrack, compiled by Jerry Buckner, of the many hits Arnie had been involved with over the years, played quietly.

I wish Arnie could have been there. He would have enjoyed moving around the room, smiling, making sure there was enough food for everyone.

You Think You Will Die

As Charles Dickens wrote in *Great Expectations*, "You think you will die, but you keep living, day after day after terrible day."

This was a grief I thought I would not survive. Mostly, I slept to quiet the repetitive old *dah-dah-dah-dah-dah-dah-dahh* refrain that again had taken a grip on my brain. When I tried to pull myself together, I did all the things the mavens of widowhood warn against, such as be careful where you walk, your balance may be off. The mavens were correct. I stumbled and fell—twice—once at home in my kitchen, hearing my head crack on a cabinet door on my way to the floor. Another when I tripped on a lonely stretch of a crooked sidewalk a few blocks from my apartment, cursing the person who had told me exercise would help assuage my grief, not exacerbate it.

Lying on the cold cracked cement, I realized that for the first time in my life, I had no one to call for help. No one to say, "I'll be right there." Samantha lived forty-five minutes away, so obviously I couldn't lie there and wait for her to show up. I had no other family in town, and I'm not exactly a gregarious person with lots of friends to impose on.

Eventually, I managed to roll over into a position that looked similar to a humpback camel and struggled to stand on one bruised knee at a time until I was able to push myself upright and drag my aching knees and battered psyche back to my apartment. There was a fog of numbness in my skull as if it had been stuffed with cotton, hay, and rags, and it wouldn't go away.

I became confused, lost my way on roads I had driven hundreds of times, misjudged the distances in my garage and scraped my car repeatedly on the same damn pole at the exit gate. I drove to one of Arnie's and my favorite restaurants, but didn't know how I got there and couldn't get out of the car. I walked into a Publix grocery store, but quickly walked out, as I didn't have anyone to buy for. And the dumbest thing—I bought myself new measuring cups.

Eventually, I became reticent to leave the apartment at all. Then suddenly, I made up my mind to move back to New York and to sell the Atlanta apartment—the home Arnie and I had lived in for thirty years. I was numb one minute, manic the next. I switched between staying in bed all day to being infused with bursts of kinetic energy at night.

Arnie and I had seen the dervishes in Egypt as they whirled to become closer to a state of ecstasy. I became the dervish of grief, whirling to get further from my despair. I cataloged, sorted, auctioned, and dispensed with, at a minimum, 90 percent of the physical items Arnie and I had collected during our travels. I saved only pocket-sized memorabilia—a chunk of the Berlin Wall, a lava rock picked up on a windy hill in Scotland—mindless, stupid stuff.

Left was my collection of blue-and-white porcelain, basic furniture, Arnie's collection of Papua New Guinea masks (he had become fascinated with them on one of our business journeys there), and 1,000 or so books—the majority about *Titanic*, which I later donated in Arnie's memory to the company that now holds the title to the ship's artifacts. I gave the rest to charity.

Too quickly our apartment sold, and I was forced to move out. Which was OK; if Arnie wasn't there, I didn't want to be there either. I took a temporary apartment in a nearby rental until I could sort myself out and fulfill my goal of finally moving back to New York.

Then COVID-19 hit. I became isolated in a supposedly temporary rental that for some decorator's bizarre reason had dark-brown, oppressive, ten-foot-high doors that to me looked like casket lids.

I was alone, in an unfamiliar space; a few months away from my eightieth birthday. *"You think you will die, but you keep living, day after day after terrible day."*

In this new environment, nothing looked as if it belonged to me. Even my favorite coffee cup looked strange standing in the different sink. Nothing had meaning. I had a closet stacked with unpacked boxes of photo albums and video tapes that, like me, had nowhere to go and no one to help with that decision.

Next, I became obsessed with our offsite storage room that Arnie and I had been talking about clearing out for fourteen years. In it were more boxes of books and memorabilia from all the stages in our lives: Samantha, *Titanic*, music, businesses, travels, even a trunk from my teenage life sixty-plus years ago. It weighed on my mind; the cost of that hording indulgence was obscene. It must be shut down. No Arnie to help?

Arnie's and my life as a couple could now only be viewed in the memories in my head and in the thousands of photographs and videos of every configuration in the boxes in the closet and the mounts of memorabilia in the storage room. I knew it all had to be dealt with, but how could I do it alone?

Eventually, I decided to begin by filling the COVID hours with sorting those thousands of photos and videos Arnie and I had taken to document our life from July 27, 1969, the day we met, to July 19 of 2019, the day he left me—18,254 days.

They were with me in the rental apartment so it would be easy, and I didn't have to be exposed to COVID and the outside world. So, I decided to digitize them all for Samantha.

Friends and family warned me not to look at the photos—it would be too painful. But as my friend Dr. Lisa Shulman, a neurologist, wrote in her book *Before and After Loss*, "Exposure to painful emotions and memories is a difficult but necessary step on the path to healing."

God yes, it was painful. I sorted and wept and wept and sorted those photos, seeing our life go by year after year—and documented them by year on six 14x11 sheets of posterboard—front and back.

The photo sorting and the charts made my life with Arnie less ephemeral and more precious. From the day we met, when he had a mustache and goatee, and I wore my sister's dress—when we were young, forward-thinking, eager to attack—through to the day we brought Samantha to our apartment on Fifty-First Street, nervous as hell. And finally, to our last visit to Venice. As people say when leaving the opening of a new play: "I laughed; I cried; I recommend you see it." However, this play was over, the curtain was down. I wouldn't recommend the death of a spouse to anyone, if it can at all be avoided.

It was then I started having the dream of the one-armed man again, and snippets of memories—one, a surprise trip to India Arnie had planned for my seventieth birthday. On our itinerary was the sacred city of Varanasi on the Ganges, where families go to cremate their loved ones after death. As we watched the sun rise over the Ganges, Arnie and I stood on opposite sides of a field of burning embers from the last cremations waiting to be collected and sprinkled into the Ganges to begin their journey to the afterlife.

Having your ashes scattered there was a sacred ritual assuring the deceased's remains would begin their cycles of birth, life, death, reincarnation. Samsara. Maybe that wasn't such a bad idea—*Sprinkle my ashes in the Ganges and get me out of this despair.*

Arnie and I were now on opposites sides of death's abyss, only there were no burning flames I could fling myself into—so I ordered wine, lots of wine, from a delivery service in Florida, and drank a glass every night with dinner, and a few glasses after dinner to put myself to sleep.

As I mentioned before, I read and read, books on religion, books on the similarities between Judaism and Buddhism, and too many memoirs about grief—how to cope with grief, what grief does to your brain, to your body, to your life. I followed that with books on reincarnation, books on the soul, books on meditation written by monks and gurus, books on tarot cards, books on seeing the deceased, and books with titles I can't remember. My Kindle runneth over. And I talked to Arnie every day, pleading with him to send me a sign that he was at peace and watching over me.

Then my eightieth birthday arrived, the first without Arnie. I woke up with a start, feeling a presence in the room. It was Arnie standing by the bed. He looked younger and rested, dressed in his usual khakis, his blue button-down chambray shirt, and his navy windbreaker with the turned-up collar—and he was smiling.

I extended my hand to touch him, and overflowing with joy I said out loud, "You're here? You're really here!"

But he wasn't. It was my mind wanting it so badly that I had manifested his image at my bedside on my birthday. Or so "they" told me. I'm still not sure "they" are correct, as something similar happened two more times.

Once, when longing for Arnie, I asked him to show me a sign; "How about a dime?" I asked. The next time I went to Samantha's condo, on the threshold, to the right of the door, was a dime, heads up in the sunlight. Then it happened again when I went into my office one early morning to write, and the overhead light, which I never use, was flickering on and off. And in front of my desk, beneath the light, on the floor looking up at me, was Arnie's passport photo. Now tell me that wasn't Arnie and his humor giving me a sign that he's looking after me, suggesting it was OK to get on with my life. But I wasn't yet ready.

I understood Ida Straus, the *Titanic* passenger traveling with her husband, Isidor, who got out of the lifeboat to stand on the deck and die with her husband. I told my internist that, no matter the physical problems I may develop, I would not do anything to rectify the situation: no more mammograms, colonoscopies, or therapists. I had already tried a therapist but quit. At eighty years old, I didn't want to go back to my childhood to figure out where my head was. I knew where my head was. Unless Arnie Geller walked through the door, I would never be OK again.

As my mom had done her "Going to Florida" vacuuming to suck all her issues out of her mind, I was on my own crazy escape to neverland, and I didn't want any advice in the process.

Finally, I could no longer survive in the disarray around me, closed in behind brown doors, surrounded by stacks of corrugated boxes, waiting for my mind to make a decision, so reminiscent of the days on Eighty-First Street when Arnie and I were at an impasse about moving back to Atlanta or staying in New York. Now, where to go was my decision alone. Arnie wasn't giving me any signs.

What to do? My dream to move back to New York would separate me from Samantha, who was also grieving the loss of her father. I agonized. And then I remembered one day in hospice, I had asked Arnie if I should move back to New York. Again, never verbalizing why. But I knew he understood. He wasn't speaking much at that point, so I told him I would say two cities and he could answer with a palms up or a palms down.

He looked at me kindly, and when I said, "Move to New York," he gave his hand a so-so shake, side to side.

When I said, "Stay in Atlanta with Samantha," he lifted his hand and turned it palm up, like, "What took you so long?"

As usual, he never told me what to do, he simply led me into the correct decision. Within a few days a smaller apartment in our old apartment building came on the market. I bought it sight unseen, knowing it was Arnie who had guided me to the right decision—bashert.

Epilogue
He Had a Hat

In May of 2024, I took what most likely would be my last trip to Venice on what would have been Arnie's and my fifty-fifth wedding anniversary. I had been reticent to visit alone but convinced myself to go by having made a promise to a friend of Arnie's and mine, Mauro, to see his palazzo. Arnie had helped him develop it into a cultural center for temporary exhibitions. Most important for me was to see the brass plaque Mauro had placed on a wall to honor Arnie.

The afternoon of the invitation, I took a walk, alone, along a fondamenta near my hotel. It was tourist season, and I needed to escape the crowds overtaking the city, so I had chosen an out-of-the-way fondamenta not on any normal tourist's must-see list. I was walking slowly, listening to the rhythm of the water in the canal lapping at its walls as the tide began to flow in from the lagoon. And then I fell. My right knee hit the ground first and then my left, and I pitched forward, causing my glasses to fly off, catching my right hearing aid and flinging it, plop, into the canal.

And there I sat—alone on the fondamenta with no one to call, again. Scared, trying to figure out my options, like that time in Atlanta when I fell soon after Arnie's death. Back then I found the strength to push myself up. This time I couldn't. I didn't want to call Mauro. His palazzo was near San Marco, quite a distance away, and it would require him to take a vaporetto to get to me. So I sat there thinking that maybe this traveling alone idea wasn't a good one.

After ten minutes or so, an Italian couple came rushing up, grabbed my arms, and pulled me to a standing position all the time saying "Ospedale? Va bene? Ospedale? Va bene?" I explained I was *va bene*, shook my head at the *ospedale* idea and continued to say: "Va bene, grazie" until they accepted that I was indeed, OK.

But obviously I wasn't. In the years since Arnie had left me, I had become less agile, not only in my walking, but in my ability to solve all the situations that come up when traveling alone: finding departure gates, walking cities alone at night, finding a restaurant that would take a single diner, which had become an absolute nightmare in Venice since Arnie and I had last visited. Maybe it had always been but, of course, I had no need to ask for a table for one back then. Everything now seemed so much harder and discouraging.

Hurting like hell, I limped back to my hotel and dressed for dinner at the opposite end of the Grand Canal. Two extra strength Tylenol, a vaporetto, two bridges, and I was there. Looking at Arnie's brass plaque etched with his image and two glasses of prosecco got me through one of those mystical soft-black nights only Venice can provide—and Arnie would have loved.

The next two days everything hurt and I stayed in bed, making notes, writing sentences: "*I have never been a people person but I was an Arnie person, and now I am a no person.*" And "*I am alone at home, alone on the road, alone, alone, alone!*" Depressed? You think?

I forced myself to remember a happier time when Arnie and I took an apartment in Venice for several months to work on a project. In our free time we rented a car and used Venice as an ideal starting place to explore the Italy south of La Serenissima.

On one of those forays, we went to Cortona. I wanted to see where Frances Mayes lived. Her book *Under the Tuscan Sun* was one of my favorites.

"Wouldn't it be fun," I asked Arnie, "if we could find a farmhouse here? We could purchase one already renovated and make it our semi-permanent home."

I tried to paint a verbal picture of how that would be. We would eat summer dinners outside on rustic, candlelit tables, surrounded by friends speaking Italian, which of course we would both have to learn. *Grazie* and *scusi* would not be enough to cut it anymore.

We would laugh and drink Antinori Chianti Classico—well, I would drink Antinori Chianti Classico. But together we would eat juicy, summer-kissed tomatoes mixed with fresh basil picked from our garden, drizzled with olive oil produced by our own trees. We would serve our handmade pasta tossed with a freshly grated Parmigiano Reggiano, finished with a squeeze or two of lemon, from Sicily, of course, where the best lemons in the world are grown.

My God! Who did I think I was? Ina Garten?

Anyway, Arnie wasn't buying it.

It all seemed possible back then, during that trip to Cortona, and possibly again for a fleeting moment on the morning of my eightieth birthday, when I had awakened to Arnie standing by the side of the bed. But when I reached out to touch him, he was gone, as was Cortona, now only a wish and a memory and entries in my notebook.

On that visit to Cortona, thirty years ago now, he was intrigued by a Panama calling his name from a shop window, and with my urging, or more likely because the sun was relentless, he agreed to enter the shop.

It was cool inside, a respite from the afternoon heat, with aged-darkened wooden shelves from ceiling to floor filled with every shape and style of hat glowing in the subtle lighting.

Arnie asked to see the hat in the window, the Panama, woven from creamy toquilla into a debonaire fedora. The dark-brown grosgrain ribbon surrounding the crown set it off smartly, making him smile as he tried it on. It was perfect. The width of the brim balanced his face and had the exact tilt to make him look Errol Flynn debonaire. It didn't take much cajoling for him to buy it and to wear it out of the shop. From that day on, when we were headed to a warm climate, that hat traveled with us. How strange that we never got to Panama. But if we ever did, he had a hat.

• • •

There is an oft-told Jewish joke about a bubbe who takes her beloved grandson to the beach one day. During some freak of nature, the boy gets sucked out to sea by an angry wave.

Standing on the shore in panic and disbelief, the bubbe wrings her hands, falls to her knees, and prays, "Please God, oh please, I will attend services every Friday evening, give to the poor, be nice to my daughter-in-law, if you will only bring my precious grandson back to me."

All of a sudden, the sky darkens, lightning flashes, and a turbulent wave comes crashing onto the shore, depositing her sweet grandson safe and sound at her feet.

Dropping to her knees, the grateful bubbe exclaims: "Oh, thank you, thank you, God. But he had a hat!"

Acknowledgments
October 21, 2025
(Arnie's Birthday)

These acknowledgments are being written on the date above. It has taken me five years to reach this point. Mostly because grieving is a Mount Everest to climb, and I still struggle to reach the top. Along the way, I kept questioning myself: *Should I do this? Can I do this? Do I have the skills and the patience to do this?* And the biggest question of all: *Why am I doing this?*

Actually, as I mentioned in the prologue, I started this book to make peace with Arnie's passing and it seemed right to begin on that day in 1969 when our eyes first met "across a crowded room," to quote a line from the Rogers and Hammerstein's song "Some Enchanted Evening." It was then Arnie took my hand and never let go and for that I am grateful to him and to the people who entered our lives along the way.

Arnie always put family first and so shall I: First, of course, is Samantha, our daughter, who joined us on that journey with her sweet spirit, humor, and devotion to her father. I have recruited her memory for many of the incidents in this book.

And speaking of family, there is Jan Despres, my sister, who never forgets a thing and who became my first reader. She is a wizard at finding spelling mistakes, checking facts, and always took my calls when I needed encouragement.

Allie Bobby, our niece, with her husband Greg, were there to provide me with dates and answers to multiple technical and exhibition questions. More importantly Allie, along with Samantha, helped me maneuver the emotional, medical, and legal matters overpowering me at the end.

Marcia and Bob Waxman belong in both the family and friends' category as they were a significant part of Arnie's and my journey for most of the fifty years and still are there for me now with much more than a brisket recipe, no matter how good it was.

Jerry Buckner and Gloria Buie, with her son, Ben, were a source of enough Arnie stories to keep me going for years to come. Paul and Bruce Hack, Arnie's cousins, filled me in with their family stories of Cousin Arnie during his formative years in Detroit and in college.

Many remarkable people filled our *Titanic* years, among them is Stacey Savatsky whom I first interviewed and then introduced to Arnie, who immediately hired her to oversee the company's laboratory and procedures required to maintain *Titanic*'s artifacts. Stacey and her husband, Joe Adams, keep up Arnie's tradition of investigating new and exciting places to dine. Without them I would never have a decent meal or leave the apartment. They, too, are part of my family now.

Over coffee, Tom Zaller, an executive in the company, helped me remember the "good old days" when we were deep in the building of the *Bodies* and *Titanic* exhibitions and touring multiples of each on different continents to present them to the world. Back then when we talked at the end of those exhausting days, it was over merlot, not coffee, that kept us going.

Ken Varana reminded me of Arnie's approval and involvement in the geographic information system (GIS), the first undersea computer mapping project of *Titanic*'s resting place, heightening its status as an important archeological site.

PH Nargeolet played a valued part in helping me recall the company's history. We spent untold hours on the telephone discussing the formation of RMS Titanic, Inc., the various dives to the wreck site, and the retrieval of the artifacts. PH's stories kept me close to Arnie and were the go-to source for that part of the memoir until

June of 2023 when the tragic, unspeakable accident in the submersible *Titan* took his life.

I believe this book would never have come to pass if Lisa Shulman hadn't urged me to press on. It was she who introduced me to Josh Isard, a developmental editor who stopped me from going off the rails with my not-so-titillating tales of growing celery in the muck flats of Muskegon, Michigan. Josh kept me on the Arnie Geller path, which was exciting enough.

And I am grateful to all at KN Literary Arts, especially Jennifer Sanders, who guided me though the publishing process with patience and good cheer.

In my heart, I still hold hope that someday Arnie and I will again see each other across a crowded room and start off on another amazing journey. But until then, as most authors say when they write their acknowledgments: If I have forgotten anyone here or failed to mention them in the text, please forgive me as I am and will be eternally grateful. And to quote an old folk song: "The old grey mare ain't what she used to be."

Historical Note: I imagine you saw the red, swallowtail flag with the five-pointed white star on the cover of this book. In 1912, RMS Titanic was owned by the White Star Line, a British shipping company. *Titanic* flew that flag, or burgee, from the mainmast as a symbol of this ownership.

Wedding Day, May 24, 1970

Titanic Expedition 1993

July 27, 1969

About the Author

Arnie and Judy found each other on July 27, 1969, at a business party when their eyes met across a crowded room. He was a seasoned bachelor. She, on that very day, had been in divorce court ending her nine year marriage. In Yiddish that would be called a *bashert*, a meant to be, even though Arnie's life philosophy was, "Everything is going to be okay" and Judy's was, "Nope, we're going to die." He liked rock 'n' roll, and she liked show tunes. He liked cheeseburgers, and she liked pasta. He was Jewish, and she wasn't. They married within a year and were inseparable for fifty more.

They lived and visited many places over the years finally landing on one of the Peachtrees in Atlanta, Georgia. It was there Arnie became the founding President of RMS Titanic, Inc., the entity responsible for the protection of *Titanic*'s artifacts. Arnie passed away on July 19, 2019, and Judy, trying to assuage her grief, began to revisit their life. During the process of searching for dates, prowling Ancestry.com, digging though newspaper archives, and sorting hundreds of photos, she thought it might be an interesting story to share, which resulted in this memoir: *It's Just Cheeseburgers, Honey.*

Judy also wrote *TITANIC Women and Children First*, which was the first book to chronicle the heart-rending stories of a cross-section of the women and children who sailed on the doomed ship and how it shaped their lives. She is also the author of the catalogue for *Titanic: The Artifact Exhibition*, which was printed in multiple languages throughout the world.